Hiking Arizona

Arizona

A Guide to the State's Greatest Hiking Adventures

Fourth Edition

Bruce Grubbs

FALCONGUIDES

GUILFORD, CONNECTICUT
HELENA, MONTANA

AN IMPRINT OF ROWMAN & LITTLEFIELD

Jan 2015

FALCONGUIDES®

is an imprint of Rowman & Littlefield
Falcon, FalconGuides, and Outfit Your Mind are registered trademarks of Rowman & Littlefield.

Distributed by NATIONAL BOOK NETWORK

Copyright © 1996, 2001, 2008, 2015 Rowman & Littlefield
First published in 1987 as *The Hiker's Guide to Arizona* by Falcon Press
Photos: Bruce Grubbs except image on page 67 by Stewart Aitchison
Maps: Bruce Grubbs © Rowman & Littlefield

British Library Cataloguing-in-Publication Information available

Library of Congress Cataloging-in-Publication Data

Grubbs, Bruce (Bruce O.)
  [Hiker's guide to Arizona]
  Hiking Arizona : a guide to the state's greatest hiking adventures / Bruce Grubbs. – Fourth edition.
      pages cm. – (FalconGuides)
  "Distributed by National Book Network"–T.p. verso.
  "First published in 1987 as The Hiker's Guide to Arizona by Falcon Press."
  Includes index.
  ISBN 978-0-7627-9156-9 (paperback : alk. paper)
  1. Hiking–Arizona–Guidebooks. 2. Arizona–Guidebooks. I. Title. II. Title: Arizona.
  GV199.42.A7A38 2014
  796.5109791–dc23
                                  2014034667

∞™ The paper used in this publication meets the minimum requirements of American National Standard for Information Sciences—Permanence of Paper for Printed Library Materials, ANSI/NISO Z39.48-1992.

Contents

The Hikes

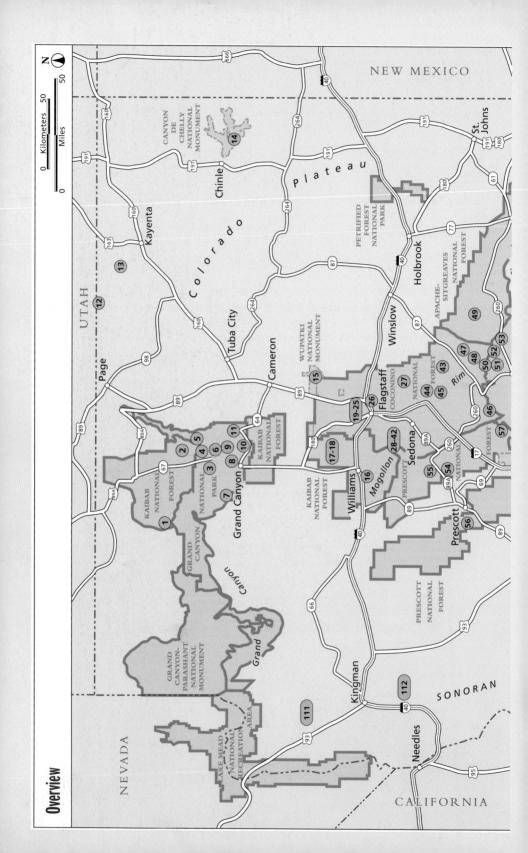

Overview

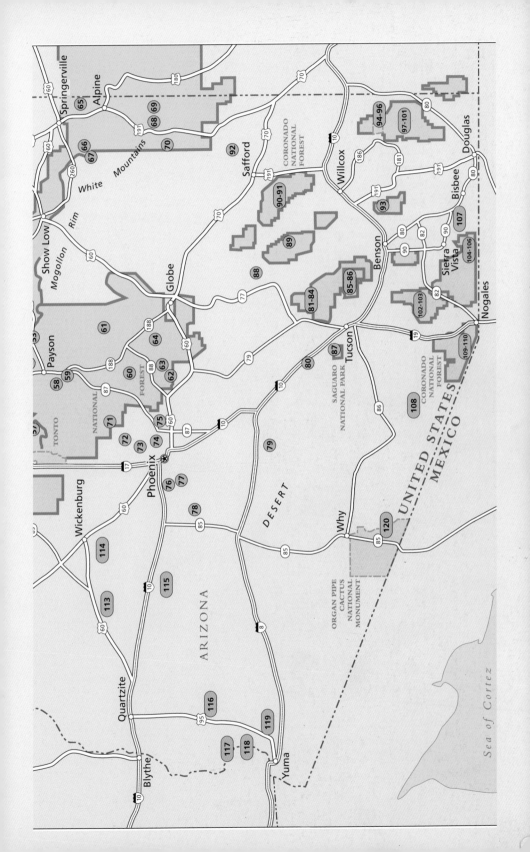

HELP US KEEP THIS GUIDE UP TO DATE

Every effort has been made by the author and editors to make this guide as accurate and useful as possible. However, many things can change after a guide is published—trails are rerouted, regulations change, techniques evolve, facilities come under new management, etc.

We welcome your comments concerning your experiences with this guide and how you feel it could be improved and kept up to date. While we may not be able to respond to all comments and suggestions, we'll take them to heart, and we'll also make certain to share them with the author. Please send your comments and suggestions to the following address:

Globe Pequot
Reader Response/Editorial Department
246 Goose Lane
Guilford, CT 06437
Or you may e-mail us at: editorial@falcon.com

Thanks for your input, and happy trails!

Acknowledgments

I would like to thank the many government employees who gave unselfishly of their time and expertise of the natural areas of Arizona. Here a just a few of those people:

Thanks to Joyce H. Wright, business manager, Arizona Strip Interpretive Association; Rick Best, chief interpreter, Navajo National Monument; and Joseph Spehar, Apache-Sitgreaves National Forests. And thanks to Forest Supervisor Conny J. Frisch, John Eavis, Charlotte Minor, and Wilderness Ranger John Neeling of Kaibab National Forest and Recreation Officer John Nelson and archaeologist Peter Pilles of Coconino National Forest.

Thanks to Fisheries Program Manager James R. Novy of the Arizona Game and Fish Department; Devin J. Wanner, public affairs specialist, Prescott National Forest; Dan Merritt, receptionist, and Beverly Blair and District Ranger Larry Widner, Globe Ranger District, for Tonto National Forest. Thanks, too, to District Ranger Tom Bonomo, Verde Ranger District, Prescott National Forest; Frank Holmes, permit sales clerk, San Carlos Apache Tribe; and David Weir, information receptionist, Coronado National Forest. And thanks to Ron Morfin, Yuma Field Office, Bureau of Land Management (BLM); Bruce Asbjorn, outdoor recreation planner, BLM Kingman Field Office; Deputy State Director Michael Ferguson, BLM Resources Division; Ken Mahoney, Arizona BLM Wilderness Program Coordinator; and Park Ranger Jackie Price, Cibola National Wildlife Refuge.

Thanks also to my hiking friends who put up with my photography and trail mapping on hikes and backpack trips. And thanks to my friend and former coauthor, Stewart Aitchison, who originally suggested that we work together to produce a hiking guide to Arizona, for all the work he did on the first two editions of this book, as well as getting me started writing outdoor books. Special thanks to Duart Martin for her unflagging support of this project, especially during the final stages of editing and map preparation.

And finally, thanks to Katie Benoit Cardoso and the rest of the staff at Falcon-Guides for their patient efforts in making this new edition a reality.

INTRODUCTION

The first edition of *Hiking Arizona* (originally titled *The Hiker's Guide to Arizona*) appeared in 1987. Since then the book has been revised several times to keep up with changes in approach roads and trails as well as contact information, a process that continues with this edition. Arizona is one of the fastest-growing states in the Union, and the number of outdoor enthusiasts has also exploded. Yet there is still no better way to explore the great state of Arizona than on foot.

This guide contains 120 different hikes—just a sample of the wide variety of hikes available in this varied state. Some trails are very popular and may require obtaining permits in advance. I've included a few of these trails because they exhibit some of the very best of what Arizona has to offer in scenery, wildlife, and adventure. Other trails are still relatively unknown and can be wonderful wilderness experiences. My intent is to offer the reader an introduction to Arizona's finest hiking, with the hope that he or she will explore beyond the coverage of this book.

All the national parks, some of the national monuments, and many of the state, county, and city parks offer a multitude of hiking trails. The national forest and Bureau of Land Management lands, which cover much of Arizona, have designated wilderness areas and nonwilderness portions that also contain many hiking trails. Use this guidebook as a starting point to discover your own favorite areas. One lifetime is not enough to exhaust all the possibilities.

Geology

In terms of geology, Arizona is one of the most diverse areas in North America. It can be divided into three topographic regions: the Colorado Plateau, the Central Highlands, and the Basin and Range Country.

The Colorado Plateau takes in most of northern Arizona, as well as much of southern and eastern Utah, western Colorado, and northwestern New Mexico. The plateau averages a mile above sea level but ranges from 4,000 to over 12,000 feet; is composed primarily of colorful horizontal layers of sandstone, limestone, and shale; and is drained by the Colorado River and its myriad tributaries. This is a land of buttes, mesas, and canyons culminating in the erosional tour de force called the Grand Canyon.

The Mogollon Rim—a 2,000-foot escarpment separating the Colorado Plateau from the Central Highlands—demarcates the plateau's southern edge. Near this landscape break is dramatic evidence of geologically recent volcanic activity. The San Francisco Peaks (officially named San Francisco Mountain but referred to as the "San Francisco Peaks," or just the "Peaks," by locals) and their neighboring 800 volcanoes make up one of the largest volcanic fields in the United States. The White Mountains form another volcanic wonderland in eastern Arizona.

◁   *Aerial view of the Mogollon Rim near Sedona*

Stretching in a broad band across the middle of Arizona are the Central Highlands. The highlands are a transition zone between the relatively flat-lying but high elevation sedimentary rocks of the Colorado Plateau and the tortured and convoluted metamorphic and igneous rocks of the Basin and Range Country. Hikers in the Central Highlands find themselves in impressively deep canyons and/or struggling up rugged but dramatic mountains.

The third major topographic region, the Basin and Range Country, covers southern and western Arizona and extends into western Utah, Nevada, eastern California, and northwestern Mexico. Here, broad desert valleys separate the numerous mountain ranges, a landscape created by rising and sinking pieces of the Earth's crust. To the west and southwest within Arizona, the small, corrugated ranges are typically desert all the way to their summit ridges. In southeastern Arizona the mountains are higher, reaching 9,000 to 10,000 feet and harboring chaparral, woodlands, and coniferous forests—literally "sky islands" of forest in a sea of desert.

Natural History

Arizona is blessed with a remarkably rich and diverse collection of habitats—everything from searing desert to alpine tundra. Each of these habitats contains special plant and animal communities.

One major factor in producing this variety of habitats is the relationship between elevation and temperature. For every 1,000 feet gained, there is a corresponding drop of about 5°F. Additionally, going higher means greater annual precipitation. Astoundingly, elevations in Arizona range from about 75 feet above sea level (where the Colorado River flows into Mexico at the southwest corner of the state) to 12,633 feet (at the top of the San Francisco Peaks in north-central Arizona).

The sun shines 85 to 90 percent of the daytime in the lower desert regions and only slightly less in the high country. Annual temperature extremes have spanned more than 160 degrees—from a low of −40°F at Hawley Lake, in the White Mountains, to a high of 128°F at Lake Havasu City, along the Colorado River. Daily fluctuations commonly exceed 40 degrees or more, which is typical of arid climes. The low humidity and clear skies allow daytime heat to radiate into space at night.

Annual precipitation can vary from almost nothing in some of the southwestern desert areas to more than 50 inches on the higher mountains. Generally the moisture comes during one of two rainy seasons—either during winter or late summer. At elevations above 5,000 feet, the winter precipitation usually falls as snow. Flagstaff, at 7,000 feet, averages about 110 inches of snow per season. This may sound like a lot of moisture, but that 100 inches of snow melts down to about 11 inches of water.

From July through mid-September, the North American Monsoon brings afternoon thundershowers, which, although generally brief, may result in heavy runoff and flash floods because of the rocky, impenetrable nature of the ground.

All of these major environmental factors, along with other minor ones, set the stage for the striking array of life in the state. Arizona contains six major biotic communities: Alpine Tundra (12,633 to 11,000 feet), Coniferous Forest including aspen groves (11,000 to 6,000 feet), Woodlands (7,000 to 4,000 feet), Chaparral (6,000 to 4,000 feet), Grasslands (7,000 to 4,000 feet), and Deserts (6,000 to 75 feet). The only major North American biotic community not represented in the state is tropical. Hiking from the summit of the San Francisco Peaks to the bottom of the Grand Canyon, a horizontal distance of less than 80 miles, is biologically similar to traveling from northern Canada to northern Mexico.

Within these six communities are found more than 3,400 species of flowering plants, ferns, and fern allies; 64 species of fish; 22 species of amphibians; 97 species of reptiles; 435 species of birds; and 140 species of mammals. Arizona has 60 percent of all the types of wildlife species found in North America. And this does not include the multitude of insects, arachnids, mosses, lichens, and other organisms that constitute the rest of the ecosystem. Arizona—considered by many to be a vast, lifeless desert—has a startling abundance of living, breathing, reproducing flora and fauna.

One special habitat that can be found within any of the major communities is the riparian, or streamside, habitat. In terms of wildlife, this is the most important habitat in the American Southwest. The vast majority of vertebrate animals utilize the riparian habitat at some point during their life cycles—either to feed, to nest, to drink, or to follow the watercourse during migration. Some biologists estimate that, unfortunately, 80 to 90 percent of Arizona's precious riparian ecosystems have been destroyed or altered in some way.

Human History

As you hike Arizona's backcountry, you will see artifacts left by the state's prehistoric peoples. The first human inhabitants were Paleo-hunters, who arrived at least 11,000 years ago, in the waning years of the last glacial period. Arizona's weather was considerably cooler and wetter than it is today, and small glaciers graced the summits of the San Francisco Peaks and the White Mountains.

Using a spear-throwing device called an atlatl, these hunters stalked mammoths, ground sloths, giant bison, Harrington's mountain goats, tapirs (piglike mammals), cameloids, and other relics of the Pleistocene era. Over several thousands of years of gradual warming and drying and, perhaps further decimated by overhunting, the great ice-age mammals disappeared. The hunters turned their attention to other game such as deer, elk, bighorn sheep, and pronghorn antelope; rabbits, squirrels, and other rodents; and birds. A greater emphasis was also placed on the gathering of wild plant foods. These people had to be opportunists to survive in this unforgiving environment.

Although maize and squash were introduced into Arizona from Mexico perhaps as long as 4,000 years ago, not until about 2,000 years later did the hunter-gatherers become serious farmers. As agriculturalists, they tended to remain in one area to work and guard their small farming plots. Permanent homes were constructed. These were usually pit houses—structures that were partially subterranean, with vertical poles running around the perimeter of the hole to support a roof. Later, aboveground stone-and-mud houses replaced the pit houses, sometimes with attached rooms and several stories. A few dwellings were located in south-facing caves or on hilltops.

Around AD 600 Arizona's native people acquired several other new items from people to the south in Mexico. Beans—pinto, lima, and tepary—were introduced, as were the technique of pottery making and the bow and arrow. These new foods, ways of preparing them, and more efficient hunting implements apparently allowed the population to increase dramatically.

Three major and distinct Indian cultures developed, along with a number of smaller groups. People in the southern part of the state, whom archaeologists call the Hohokam, engineered complex irrigation canals to carry river water onto the hot desert plains. The Anasazi (sometimes called the Ancestral Puebloans) lived on the Colorado Plateau and relied on rainstorms to water their crops. The Mogollon people lived throughout the Central Highlands and practiced both irrigation and dry farming.

After six or seven centuries of prosperity, the Anasazi began to abandon their lands. What caused their departure is not fully understood but was probably a combination of drought, overuse of natural resources, overpopulation, and perhaps disease and warfare. By the mid-1400s the Mogollon and Hohokam peoples had also left their villages.

Where did everybody go? Some probably moved out of the Arizona region entirely, while others resumed a hunting-and-gathering lifestyle. A few, such as the Hopi (who are likely direct descendants of the Anasazi), found different locations favorable to their dry-farming methods and continued their agricultural tradition. About this same time, new people from the north entered the American Southwest, including the Navajo and Apache.

Arizona's historic period begins in 1539 with Estévan, a black Moor, who was with the Spaniard Fray Marcos de Niza exploring north toward the American Southwest. Estévan had gone ahead of the padre and sent back word of "seven very rich great cities." Unfortunately, Zuni Indians killed Estévan. Hearing this news, Niza retreated to Mexico, where his report of a collection of cities of unbelievable riches led Francisco Vásquez de Coronado to mount an expedition the next year to find the Seven Cities of Cíbola. The Spaniards were disappointed to discover that legendary Cíbola was in reality the stone-and-mud pueblos of the Zuni. However, a small detachment of Coronado's men led by García López de Cárdenas is credited with being the first Europeans to see the Grand Canyon in 1542. Not long after this foray came Spanish padres seeking Indian souls instead of gold. Some Native Americans fared better than others under the Spanish invasion.

By the 1820s, fur trappers such as James Ohio Pattie, Jedediah Smith, Bill Williams, Pauline Weaver, and Kit Carson were traipsing along Arizona's streams and rivers, even though the land was under Spanish and then Mexican rule. After the Mexican War of 1847–48, Arizona north of the Gila River was ceded to the United States. Within a few years, prospectors, ranchers, and settlers followed, displacing the original Indian residents. In 1854 the Gadsden Purchase completed the acquisition of present-day Arizona. Originally part of New Mexico Territory, Arizona became a separate territory in 1863.

Conflict erupted as these different groups fought over Arizona's limited natural resources. However, by the end of the nineteenth century, the Old West was quickly becoming a memory. On Valentine's Day 1912, Arizona became the nation's forty-eighth state.

Preserving Arizona's Archaeological and Historic Heritage

Arizona is fortunate to have some of the best-preserved prehistoric structures and artifacts in the world. Unfortunately, many of these sites have been vandalized to some degree. Disturbing archaeological sites or collecting artifacts not only lessens their scientific value but also deeply upsets Native Americans whose ancestors left these things behind.

Two federal laws, the Antiquities Act and the Archaeological Resources Protection Act, forbid removal or destruction of archaeological and historical resources on federal land. The Arizona State Antiquities Act provides similar protection on state lands. Failure to comply with these laws can result in stiff fines and imprisonment, not to mention many years of bad luck and terrible nightmares inflicted by ancient spirits. Any vandalism should be immediately reported to the nearest federal or state resource office or law enforcement agency.

Wildfires

In recent years Arizona has suffered a number of unusually large and destructive wildfires. While fire has always been part of the natural forest ecology in Arizona, a combination of drought, tree-killing insect epidemics, and overdense forests caused by more than a century of poor management practices has led to fires not only burning hundreds of thousands of acres of forest but also burning large areas of desert as well. Recent large fires have affected a number of the hikes in this book, and more are sure to be affected in the future. Always call or e-mail the appropriate land-management agency before your hike, or at least check their website, for current conditions and possible area or trail closures.

The Arizona National Scenic Trail

The Arizona National Scenic Trail, the dream of Flagstaff teacher and hiking enthusiast Dale Shewalter, is an 800-mile nonmotorized trail that traverses the state from Mexico to Utah. The Arizona Trail is intended to be a primitive, long-distance trail that highlights the state's topographic, biologic, historic, and cultural diversity.

The primary users are hikers, equestrians, and mountain bicyclists (outside wilderness or other specially managed areas). Government agencies, volunteers, and private groups and businesses are working together to maintain and improve the Arizona Trail.

Pronghorn, also known as antelope

In most cases the Arizona Trail utilizes existing trails that are also known by their original names and agency numbers. Primitive roads are temporarily being used in certain areas to connect sections of trail and are gradually being replaced by new trail construction to maintain the vision of a nonmotorized trail. The Arizona Trail has already become one of the premier long-distance trails in the country.

Some of the hikes in this book follow portions of the Arizona Trail. While I use the original trail name for clarity, I also mention when a hike follows part of the Arizona Trail.

In late 1993 an intergovernmental agreement was established between Arizona State Parks, the USDA Forest Service, the National Park Service, and the Bureau of Land Management (known as the Arizona Trail Partners) that allows these agencies to cooperatively plan for the development and completion of the Arizona Trail. In 1995 Pima County, Walnut Canyon National Monument, and the Arizona Trail Association joined the Arizona Trail Partners.

In 1994 the Arizona Trail Association was founded to promote the Arizona Trail as a unique and outstanding recreational and educational resource and to provide opportunities for citizens to become involved in the development, maintenance, use, and enjoyment of the Arizona Trail. Volunteers are always welcome; contact the ATA at www.aztrail.org.

Tips for Hiking in Arizona

Walking is a lost art among urban dwellers. Walking on trails and cross-country, on surfaces that may be far from smooth and flat, is not just a matter of "picking 'em up and putting 'em down"! Learning how to walk in the backcountry adds greatly to your endurance and pleasure.

Technique

Most novice hikers try to go too fast and then find themselves out of breath and stopping frequently. The group should move at a speed that allows easy (not breathless!) conversation among all members. Long hikes, especially uphill sections, should be paced so that rest breaks are needed only about once an hour. That's not to say you shouldn't stop at scenic viewpoints or when you find something else that is interesting. But if you find yourself taking a great many breaks, you're probably going too fast. Keep rest stops short so you don't become chilled. It's harder to get going after a long break.

As you walk, always pay attention to the stretch of ground immediately in front of you. Hazards such as spiny plants, overhanging sharp branches, and sunbathing rattlesnakes are easy to miss if you only have eyes for the scenery on the horizon. On the other hand, daydreaming is an important part of hiking. There are always sections of trail that aren't very interesting. The experienced hiker can let his or her mind wander far away but still pay attention to the trail underfoot and the route ahead. Or one can focus on aspects of the environment such as birdsong or identifying trees from a distance by their general shape. Either technique helps the miles pass almost unnoticed.

Hikes taken with young children should have extremely modest goals. A day hike of a few hundred yards may be far enough. Children find all sorts of interesting things in a small area that adults would never notice. Seeing the natural world anew through a child's eyes is a wonderful and enlightening experience.

Equipment

Good equipment, along with the skill and technique to use it, makes hiking safer and more enjoyable. Day hiking is very popular because it can be enjoyed with a minimum of specialized equipment. On the other hand, overnight or longer backpack trips require a good pack, tent or other shelter, sleeping bag, and boots.

Essentials

On all hikes that are more than a casual stroll, you should carry certain essentials—water, food, rain/wind gear, sunglasses, sunscreen, a knife, a lighter or other reliable fire starter, a map, a compass, and a flashlight. These items can easily be carried in a small fanny pack, and they may save your life if you are delayed or the weather suddenly changes.

Footwear

For short, easy hikes on good trails, nearly any comfortable, good-fitting footwear with plenty of toe room, such as tennis or running shoes, will work. For difficult hiking with heavy loads, some hikers prefer all-leather boots. Many of us still prefer lightweight hiking boots even for very difficult cross-country hiking, trading durability for lighter weight on our feet.

Good quality, well-fitting socks are critical to hiking comfort. A good combination is a light inner sock of cotton, wool, or polypropylene, with an outer medium- or heavyweight sock of wool with nylon reinforcing. The outer sock will tend to slide on the inner sock, rather than directly on your skin, reducing the chance of blisters. Incipient blisters should be treated before they happen. A hot spot can be protected with a piece of felt moleskin. Often a change of socks will help as well.

Clothing

Nearly any durable clothing will do for hiking in good, stable weather. On hot, sunny days keep your skin covered and use a good sunscreen. Long pants will also protect your skin from scratches when hiking a brushy trail.

Use the layer system when hiking in cold or stormy weather. The layer system also saves weight while backpacking, because layers can be combined as needed. In cold, wet weather the four-layer system works well. The inner layer consists of lightweight, synthetic, wicking long underwear. The next layer consists of sturdy pants and a sturdy shirt that will hold up to brush and rocks. The third layer consists of an insulating jacket or parka, and the fourth layer is your rain gear.

Don't put up with being overheated or chilled while hiking. Stop to add or subtract layers as necessary to stay comfortable.

Food

You should bring some food on all but the shortest hikes. High-calorie food keeps your energy level high. Make sandwiches or bring fruit, cheese, crackers, nuts, and drink mixes.

Some suggestions for a backpacker's breakfast include low-bulk cold cereals with powdered milk, hot cereals, dried fruit, breakfast bars, hot chocolate, tea, and coffee bags. For lunch try munchies such as nuts, cheese, crackers, dried fruit, candy bars, energy bars, dried soup, hard candy, beef or turkey jerky, sardines, and fruit-flavored drink mixes. For dinner try dried noodle or rice-based dishes supplemented with margarine and a small can of tuna, turkey, or chicken.

Water

On day hikes bring water from home. Water is the most important item in your pack—be sure you have enough. Each hiker may drink a gallon or more during a long, difficult hike, and hot weather increases that to two gallons or more. On backpack trips you will have to use water from wilderness springs, streams, or lakes; always purify it with a proven water-purification system.

Always drink more water than required to slake your thirst. In this dry climate with low humidity, your skin loses a great deal of moisture without actually sweating. At the same time, your body is losing salt and other essential electrolytes. Sports drinks can help replenish water and electrolytes at the same time, and eating salty, nutritious snacks such as nuts also replaces electrolytes.

Dehydration and loss of electrolytes rapidly bring on heat exhaustion and can lead to sunstroke, a serious medical emergency requiring evacuation to a hospital. Because it is almost impossible to recognize the onset of heat exhaustion in oneself, it is essential that each member of the hiking party know the symptoms (excessive thirst, weakness, headache, disorientation, muscle cramps, nausea, and ultimately loss of consciousness) and be on the lookout for them.

Pack

A well-fitting, well-made daypack goes a long way toward making your hike a pleasant experience. Better daypacks have a rigid back panel and a waistbelt to help support and stabilize your load.

Packs for backpacking fall into two categories—internal frame and external frame. A good backpack of either type carefully distributes the load between your shoulders, back, and hips, with most of the weight on your hips. It is critical that your backpack be correctly fitted by an expert. The only thing worse than a badly fitted backpack is a pair of badly fitted hiking boots.

Walking sticks are helpful, especially at stream crossings and on rough trails and terrain. I prefer a single stick to leave a hand free for photography, and others like a pair of trekking poles. In either case, you'll find that rubber tips (usually available as an option on trekking poles) grip much better than metal tips on Arizona's rocky trails. Rubber tips are also quieter. If you hike with metal-tipped poles, you will never see any wildlife!

Sleeping Bag

As a backpacker, your sleeping bag is one of the most important items in your pack. With a good one, you'll probably have a good night's sleep; a poor bag will guarantee a miserable, sleepless night. The occasional user may be happy with a backpacker-style mummy bag insulated with one of the current synthetic fills. People who do extended backpack trips often prefer down bags because of their lighter weight and easier packing. Sleeping bags are rated by temperature and sometimes by recommended seasons.

Sleeping Pad

Since lightweight sleeping bags don't provide much insulation or padding underneath, you'll need a sleeping pad. Closed-cell foam pads are cheap and durable but not very comfortable. Self-inflating foam pads are comfortable, but check carefully for cactus spines on the ground before you put one down. Avoid air mattresses as they provide no insulation and puncture very easily.

Shelter

Most hikers depend on a tent for shelter. Sound construction and high quality are important. A three-season, two-person dome or freestanding tent is the most versatile. Some hikers avoid the weight and expense of a tent by carrying a tarp with a separate groundsheet.

First-Aid Kit

A small first-aid kit will do for day hikes, but you'll definitely need a more complete kit for backpacking. Make sure you get one intended specifically for wilderness sports. And take a first-aid course. Knowledge is your best defense.

Equipment Sources

Local outdoor shops staffed by people who actually use the gear and are willing to share their knowledge with you are a valuable resource that you should support. If you can't find a good local shop, ordering by mail or online is a good alternative. Check the ads in outdoor magazines for addresses, phone numbers, and websites.

Making It a Safe Trip

Wilderness can be a safe place—if you are willing to respect your limitations. You'll safely gain confidence and self-reliance if you start out with easy hikes and progress to more difficult adventures.

Trip Planning

Individuals or parties pushing too hard often suffer wilderness accidents. Instead, set reasonable goals, allowing for delays caused by weather, deteriorated trails, unexpectedly rough country, and dry springs. Remember that your group moves at the speed of the slowest member. Be flexible enough to eliminate part of a hike if your original plans appear too ambitious. Do not fall into the trap of considering a trip plan "cast in stone"—instead, take pride in your adaptability. Plan your trip carefully using maps, guidebooks, and information from reliable sources such as experienced hikers and backcountry rangers.

When backpacking, consider alternatives to traditional campsites. Dry camping—that is, away from water sources—virtually eliminates the possibility of contaminating wilderness streams and lakes. You can also avoid heavily used campsites and their camp-robbing animal attendants such as skunks, mice, rock squirrels, jays, and insects. The technique is simple: Use collapsible water containers to pick up water at the last reliable source of the day, and use minimal water for camp chores. With practice, dry camping will become second nature and you'll be able to enjoy many beautiful, uncrowded campsites.

Water Essentials

Backcountry water sources are not safe to drink. Infections from contaminated water are uncomfortable and can be disabling. Giardiasis, for example, is a severe gastrointestinal infection caused by cysts that can result in an emergency evacuation of the infected hiker. Purify all backcountry water sources. The newer chlorine dioxide tablets are effective against viruses, bacteria, and cysts, and they are the lightest water-purification system.

Water filters are popular, but few of them filter and/or kill viruses. Water filters remove bad tastes as well as bacteria and cysts, but they do not remove viruses. Filters labeled "water purifier" have an active iodine element that does kill viruses.

You can also purify water by bringing it to a rolling boil. This technique produces safe water at any altitude. After boiling, pour the water back and forth between containers to cool it and improve its taste.

Coffee filters plus iodine or chlorine tablets make a very lightweight water-purification system for backpackers.

Backcountry Navigation

Maps are essential for finding your way in the backcountry. Don't depend on trail signs, which are often missing or misleading

Topographic maps are the most useful type of map for backcountry navigation because they show the elevation and shape of the land using contour lines. All of Arizona is covered by the 7.5-minute quadrangle series published by the US Geological Survey, which are available for sale from the USGS and retailers. You can download these maps for free directly from USGS at usgs.gov. Each hike description in this book lists the USGS topographic maps that cover the hike. Keep in mind that USGS maps are not updated very often, so man-made details such as trails and roads may be inaccurate.

The US Forest Service and several private companies publish recreational and wilderness-area topographic maps with more up-to-date trail information. The Forest Service and the Bureau of Land Management publish a series of road maps that cover national forests and other public lands. These maps are useful for navigating roads and finding the trailhead.

Before entering the backcountry, study the maps to become familiar with the general lay of the land. This is a good time to establish a baseline—a long, unmistakable landmark such as a road or highway that borders the area. In the rare event that you become totally disoriented, you can always use your compass to follow a general course toward your baseline. Although hiking to your baseline will probably take you out of your way, it's comforting to know you can always find a route back to known country.

Refer to the map often while hiking, and locate yourself in reference to visible landmarks. Use trail signs to confirm your location. If you do this consistently, you will never become lost.

The satellite-based Global Positioning System (GPS) is very useful in areas where landmarks are few, such as piñon-juniper flats, dense forest, and when bad weather hides landmarks. Although GPS makes it possible to find your location nearly anywhere, a GPS receiver is no substitute for a good map and a reliable compass. With GPS alone, you'll know your coordinates to a few feet but still not know where you are, let alone where you need to go. You'll need a map and compass to plot your location and determine the route you need to travel. Also, as with any other mechanical or electronic device, a GPS unit can fail. Bring spare batteries. GPS works especially well in combination with computer-based topographic maps. Several companies produce regional and statewide coverage, usually based on the government topo maps but enhanced with more up-to-date data. There are also free sources for maps. With computer and online maps, you can plot GPS waypoints on the computer and then download them to your GPS receiver. You can also use a variety of on-screen tools to measure distances and elevations, which can be of great help in planning your hike. You can then print custom maps for your trip.

The GPS coordinates given for all the trailheads and selected points in the "Miles and Directions" sections of the hike descriptions use latitude and longitude (lat/long) because it is the most universal coordinate system. Unfortunately lat/long is difficult to use on printed maps without a special plotter. The Universal Transverse Mercator (UTM) coordinate system is much easier to use in the field and all GPS receivers and many printed maps use it. You can convert between UTM and lat/long using a number of websites, including http://www.ngs.noaa.gov/tools/utm.shtml. If this site is down, search for "UTM conversion."

Most computer-based maps are based on the WGS84 datum, which is the standard for GPS land navigation. The coordinates in this book use WGS84. Most USGS topo maps use the older NAD27 datum. Since the datum provides the reference points on which the maps are drawn, using the wrong datum can cause large errors—miles in some cases. Be sure to set your GPS receiver accordingly before using the coordinates in this book or from a paper map.

A number of sources on the web provide GPS data, including waypoints, routes, and tracks, for trails and hiking routes. Use caution and don't rely on such data for your only means of navigation in the backcountry. There's no way to tell how reliable GPS data is unless you collected it yourself or it comes from a source that you know you can trust; always cross-check with a topo map and a written trail description.

Also, don't walk along with your face buried in your GPS or cell phone screen, following a detailed track or route. That's a really good way to blunder into a cactus or, worse, a sunbathing rattlesnake! Instead, leave your GPS off while walking, and take it out at rest stops to check your location and progress. Doing so also greatly extends the battery life, from hours to days.

Trail Courtesy

Don't cut switchbacks. It takes more effort and increases destructive erosion of the trail and landscape. Give horses and pack animals the right-of-way by stepping off the trail on the downhill side. Avoid sudden movements or loud noises, and follow any instructions given by the wrangler. You will encounter mountain bikes outside designated wilderness areas. Since they're less maneuverable than you, it's polite to step aside so that the riders can pass without having to veer off the trail, even though you have the right-of-way.

Smokers should stop at a bare spot or rock ledge, then make certain that all smoking materials are extinguished before continuing. Due to fire hazard, it may be illegal to smoke while traveling on public land. Never smoke or light any kind of fire on windy days or when the fire danger is high—wildfires can start easily and spread explosively.

Although dogs are allowed in most national forests and designated wilderness, it is your responsibility to keep them from bothering wildlife or other hikers. In national parks and monuments, dogs are generally not allowed on trails. In national forests dogs must be kept under control on a leash.

Don't cut live trees or plants of any kind, carve on trees or rocks, pick wildflowers, or build structures such as rock campfire rings.

Motorized vehicles and bicycles, including mountain bikes, are prohibited in all designated wilderness areas. State parks and other areas may also have restrictions.

Camping

Choose campsites on durable, naturally drained surfaces, such as forest duff, sand, gravel, or rock. In the forest look above you for dead branches that could break off. Avoid fragile meadows and sites next to springs and creeks. Never dig drainage ditches or make other "improvements." Rangers sometimes close specific areas to camping or entry to allow them to recover from heavy use.

Campfires

Don't build campfires except in an emergency. There are far too many fire scars in Arizona's backcountry. If you have good equipment, you'll be warmer without a fire.

Campfires are prohibited in certain areas at all times and during periods of high fire danger in other areas. Be aware that when fires are prohibited, the fire danger is so extreme that fires will spread explosively. Check with the land management agency listed with each hike for current regulations.

Trash

If you carried it in, you can also carry it out. Do not bury food or trash. Animals will always dig it up. Don't feed wild creatures. They become dependent on human food, which can lead to unpleasant encounters and cause the animals to starve during the off-season.

Sanitation

A short walk in any popular recreation area will show you that few people seem to know how to answer the call of nature away from facilities. Many diseases such as giardiasis are spread by poor human sanitation. If facilities are available at places such as trailheads, always use them. In the backcountry select a site at least 100 yards from streams, lakes, springs, and dry washes. Avoid barren, sandy soil, if possible. Dig a small "cat-hole" about 6 inches down into the organic layer of the soil. (Some people carry a small plastic trowel for this purpose.) When finished, refill the hole, covering any toilet paper. In some areas regulations require that you carry out used toilet paper.

Weather

Summer heat is a serious hazard at lower, desert elevations. Protection both from the heat and the sun is important: A lightweight sun hat is essential. During hot weather hike in the mountains at higher elevations, or hike early in the day to avoid the afternoon heat.

Afternoon thunderstorms, which bring high winds, heavy rain and hail, and lightning, are common from July through mid-September and may occur any time of year. When thunderstorms form, stay off exposed ridges and mountaintops and away from lone trees. Also avoid camping or parking your vehicle in dry washes and drainages. Flash floods can appear suddenly from heavy rains falling many miles away. Never try to cross a flooded wash, either by vehicle or on foot.

Hypothermia is a life-threatening condition caused by continuous exposure to chilling weather. Rainy, windy weather causes an insidious heat loss and is especially dangerous. Snowfall and blizzard conditions can occur at any time of year in the higher mountains. Extended wet weather occasionally occurs during the winter in the desert. Hypothermia may be prevented by adjusting your clothing layers to avoid chilling or overheating and by eating and drinking regularly so that your body continues to produce heat.

Insects and Their Kin

A few mosquitoes may appear in the desert after wet spring weather and in the mountains during the late summer rains. Since Arizona mosquitoes are known to carry West Nile virus, use repellent and sleep in a tent when mosquitoes are out.

Although most scorpions can inflict a painful sting, only the bark scorpion, a small, straw-colored scorpion found in the lower deserts, is dangerous. Black widow and brown recluse spiders can also be a hazard, especially to young children and adults who are allergic. Susceptible individuals should carry insect-sting kits prescribed by their doctors. Kissing bugs and other obnoxious insects are dormant during cool weather but are active in warm weather. Use a net tent to keep nighttime prowlers away when camping in warm weather in the deserts. You can avoid most scorpion and spider encounters by never placing your hands or bare feet where you can't see. Kick over rocks and logs before picking them up.

A flash flood during late summer is a common occurrence. ▶

A rare sighting of a Gila monster

Aggressive Africanized bees are found throughout the state and are indistinguishable from domesticated honeybees. The best way to avoid being stung is to give all bees a wide berth. If attacked, drop your pack, protect your eyes, and head for dense brush or a building or vehicle if one is nearby.

Snakes

Arizona boasts more species of rattlesnakes than any another state—eleven species and several varieties. Rattlesnakes are most common at lower elevations but may be encountered anywhere. Since rattlesnakes can strike no farther than approximately half their body length, avoid placing your hands and feet in areas that you cannot see, and walk several feet away from rock overhangs and shady ledges. Because bites often occur on feet, ankle-high hiking boots and loose-fitting long pants offer some protection. Snakes, which are cold-blooded, prefer surfaces at about 80°F, so during hotter weather watch for snakes in shady places. In cool weather be alert for sunning snakes on open ground.

Wildlife

Wild animals normally leave you alone unless molested or provoked. Black bears, mountain lions, wolves, and coyotes are shy around people and usually not a problem. Do not feed any wild animal—they rapidly get accustomed to handouts and will then vigorously defend their new food source. Around camp, rodent problems can be avoided by hanging your food from rocks or trees.

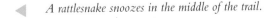 *A rattlesnake snoozes in the middle of the trail.*

Plants

Poison ivy grows along streams and dry washes at intermediate elevations. Poison ivy is easily recognized by its leaves, which grow in groups of three. Contact with the leaves, stems, and berries sometimes causes a rash that later starts to blister. Unless large areas of skin are involved, or the reaction is severe, no specific treatment is required other than calamine lotion to relieve the itching. Cacti and other spiny plants occur at all but the highest elevations. Some cacti, especially cholla, have tiny barbs on their spines, which cause the burrs to cling ferociously. Use a pair of sticks to quickly pluck the burr or joint from your skin or clothing. A pair of tweezers is essential for removing spines.

Never eat any wild plant unless you know its identity. Many common plants, especially mushrooms, are deadly.

Rescue

Anyone entering remote country should be self-sufficient and prepared to take care of emergencies such as equipment failure and minor medical problems. Very rarely, circumstances may create a life-threatening situation that requires a search effort or an emergency evacuation. Always leave word of your hiking plans with a reliable individual. For backpack trips, you should provide a written itinerary and a map. In your instructions allow extra time for routine delays, and always make contact as soon as you are out. The responsible person should be advised to contact the appropriate authority if you become overdue. County sheriffs are responsible for search and rescue except in the national parks, where you should contact a park ranger. Calling 911 is the best way to initiate a rescue in all areas.

If you have a cell phone, it's worth trying to use it in an emergency situation. It may work, especially if you are on a ridge or other high point. But don't count on a cell phone for communications in the backcountry. The supporting system is designed to cover populated areas such as major highways and cities.

Open mine shafts are found throughout Arizona and are extremely dangerous.

How to Use This Guide

The hikes are presented in an easy-to-read format with at-a-glance information at the start. Each hike description contains the following information:

Hike number and name: The hike number is also shown on the location map to help you visualize the general location of the hike. I've used the official, or at least the commonly accepted, name for a trail or hike wherever possible. Loop hikes or other routes that use several trails are usually named for the main trail or for a prominent feature along the way.

Each hike description starts with a **general description** of the hike, including special attractions and the name of the wilderness area, if any.

Distance: This indicates the total distance of the hike in miles. Distances were carefully measured using digital topo maps, which is the most accurate method of measuring trail distances short of physically rolling a trail wheel over the route. Both methods are more accurate than measuring distance with the odometer in a GPS receiver, because of the 10-meter accuracy limit of civilian GPS. Hikes may be loops, which use a series of trails so that you never retrace your steps; out and back, which return along the same trails used on the way out; point-to-point hikes, which normally require a car shuttle between trails; and lollipop, which are hikes with an out-and-back section leading to a loop.

Hiking time: This time in hours is necessarily based on average hiking times for a reasonably fit person. Nonhikers will take longer, and very fit, seasoned hikers will take less time.

Difficulty: All the hikes are rated as easy, moderate, or strenuous, along with the reason for the rating. This is a subjective rating, but in general, easy hikes can be done by nearly anyone and take a few hours at most. Moderate hikes take all or most of a day and require moderate physical abilities and/or wilderness route-finding skills. Strenuous hikes are long with significant elevation change, requiring a full day or several days to accomplish, and may involve cross-country hiking and route finding. These hikes should be attempted only by experienced hikers in good physical condition.

Trail surface: Paved, dirt and rocks, sand, etc.

Best season: This is the recommended season to do the hike. The season may be longer or shorter in some years. "Year-round" hikes may be hot in summer; you may want to hike early in the morning. And remember that individuals vary in their tolerance to heat or cold. A temperature that may be comfortable for one hiker may be unpleasant for another.

Water: Since this is generally arid country, you should always be aware of water sources along the trail, even for day hikes on which you'll normally carry all the water you'll need from home. Dehydration occurs quickly in the low-humidity conditions that are common here, and running out of water can quickly result in a medical emergency, especially during the hotter half of the year. And of course, backpackers must plan their entire trip around water sources. This section lists known sources, including springs, creeks, rivers, and natural water tanks and pockets. Very few water sources in this dry country can be considered absolutely reliable. Don't ever depend on a single water source, no matter how reliable it has been in the past. And remember that *all backcountry water should be purified.*

Other trail users: Inside the three wilderness areas, you may encounter horses. On trails outside the wilderness areas, you may also encounter mountain bikes or all-terrain vehicles.

Canine compatibility: This section tells you if dogs are permitted or not, and whether they must be on a leash.

Land status: When hiking the trails described in this book, you'll be hiking in the Tonto National Forest. All but a few of the hikes are within one of the three wilderness areas: Superstition, Four Peaks, or Mazatzal.

Nearest town: This section lists the nearest town with at least a gas station and basic supplies.

Fees and permits: This section lists if a fee is required for trailhead parking or backcountry travel, and whether or not a permit is required.

Schedule: This section lists dates that the hike is open.

Maps: The appropriate USGS 7.5-minute topographic quadrangles are always listed, because they are the most detailed maps available. The quadrangle name may also help you find the appropriate area when using digital maps. Hikers planning to follow faint trails or cross-country routes should always carry the 7.5-minute maps and be skilled in reading them. I make note of such hikes in the trail or route description. Other maps are listed if they are useful for the hike.

Trail contacts: This section lists the name and contact information for the land-management agency that has jurisdiction over the hike. It's always a good idea to contact the agency before you hike to learn of trail closures or other unusual conditions.

Finding the trailhead: These driving directions are given in miles from the nearest large town for all of the hikes, followed by the GPS coordinates of the trailhead. To use these coordinates with a map, you must set your GPS to the datum used by your map. For paper USGS topo maps, use NAD27. For most other maps, use WGS84. The coordinates are in latitude and longitude—if you prefer UTM, you can convert from lat/long to UTM at a number of websites, including http://www.rcn.montana.edu/resources/converter.aspx. These sites seem to come and go—to find more, use your web browser to search for "convert lat/long to UTM."

The Hike: In this narrative the hike is described in detail, along with interesting natural and human history. The description uses references to landmarks rather than distances wherever possible, since distances are listed under key points. Many summits remain unnamed but are useful as landmarks. I refer to these by their official elevations as shown on the USGS 7.5-minute topographic maps; for example, "Peak 1,234."

Miles and Directions: This is a listing of key points along the hike, including trail junctions and important landmarks. You should be able to follow the route by reference to this section; however, the key points are not a substitute for thoroughly reading the hike narrative before taking the trip. Distances are given from the start of the hike in miles.

Trail Finder

Number	Hike	Easy Day Hikes	Hikes with Children	First Night in the Wilderness	Long Day Hikes	Hikes for Photographers	Hikes with Side Trips and Exploring	Hikes for Peak Baggers	Hikes for Backpackers
1	Ranger Trail					•			•
2	Dog Lake				•				•
3	Widforss Trail				•				
4	Ken Patrick Trail				•				
5	Nankoweap/Saddle Mountain Trail				•	•	•		•
6	North Kaibab Trail			•					•
7	Boucher-Hermit Loop					•	•		•
8	South Kaibab and Bright Angel Trails			•		•	•		•
9	Clear Creek					•	•		•
10	Horseshoe Mesa				•	•	•		•
11	Tanner to Grandview					•	•		•
12	Rainbow Bridge Trail					•	•		•
13	Keet Seel Trail					•			•
14	White House Ruin Trail	•	•			•			
15	Wupatki Ruin	•	•			•			
16	Bill Williams Mountain Trail				•			•	
17	Bull Basin–Pumpkin Trails				•			•	•
18	Kendrick Peak Trail				•			•	
19	Walker Lake	•	•						
20	Bear Jaw–Abineau Canyon Loop				•	•			
21	Humphreys Peak Trail				•	•		•	
22	Kachina Trail				•	•			
23	Weatherford Trail				•	•	•		
24	Inner Basin Trail				•	•	•		
25	Sunset-Brookbank Loop				•		•		
26	Walnut Canyon Rim				•				
27	Mormon Lake	•				•			

Number	Hike	Easy Day Hikes	Hikes with Children	First Night in the Wilderness	Long Day Hikes	Hikes for Photographers	Hikes with Side Trips and Exploring	Hikes for Peak Baggers	Hikes for Backpackers
28	Sycamore Rim Trail				•		•		
29	Kelsey-Dorsey Loop				•	•			
30	Taylor Cabin Loop				•	•			•
31	Parsons Trail					•			•
32	Secret Mountain Trail				•	•	•	•	•
33	Loy Canyon Trail				•	•			
34	Secret Canyon				•	•			
35	Bear Sign Canyon				•	•			
36	Thomas Point Trail	•	•			•			
37	West Fork Trail	•				•	•		
38	AB Young Trail				•			•	
39	North Wilson Mountain Trail				•		•	•	
40	Wilson Mountain Trail				•			•	
41	Huckaby Trail				•	•			
42	Munds Mountain Trail				•			•	
43	Tramway Trail	•				•	•		
44	Bell Trail				•	•	•		
45	West Clear Creek Loop				•	•	•		•
46	Fossil Springs Trail	•	•			•	•		
47	Kinder Crossing Trail	•	•				•		
48	Cabin Loop			•			•		
49	Chevelon Canyon					•			•
50	Tunnel Trail	•	•						
51	Highline National Recreation Trail						•		•
52	Horton Creek				•				
53	Hells Gate Trail				•				•
54	Yaeger Canyon Loop				•				

Number	Hike	Easy Day Hikes	Hikes with Children	First Night in the Wilderness	Long Day Hikes	Hikes for Photographers	Hikes with Side Trips and Exploring	Hikes for Peak Baggers	Hikes for Backpackers
55	Woodchute Trail				●				
56	Granite Mountain Trail				●				
57	Pine Mountian			●	●		●	●	●
58	Y Bar Basin–Barnhardt Canyon Loop			●	●		●	●	●
59	Deer Creek			●	●		●		●
60	Browns Peak				●			●	
61	Hells Hole				●	●			●
62	Barks Canyon				●	●			
63	Dutchmans Loop			●	●	●	●		●
64	Fireline Loop				●	●	●		●
65	Escudilla Mountain				●			●	
66	Apache Railroad Trail			●	●	●			●
67	Mount Baldy				●	●		●	
68	KP Creek						●		●
69	Bear Mountain						●		●
70	Bear Wallow Trail				●				●
71	Cave Creek Trail				●		●		
72	Go John Trail				●				
73	Lookout Mountain	●	●				●		
74	Cholla Trail	●						●	
75	Pass Mountain Trail				●				
76	Baseline Trail	●							
77	Quartz Peak Trail				●			●	
78	Margies Cove Trail				●	●			
79	Table Top Trail					●		●	
80	Hunter Trail				●	●		●	
81	Wilderness of Rocks	●				●	●		

Number	Hike	Easy Day Hikes	Hikes with Children	First Night in the Wilderness	Long Day Hikes	Hikes for Photographers	Hikes with Side Trips and Exploring	Hikes for Peak Baggers	Hikes for Backpackers
82	Butterfly Trail			•	•				•
83	Finger Rock Trail				•	•	•	•	•
84	West Fork Sabino Canyon				•	•	•		
85	Mica Mountain				•		•	•	•
86	Tanque Verde Ridge				•		•		•
87	Hugh Norris Trail				•			•	
88	Aravaipa Canyon				•	•			
89	Powers Garden				•		•		•
90	Ash Creek Falls	•	•						
91	Webb Peak	•	•					•	
92	Safford-Morenci Trail								•
93	Cochise Stronghold East				•	•			
94	Sugarloaf Mountain	•	•			•			
95	Echo Canyon	•	•			•			
96	Heart of Rocks					•			
97	Buena Vista Peak	•	•		•	•		•	
98	Silver Peak				•			•	
99	Chiricahua Peak				•		•		•
100	Monte Vista Peak				•			•	
101	Rucker Canyon				•				
102	Mount Wrightson			•	•		•	•	•
103	Santa Rita Crest Trail				•			•	•
104	Carr Peak				•			•	
105	Ramsey Canyon				•		•	•	
106	Miller Peak				•			•	
107	San Pedro River Trail				•	•			•
108	Summit Trail				•	•			

Number	Hike	Easy Day Hikes	Hikes with Children	First Night in the Wilderness	Long Day Hikes	Hikes for Photographers	Hikes with Side Trips and Exploring	Hikes for Peak Baggers	Hikes for Backpackers
109	Sycamore Creek					●			
110	Atascosa Lookout				●			●	
111	Cherum Peak Trail				●			●	
112	Wabayuma Peak				●			●	
113	Harquahala Mountain Trail				●			●	
114	Vulture Peak				●			●	
115	Ben Avery Trail				●	●			
116	Palm Canyon	●	●			●			
117	Squaw Lake Nature Trail	●	●						
118	Betty's Kitchen Interpretive Trail	●	●						
119	Muggins Peak				●	●		●	
120	Bull Pasture				●	●			

Map Legend

Municipal

≡⟨17⟩≡ Interstate Highway

≡⟨60⟩≡ US Highway

≡⟨264⟩≡ State Road

≡⟨449A⟩≡ Local/County Road

≡⟨356⟩≡ Forest Road

= = = = Unpaved Road

— ·· — ·· — State Boundary

Trails

━ ━ ━ ━ Featured Trail

- - - - - Trail

· · · · · · · · · Off-Trail

Water Features

Body of Water

Marsh or Swamp

River/Creek

Intermittent Stream

Waterfall

Rapids

Spring

Land Management

National Park/Forest

National Monument/Wilderness Area

Symbols

≍ Bridge

▲ Backcountry Campground

Boat Launch

■ Building/Point of Interest

Λ Campground

∩ Cave

🅿 Parking

≍ Pass

▲ Peak/Elevation

🛆 Picnic Area

——•—— Powerline

Ranger Station/Park Office

🚻 Restroom

Scenic View

Tower

○ Town

⟨20⟩ Trailhead

❓ Visitor/Information Center

Grand Canyon

Nearly 300 miles long and averaging 10 miles wide, the Grand Canyon is truly the master canyon of the Colorado Plateau. A lifetime can easily be spent exploring its depths. As you descend through the layered geology of the canyon, you'll also be traveling southward in climate. On the South Rim mixed ponderosa pine and piñon–juniper forest identify the transition life zone. Midway in your descent you'll be passing through the upper Sonoran life zone, identifiable by its pygmy forest of junipers. Near the river you'll be hiking in the lower Sonoran life zone, characterized by low desert shrubs and grasses. The North Rim of the canyon is formed by the south edge of the Kaibab Plateau, a scenic alpine plateau that is 8,000 to 9,000 feet in elevation. The plateau receives more rain and snow than the South Rim and so is covered with a forest of ponderosa pine, Douglas fir, and quaking aspen.

Along the Nankoweap Trail

Spanish conquistadors under the command of Coronado, who rode north from Mexico City in 1540, were the first Europeans to visit the Grand Canyon. They reached the South Rim in 1542, most likely somewhere between the present Tanner and Grandview trailheads. They spent a number of days trying to find a way to the Colorado River, without success. Undoubtedly their native guide knew of several routes but chose to keep the information to himself. More than 200 years would pass before Europeans would see the canyon again. During the 1820s mountain men roamed the Southwest in search of beaver, but apparently none of these intrepid explorers got below the rims of the canyon. Major John Wesley Powell carried out the first scientific exploration of the great canyon system on two Colorado River float trips between 1869 and 1871. His group, one of several government-sponsored surveys of the West, also extensively explored the region surrounding the canyon. Powell named the Grand Canyon and many of its features. After Powell's explorations, miners and prospectors began to establish trails into the canyon. Most of them eventually found that guiding tourists into the canyon was more profitable than mining. This last wave of miners improved their trails to accommodate tourists, and many of their trails are still popular with hikers today.

Several hikes on the Kaibab Plateau are featured in this section. These are great hikes for summer or early fall, as the plateau is high enough to be pleasantly cool even during the hottest summer days. Several of the best hikes into the canyon also are featured. These routes are historic trails that have been abandoned and now receive only minimum maintenance. It is strongly suggested that hikers carry the appropriate topographic maps on these hikes, as sections of trail may not be obvious. The hikes listed are within Grand Canyon National Park, and overnight camping requires a permit that can be obtained from the backcountry office on the South Rim. Reservations can be made in person at the backcountry office or in advance by mail. For information contact the National Park Service office listed under Trail Contacts with each hike. Campfires are not allowed in the park backcountry, so plan to cook on a backpacking stove.

1 Ranger Trail

This is an overnight backpack trip into the Kanab Creek Wilderness on a historic trail through interesting sandstone formations. There are opportunities to explore nearby canyons such as Jumpup and Kanab Canyons.

Distance: 9.6 miles out and back
Hiking time: About 6 hours
Difficulty: Strenuous
Trail surface: Dirt trails
Best seasons: Mar through May and Sept through Nov
Water: Upper Jumpup and Lower Jumpup Springs
Other trail users: None
Canine compatibility: Dogs under control on leashes allowed in national forest; dogs not allowed in Grand Canyon National Park

Land status: Kanab Creek Wilderness, Kaibab National Forest
Nearest town: Fredonia
Fees and permits: None required for wilderness area; permit required if you continue south into Grand Canyon National Park
Schedule: Open all year
Maps: USGS Jumpup Point; North Kaibab National Forest
Trail contacts: Kaibab National Forest, 800 S. Sixth St., Williams, AZ 86046; (928) 635-8200; www.fs.usda.gov/kaibab

Finding the trailhead: From Fredonia drive south on FR 422 (Ryan Road) about 23.3 miles, then turn right (west) onto FR 423. Follow FR 423 for 3.3 miles to FR 235. Continue on FR 235 about 7 miles until it becomes FR 423 again. Drive another 8 miles to the end of the road at Jumpup Cabin and the Ranger trailhead. A high-clearance vehicle is recommended; the dirt forest service roads may be impassible when wet. GPS: N36 35.12'/W112 32.84'

The Hike

The Ranger Trail is one of a number of routes into the magnificent Kanab Creek Wilderness. The trail begins at an old cabin and quickly drops into Jumpup Canyon. After a few switchbacks through the cross-bedded Coconino sandstone, the trail reaches the canyon bottom where a side canyon joins from the east. Upper Jumpup Spring emerges here and is piped into a concrete trough. This is a lovely spot, with large box elders and fragrant big sage. There are stands of wolfberry, which often indicates that American Indians once frequented the location. They liked to eat the juicy, tart berries and probably encouraged their growth.

The trail continues down the main canyon bottom, in places climbing up on the right or left bank, or bench. But if you don't notice the trail leaving the dry streambed, don't worry. Simply continue along the bottom.

Scan the cliff faces, especially under overhangs, and you might discover some intriguing prehistoric rock art. There are pictographs (paintings) dating as far back as several thousand years ago, as well as historic Southern Paiute drawings. Please do not touch them. Oils from your fingers can degrade the images.

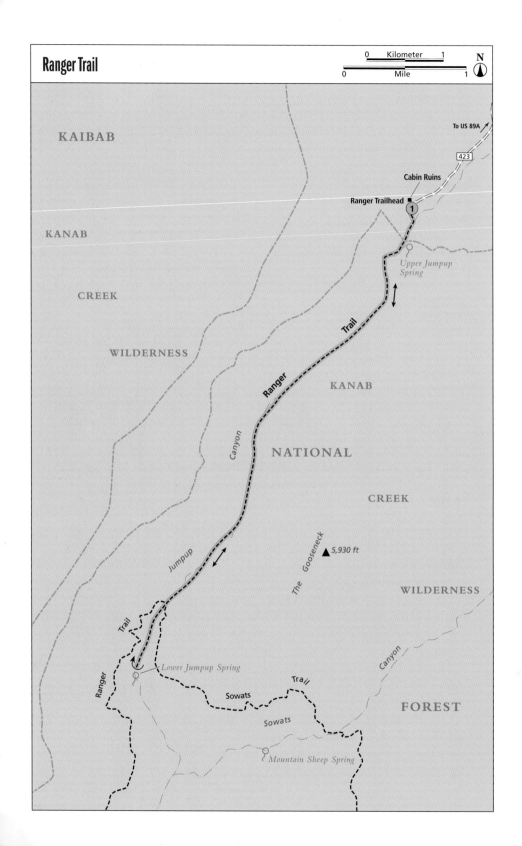

Ranger Trail

0   Kilometer   1

0   Mile   1

N

To US 89A

423

Cabin Ruins

Ranger Trailhead

1

KAIBAB

KANAB

CREEK

WILDERNESS

Upper Jumpup Spring

Ranger

Trail

KANAB

Canyon

NATIONAL

CREEK

The Gooseneck

▲ 5,930 ft

WILDERNESS

Jumpup

Canyon

Trail

Ranger

Lower Jumpup Spring

Sowats

Trail

FOREST

Sowats

Mountain Sheep Spring

Continuing downcanyon, the walls rise higher and higher. Beneath the buff Coconino sandstone, the dark-red Hermit shale appears and begins to form a slope down to the canyon bottom. After about 4 miles the canyon walls fold back, revealing the grand expanse called the Esplanade. This relatively flat bench covers hundreds of square miles in the western Grand Canyon. The resistant upper member of the Supai Group—a collection of sandstones, shale, and limestone—has created this remarkable feature.

Keep a sharp lookout for a sign and/or rock cairns that signal the Ranger Trail's exit from the canyon floor to head southwest along the Esplanade. To the southeast the Sowats Trail follows the Esplanade. For now, though, continue downstream to a stand of Fremont cottonwoods, the site of Lower Jumpup Spring. The exact point of emergence for this spring varies from year to year. Sometimes water is seeping out just below the first trees. Other years you may have to walk another 0.5 mile to find water. However, the best camping is around the area where you first encounter the cottonwoods.

The Ranger Trail across the Esplanade and the Sowats Trail both make great day hikes or longer hikes. But remember to carry plenty of water. Many of the springs shown on the topo maps are unreliable. Get the latest information from the North Kaibab Ranger District Office.

Miles and Directions

0.0 Start at the Ranger trailhead.

0.4 Reach Upper Jumpup Spring.

4.2 Reach junction of Ranger and Sowats Trails. Continue downstream on the Ranger Trail.

4.8 Arrive at Lower Jumpup Spring, your campsite or turnaround point.

9.6 Arrive back at the trailhead.

2 Dog Lake

This is a scenic walk on a section of the Arizona Trail through cool alpine meadows on the Kaibab Plateau. It's a great midsummer hike when lower elevations are scorching hot.

Distance: 3.8 miles out and back
Hiking time: About 2 hours
Difficulty: Easy
Trail surface: Dirt trails
Best seasons: Summer and fall
Water: No water available
Other trail users: Mountain bikes and horses
Canine compatibility: Dogs under control allowed

Land status: Kaibab National Forest
Nearest towns: Kanab, Utah; Page, Arizona
Fees and permits: None
Schedule: Open all year
Maps: USGS Dog Point; Kaibab National Forest (North Kaibab Ranger District)
Trail contacts: Kaibab National Forest, 800 S. Sixth St., Williams, AZ 86046; (928) 635-8200; www.fs.usda.gov/kaibab

Finding the trailhead: From Jacob Lake go south approximately 26 miles on Highway 67, then turn left (east) onto FR 611. (This signed turnoff is 0.9 mile south of Kaibab Lodge.) Follow FR 611, a maintained dirt road, 1.4 miles, then turn right (east) to remain on FR 611. After a few yards, turn left to remain on FR 611. This road is signed East Rim View. Continue 2.5 miles to the signed trailhead, which is about 0.25 mile past the East Rim Viewpoint. GPS: N36 35.37'/W112 5.18'

The Hike

Before starting the hike, walk to the rim of North Canyon for the great view from the east side of the Kaibab Plateau. This hike follows a portion of the Arizona Trail, which traverses Arizona from Utah to Mexico, a distance of over 800 miles. The northernmost section has been completed across the Kaibab Plateau from the Utah border to the Grand Canyon National Park boundary. This section of the trail is especially scenic, traversing two of the alpine meadows that grace the high plateau.

The trail crosses FR 611 here and is signed Kaibab Plateau Trail and marked with small Arizona Trail signs. Follow the trail across the road to the northwest. After about 0.2 mile through the fir forest, the trail (an old road) passes Dog Lake, a small shallow pond ringed by aspen. Although the Kaibab Plateau lies at 8,000 to 9,000 feet above sea level and receives much more precipitation than the surrounding desert, the limestone bedrock is porous and soaks up all the moisture. There are no running streams

The hooves of the desert bighorn sheep are uniquely adapted for climbing the steep, rocky terrain of desert mountains.

on the plateau; the only water sources are a few springs and small ponds. Just after the pond the trail enters a meadow and then crosses a road that comes down Dog Canyon. The trail, still marked by Arizona Trail posts, continues northwest and enters the forest again after over a mile of meadow, then crosses the east ridge of Upper Tater Canyon and FR 610. It descends into Upper Tater Canyon via a series of switchbacks and enters another fine meadow. This expansive alpine setting makes a good stopping point for an easy day hike.

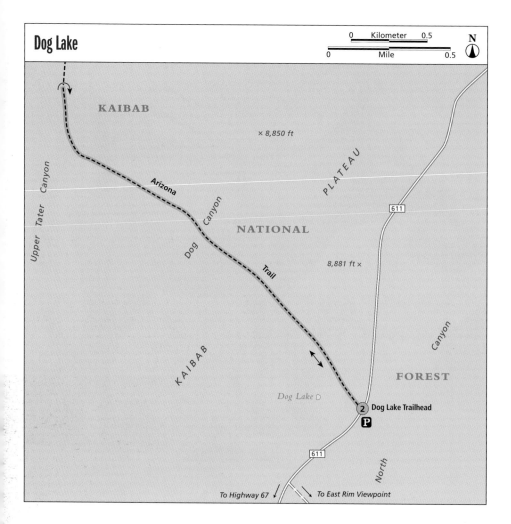

Miles and Directions

0.0   Start at the Dog Lake trailhead.

0.2   Pass Dog Lake.

0.5   Cross Dog Canyon.

1.3   Cross the east rim of Upper Tater Canyon.

1.9   Following a descent via switchbacks, reach Upper Tater Canyon, your turnaround point.

3.8   Arrive back at the trailhead.

3 Widforss Trail

This fine hike along the North Rim of the Grand Canyon is a good choice if you want some great views of the Grand Canyon without the typical viewpoint crowds.

Distance: 8.8 miles out and back
Hiking time: About 5 hours
Difficulty: Moderate
Trail surface: Dirt trails
Best seasons: Summer and fall
Water: No water available
Other trail users: None
Canine compatibility: Dogs prohibited on trails in Grand Canyon National Park

Land status: Grand Canyon National Park
Nearest towns: Kanab, Utah; Page, Arizona
Fees and permits: None
Schedule: Open May 15 through Oct 15
Maps: USGS Bright Angel Point
Trail contacts: Grand Canyon National Park, PO Box 129, Grand Canyon, AZ 86023; (928) 638-7888; www.nps.gov/grca

Finding the trailhead: From Jacob Lake drive south approximately 40 miles on Highway 67, then turn right on the signed road for the Widforss Trail. (If you miss this turnoff, turn around at the better-marked North Kaibab trailhead, about 0.5 mile farther.) Continue 0.5 mile to the signed trailhead for the Widforss Trail, with parking on the left. GPS: N36 13.43'/W112 3.91'

The Hike

The well-maintained trail climbs along a slope, then skirts along a drainage that soon opens out into the Transept, a side canyon. The trail continues along the rim, with occasional views through the dense forest, and then crosses a shallow drainage at the head of the Transept. Shortly after this point, the trail veers away from the rim and continues to Widforss Point at the head of Haunted Canyon. Although the views are more limited than some of the famous viewpoints, the opportunity to enjoy the Grand Canyon without the noise and crowds makes this hike very rewarding.

The Mexican poppy adds a bright yellow splash to hillsides after a wet winter.

Widforss, Ken Patrick, Nankoweap/Saddle Mountain, North Kaibab Trails

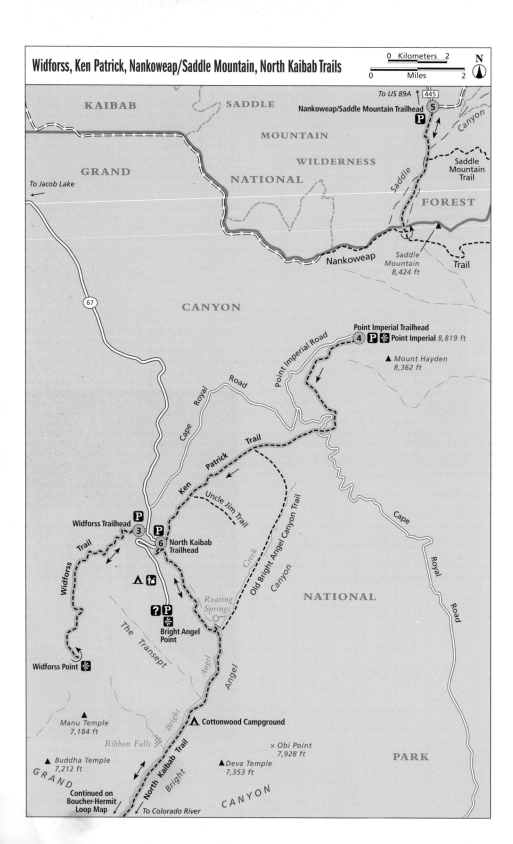

0 Kilometers 2
0 Miles 2

N

KAIBAB

SADDLE

To US 89A 445

Nankoweap/Saddle Mountain Trailhead
P **5**

MOUNTAIN

WILDERNESS

Saddle
Mountain
Trail

GRAND

NATIONAL

Saddle

FOREST

To Jacob Lake

Nankoweap

Saddle
Mountain
8,424 ft

Trail

67

CANYON

Point Imperial Trailhead
4 **P** **Point Imperial** 8,819 ft

Point Imperial Road

▲ Mount Hayden
8,362 ft

Cape
Royal
Road

Ken   Patrick   Trail

Uncle Jim Trail

Old Bright Angel Canyon Trail

Cape

Royal

Road

Creek

Widforss Trailhead
P
3   **P**

Widforss
Trail

North Kaibab
Trailhead
6

Canyon

NATIONAL

Roaring
Springs

▲ **?** **P**

Bright Angel
Point

The   Transept

Widforss Point

Angel

Bright

Angel

Manu Temple
7,184 ft

▲ Cottonwood Campground

× Obi Point
7,928 ft

PARK

Ribbon Falls

▲ Buddha Temple
7,212 ft

GRAND

North Kaibab Trail

Bright

▲ Deva Temple
7,353 ft

Continued on
Boucher-Hermit
Loop Map

To Colorado River

CANYON

Quaking aspen are resplendent in fall color on the North Rim.

Miles and Directions

0.0 Start at the Widforss trailhead.

0.4 Arrive at the first view of the Transept.

1.8 Cross a drainage at the head of the Transept.

2.4 The trail leaves the rim.

4.4 Reach Widforss Point, your turnaround point.

8.8 Arrive back at the trailhead.

4 Ken Patrick Trail

This is a cool and scenic hike along the North Rim of the Grand Canyon in Grand Canyon National Park. A car shuttle is required if you hike the entire trail one-way.

See map on page 36.
Distance: 7.4-mile one-way shuttle
Hiking time: About 4 hours
Difficulty: Moderate
Trail surface: Dirt trails
Best seasons: Summer and fall
Water: No water available
Other trail users: None
Canine compatibility: Dogs prohibited on trails in Grand Canyon National Park

Land status: Grand Canyon National Park
Nearest towns: Kanab, Utah; Page, Arizona
Fees and permits: None for day hiking
Schedule: Open May 15 through Oct 15
Maps: USGS Bright Angel Point, Wahalla Plateau, and Point Imperial
Trail contacts: Grand Canyon National Park, PO Box 129, Grand Canyon, AZ 86023; (928) 638-7888; www.nps.gov/grca

Finding the trailhead: If you walk the entire hike, you'll need to shuttle a vehicle to the end of the hike or arrange for a pickup. From Jacob Lake drive south approximately 40 miles on Highway 67. Turn left into the North Kaibab trailhead, just before entering the North Rim village. GPS: N36 13.03'/W112 3.40'

To reach the start of the hike, go north on Highway 67 about 1 mile (retracing the last mile of the drive), then turn right onto Cape Royal Road. Drive about 5 miles, turn left onto Point Imperial Road, and continue 2.5 miles to Point Imperial. GPS: N36 16.74'/W111 58.75'

The Hike

The trail, named for a park ranger killed in the line of duty, follows the rim west from Point Imperial. There are occasional views, but the thick alpine forest grows right to the edge most of the way. Nevertheless, you'll see tooth-shaped Mount

AWESOME VIEW

While you're visiting the Grand Canyon's North Rim, don't miss the view from Cape Royal, regarded by many as the best viewpoint on either rim that is accessible by paved road. Located at the end of the Cape Royal Road, the viewpoint is an easy 0.5-mile walk. From the overlook the Grand Canyon spreads out before you in a 270-degree panorama, and the depth of the canyon is accentuated by the proximity of several major buttes, including Vishnu Temple and Wotan's Throne.

Hayden and the sharp spire of Sullivan Peak. This section of the trail skirts the many heads of Nankoweap Canyon, a major side canyon. The trail follows the rim around the head of the arm west of Sullivan Peak and heads southeasterly. After passing a point where the Cape Royal Road nearly touches the rim, the trail veers west, away from the rim, and crosses the road. (**Note:** This would be a good goal for an easy day hike.)

After crossing the road the trail gets less use and can be hard to follow through the fir-and-spruce forest. The trail drops down to cross the head of Bright Angel Creek and then loosely follows the rim of Bright Angel Canyon southeast. Most of the time the trail stays on the top of the broad ridge back from the rim. You'll pass the junction with the Old Bright Angel Canyon Trail, which goes left and descends into the canyon. After a couple more miles, the Uncle Jim Trail joins from the left, and the trail becomes more distinct. It dips into the head of Roaring Springs Canyon and then ends at the North Kaibab trailhead.

Mount Hayden is seen from the Ken Patrick Trail.

Miles and Directions

0.0   Start at the Point Imperial trailhead.

2.7   The trail leaves the rim. (**Option:** This is a good turnaround point for an easy out-and-back day hike.)

3.2   Cross Cape Royal Road.

3.6   Cross the head of Bright Angel Canyon.

4.7   Pass junction with Old Bright Angel Canyon Trail on the left.

6.6   Pass the Uncle Jim Trail on the left.

7.0   Cross the head of Roaring Springs Canyon.

7.4   Arrive at the North Kaibab trailhead, your shuttle or pickup point.

5 Nankoweap / Saddle Mountain Trail

This is a great day hike to a little-visited overlook of the Grand Canyon. Access is not as easy as the hikes near North Rim Village, but the remote feeling is well worth the effort.

Distance: 6.0 miles out and back
Hiking time: About 4 hours
Difficulty: Moderate
Trail surface: Dirt trails
Best seasons: Spring and fall
Water: No water available
Other trail users: None
Canine compatibility: Dogs under control allowed

Land status: Saddle Mountain Wilderness, Kaibab National Forest
Nearest towns: Kanab, Utah; Page, Arizona
Fees and permits: None
Schedule: Open all year
Maps: USGS Point Imperial; Kaibab National Forest (North Kaibab Ranger District)
Trail contacts: Kaibab National Forest, 800 S. Sixth St., Williams, AZ 86046; (928) 635-8200; www.fs.usda.gov/kaibab

Finding the trailhead: Turn off US 89A about 20 miles east of Jacob Lake. Head south 27 miles on the House Rock Valley / Buffalo Ranch Road (FR 445) to the wilderness boundary and signed trailhead. GPS: N36 20.78' / W111 57.14'

The Hike

At the end of FR 445, a sign marks the beginning of the Nankoweap / Saddle Mountain Trail. The trail starts off as an old road heading uphill. Piñon pines and junipers grow along the rocky slope. Eventually the trail turns left and traverses the slope before dropping into the upper reaches of Saddle Canyon. Already the scenery is taking on a grand scale. Off to the north are the Vermilion Cliffs. To the east are the Echo Cliffs. Between the two sets of cliffs and slicing into the Marble Platform is Marble Canyon, the beginning of the Grand Canyon.

Closer at hand, mule deer tracks are common on the trail. Also be on the alert for mountain lion tracks and scat. These magnificent predators are rarely seen. From the canyon bottom the Saddle Mountain Trail ascends to the east (and is a delightful 5-mile one-way walk to Marble Canyon). The Nankoweap Trail begins to work its way upstream. Rock cairns and blazes on tree trunks mark the route.

After another 2 miles and a climb of a thousand vertical feet, the trail tops out in the saddle of Saddle Mountain overlooking Nankoweap Canyon, a major drainage into the Grand Canyon. You have also entered Grand Canyon National Park and reached the point where the Nankoweap Trail starts its descent into the Grand Canyon. This is a difficult route into Nankoweap Creek. On the right, a seldom-hiked branch of the Nankoweap climbs west up the ridge to the Kaibab Plateau.

Remember that there is no camping allowed within the park without a Park Service permit. No permit is required in the Saddle Mountain Wilderness Area.

Miles and Directions

0.0 Start at the Nankoweap / Saddle Mountain trailhead.

0.8 The trail traverses a hill, where piñon pines and junipers grow along the slope.

1.3 Reach the bottom of Saddle Canyon and junction with Saddle Mountain Trail going east. Continue upstream on the Nankoweap Trail. (***Option:*** Follow Saddle Mountain Trail 5 miles one-way to Marble Canyon.)

3.0 Reach the rim of the Grand Canyon at the saddle west of Saddle Mountain, your turn-around point.

6.0 Arrive back at the trailhead.

6 North Kaibab Trail

This is a strenuous but rewarding backpack to the Colorado River at the bottom of the Grand Canyon, following the famous transcanyon Kaibab Trail. This route is also used by the Arizona Trail.

See map on pages 36 and 48.
Distance: 28.4 miles out and back
Hiking time: About 2 to 3 days
Difficulty: Strenuous
Trail surface: Dirt trails
Best seasons: Fall and late spring
Water: Roaring Springs, Cottonwood Camp, Phantom Ranch, and Bright Angel Campground
Other trail users: Mule pack trains
Canine compatibility: Dogs prohibited on trails in Grand Canyon National Park

Land status: Grand Canyon National Park
Nearest towns: Kanab, Utah; Page, Arizona
Fees and permits: Permit required for camping in the canyon
Schedule: Open May 15 through Oct 15
Maps: USGS Bright Angel Point and Phantom Ranch
Trail contacts: Grand Canyon National Park, PO Box 129, Grand Canyon, AZ 86023; (928) 638-7888; www.nps.gov/grca

Finding the trailhead: From the Grand Canyon Lodge on the North Rim, drive about 2 miles north on the main entrance road (Highway 67) to the trailhead parking area on the right. GPS: N36 13.03' / W112 3.40'

The Hike

The first 4.7 miles of the North Kaibab Trail quickly descend into Roaring Springs Canyon to meet Bright Angel Creek. Roaring Springs, as the name suggests, can be heard long before it is seen. Water gushes out of a cave in the redwall limestone and cascades down to Bright Angel Creek. Water from the springs is pumped to both the North and South Rims to serve tourists and residents.

About 2 miles down the creek is Cottonwood Campground, a good destination for first-time canyon hikers. Fremont cottonwood, box elders, pale hoptree, Knowlton hop, and coyote willows line the creek banks. American dippers may be seen doing their "kneebends" on boulders in the stream or "flying" underwater in search of aquatic invertebrates to eat.

Back on the main trail, travel another 3 miles to reach the entrance of the Box, where vertical walls of black Precambrian schist tower 1,000 feet above the creek. After 3 miles more you reach Phantom Ranch, built in 1922 and the only lodge within the Grand Canyon. Mail sent out from the ranch will be postmarked "Mailed

Hiker on the North Kaibab Trail ▶

from the bottom of the Canyon." The delightful booklet *Recollections of Phantom Ranch* by Elizabeth Simpson delves into the fascinating history of this isolated guest ranch.

Bright Angel Campground and the Colorado River are about a mile beyond Phantom Ranch.

Strong hikers could do this as a two-day backpack, but breaking it up into three or four days will give you more time to enjoy this remarkable place.

Miles and Directions

0.0 Start at the North Kaibab trailhead.

4.7 Reach Roaring Springs.

6.8 Pass Cottonwood Campground.

14.2 Reach the Colorado River, your turnaround point.

28.4 Arrive back at the trailhead.

Option

About 1.5 miles downstream from Cottonwood Campground is a short side trip to Ribbon Falls. The waters of Ribbon Creek are highly mineralized with calcium carbonate derived from the limestone formations above. As the mineral slowly precipitates out of the creek water, an apron of calcium carbonate, or travertine, is formed behind the falls. Moss, maidenhair ferns, yellow columbine, and scarlet monkey flowers thrive in the spray from the falls.

7 Boucher-Hermit Loop

This is an excellent three-day hike on historic trails in Grand Canyon National Park.

Distance: 19.7-mile loop
Hiking time: About 3 days
Difficulty: Strenuous
Trail surface: Dirt trails
Best season: Fall through spring
Water: Boucher Creek, Hermit Creek
Other trail users: None
Canine compatibility: Dogs prohibited on trails in Grand Canyon National Park

Land status: Grand Canyon National Park
Nearest town: Grand Canyon Village
Fees and permits: Permit required for back-country hiking/camping
Schedule: Open all year
Maps: USGS Grand Canyon
Trail contacts: Grand Canyon National Park, PO Box 129, Grand Canyon, AZ 86023; (928) 638-7888; www.nps.gov/grca

Finding the trailhead: From Grand Canyon Village drive west 4.5 miles to the end of Hermit Road. The signed trailhead for the Hermit Trail is west of the main parking area. During summer the road is closed to private vehicles, and access is via the free West Rim Shuttle. Check with the Park Service when you get your hiking permit for the shuttle schedule. Usually there is a hiker's special, which runs early in the morning. GPS: N36 3.63'/W112 12.73'

The Hike

In hot weather carry plenty of water—it is a long hike to the first water at Boucher Creek. Keep in mind that the temperature rises as you descend. One gallon per person is not excessive. In cool weather two quarts per person is sufficient.

Descend into the canyon on the Hermit Trail, which is named for Louis Boucher. Boucher was a solitary prospector who developed a small mine at nearby Boucher Creek. After a few switchbacks through the cliff-forming Kaibab limestone and the sloping Toroweap Formation, the trail turns west and descends into Hermit Basin. Impressive trail construction was done in the Coconino sandstone, where the trail was paved with slabs of rock set on edge. Cross-bedded layers of rock and sandblasting of the individual grains of sand prove that the Coconino sandstone had its origin in a Sahara-like sand dune desert. Watch for fossil dinosaur tracks along this section of the trail.

In Hermit Basin the trail passes the junction with Waldron Trail and then meets Dripping Spring Trail. Turn left (west) and follow the Dripping Spring Trail as it contours around the head of Hermit Canyon. There are impressive views down this narrow gorge. After heading several bays, you'll meet the Boucher Trail, where you'll turn right. (**FYI:** Dripping Spring is about 0.4 mile west of the junction.) Louis Boucher constructed this trail to reach his mines at Boucher Creek. The Boucher Trail stays on the same level past Yuma Point, giving a view of the Hermit Trail and Hermit Canyon to the east. The soft, red Hermit shale forms this terrace, which the trail remains on

Backpacking along the Trail

until it takes advantage of a break in the cliffs below to descend. About 0.6 mile west of Yuma Point, the trail finds the break and descends abruptly through the layered red Esplanade and Supai sandstones as it drops into the head of Travertine Canyon. After passing through the saddle south of Whites Butte, it descends the massive redwall limestone cliff through a fault to the north. Redwall limestone is actually a translucent gray rock composed entirely of the shells of millions of microscopic animals. These tiny ocean animals died and fell to the deep seafloor as a constant rain. The redwall gets its name from the red stain that seeps down from the overlying red formations and coats the surface of the cliff.

As the slope moderates, the Boucher Trail descends through the greenish Muav limestone and ends at the junction with the Tonto Trail. Turn left (west) to descend about 0.2 mile to Boucher Creek, where there is water and campsites.

The loop hike continues on the Tonto Trail to the north and east. From the rim the Tonto Trail looks flat, but it is constantly climbing and descending to avoid small drainages. It zigs into side canyons and zags back out again. The Tonto Trail typically covers much more distance than the horizontal distance would suggest. Allow plenty of time when hiking this section, especially since you'll be distracted by the occasional spectacular views of Granite Gorge and the Colorado River. The Tonto Plateau, which the trail follows, is formed by the greenish-purple Bright Angel shale, which is soft and erodes into slopes rather than cliffs. The trail crosses Travertine Canyon, where huge deposits of travertine rock indicate the former presence of a large natural spring, now dry. After Travertine Canyon the trail swings into Hermit Canyon and drops into Hermit Creek.

There is always water in Hermit Creek, and there is designated camping at the Park Service campsite on the east side of Hermit Creek at the start of Tapeats Gorge. Until about 1930, Hermit Camp on the Tonto Trail at Hermit Creek was the primary tourist resort in the Grand Canyon. A long aerial tram from Pima Point was used to ferry supplies to the camp. A Model T Ford was even sent down and used on a short network of roads. When the transcanyon Kaibab Trail was completed, the tourism focus quickly switched to the Bright Angel Creek area, the present site of Phantom Ranch resort.

From Hermit Camp start the ascent out of the canyon by hiking northeast on the Tonto Trail. The Hermit Trail is clearly visible ahead, climbing the slopes above the Tonto Plateau. When you reach the junction, turn right (east). At first the climb is gentle, but the grade rapidly becomes steeper as the trail picks its way up the shale slopes. At the foot of the redwall limestone, the trail begins a series of short switchbacks known as the Cathedral Stairs. At the top of the redwall, the trail swings southwest around Breezy Point and passes a section where the original horse trail was destroyed by a landslide. The trail climbs slowly until south of Breezy Point, where it takes advantage of a weakness in the Supai sandstone cliffs and abruptly climbs to the base of the Esplanade sandstone. (Breezy Point is an easy, short side hike with great views of Hermit Camp.) An old rest house marks Santa Maria Spring, which usually has water. Shortly after the spring, the Hermit Trail climbs through the Esplanade sandstone and passes the Dripping Spring Trail junction. Turn left (east) and continue on the Hermit Trail to the rim and the trailhead.

Miles and Directions

0.0 Start at the Hermit trailhead.

1.2 Pass junction with Waldron Trail.

1.5 Turn left onto Dripping Spring Trail. (*FYI:* Dripping Spring is about 0.4 mile west of the junction.)

2.4 Turn right onto Boucher Trail.

5.2 Start the Supai descent.

6.0 Cross Travertine Canyon.

6.7 Start the redwall descent.

7.6 Turn right onto Tonto Trail.

10.3 Cross Travertine Canyon.

12.2 Reach Hermit Creek. (*FYI:* There is a designated Park Service campsite on the east side of Hermit Creek.)

13.1 Turn right onto Hermit Trail.

14.3 Reach top of the redwall.

16.9 Reach Santa Maria Spring.

17.3 Pass junction with Dripping Spring Trail. Turn left (east) and continue on Hermit Trail.

18.5 Pass junction with Waldron Trail.

19.7 Arrive back at the trailhead.

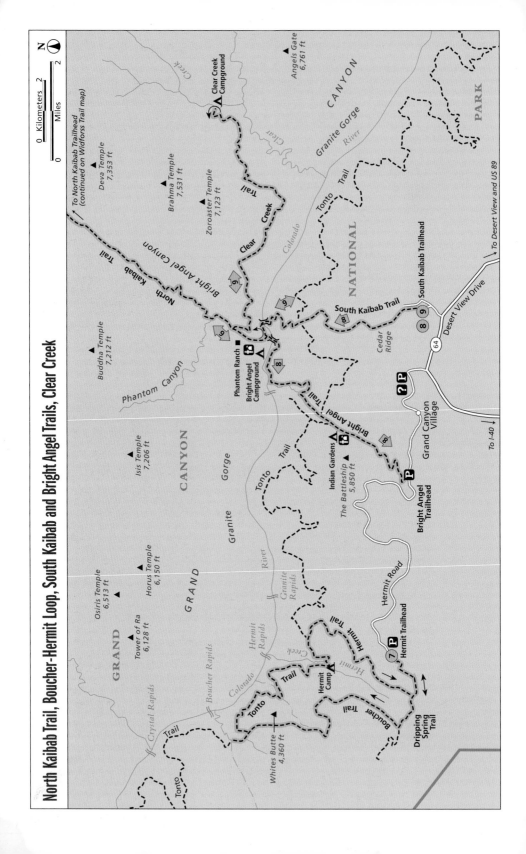

North Kaibab Trail, Boucher-Hermit Loop, South Kaibab and Bright Angel Trails, Clear Creek

N

0 Kilometers 2
0 Miles 2

To North Kaibab Trailhead
(continued on Widforss Trail map)

Clear Creek Campground

Angels Gate
6,761 ft

Deva Temple
7,353 ft

Brahma Temple
7,531 ft

Zoroaster Temple
7,123 ft

GRANITE GORGE

Granite Gorge River

Clear Creek Trail

Clear Creek

Tonto Trail

NATIONAL

South Kaibab Trailhead

South Kaibab Trail

Cedar Ridge

Desert View Drive

To Desert View and US 89

64

Buddha Temple
7,212 ft

Phantom Canyon

North Kaibab Trail

Bright Angel Canyon

Phantom Ranch

Bright Angel Campground

9

9

9

8

8

P

P

Grand Canyon Village

To I-40

Isis Temple
7,206 ft

CANYON

Gorge

Granite

Tonto Trail

Bright Angel Trail

Indian Gardens

The Battleship
5,850 ft

Hermit Road

Bright Angel Trailhead

P

8

Osiris Temple
6,513 ft

Horus Temple
6,150 ft

Tower of Ra
6,128 ft

GRAND

GRAND

CANYON

River

Granite Rapids

Colorado

Hermit Rapids

Boucher Rapids

Crystal Rapids

Hermit Creek

Tonto Trail

Hermit Trail

Hermit Camp

Boucher Trail

Hermit Trail

Dripping Spring Trail

Hermit Trailhead

P

7

Whites Butte
4,360 ft

Tonto Trail

Tonto

PARK

Options

Option 1: From the junction of the Boucher and Tonto Trails at Boucher Creek, it is an easy 2-mile cross-country hike to the Colorado River by descending Boucher Creek into Granite Gorge. As you near the river, you'll be greeted by the roar of Boucher Rapids—small on the Grand Canyon scale but impressive nevertheless.

Option 2: Another great cross-country side hike starts from the campground in Hermit Creek and descends 1.5 miles along Hermit Canyon to the Colorado River. The Tapeats sandstone, a rock that was derived from beach sand, forms the rim of lower Hermit Creek. The somber dark-gray rocks of the gorge are Vishnu schist, one of the oldest rocks on Earth. The hard, twisted schist is the root of an ancient mountain range that was entirely eroded away, leaving the nearly flat surface on which rests the Tapeats sandstone. The side canyon ends at Hermit Rapids, one of the largest in the Grand Canyon. For modern river craft, Hermit Rapids is fun but not difficult—the water is deep and free of rocks. At high water the waves reach heights of 20 feet or more. During the walk along Hermit Creek, you'll see sections of trail construction from the tourist resort days.

8 South Kaibab and Bright Angel Trails

This is the classic overnight hike in the Grand Canyon, using the only two maintained trails that descend into the canyon within the national park.

See map on page 48.
Distance: 16.1 miles one-way with a shuttle
Hiking time: About 2 days
Difficulty: Strenuous
Trail surface: Dirt trails
Best season: Fall through spring
Water: Bright Angel Campground, Indian Gardens; in summer only, Three-Mile and One-and-a-Half Mile Rest Houses
Other trail users: Mule pack trains

ELEVATION CHANGE: 4780 FT.

Canine compatibility: Dogs prohibited on trails in Grand Canyon National Park
Land status: Grand Canyon National Park
Nearest town: Grand Canyon Village
Fees and permits: Entrance fee; permit and fee required for backcountry camping
Schedule: Open all year
Maps: USGS Phantom Ranch
Trail contacts: Grand Canyon National Park, PO Box 129, Grand Canyon, AZ 86023; (928) 638-7888; www.nps.gov/grca

Finding the trailhead: The hike starts at the South Kaibab trailhead near Yaki Point. GPS: N36 3.19'/W112 5.02'. Access is via the park shuttle bus. The exit, at Bright Angel trailhead at the west end of Grand Canyon Village, is also accessible via the park shuttles, so the best place to leave your vehicle is in Grand Canyon Village near the Bright Angel trailhead.

The Hike

This is the backpack loop that many first-timers to the Grand Canyon give a try. Most go down the South Kaibab, since it is steeper than the Bright Angel. This loop can be done as an overnight, but you will have more time to look around (and rest those sore muscles) as a three-day trip.

Start by descending South Kaibab Trail. Like most Grand Canyon trails, this one starts by steeply switchbacking through the upper cliffs of the Kaibab, Toroweap, and Coconino Formations. At about 1.3 miles you reach Cedar Ridge, where there is a toilet. The ridge makes a good turnaround spot for day hikers.

The South Kaibab Trail leaves Cedar Ridge, circles under O'Neil Butte, and then plunges through the Redwall, Muav, and Bright Angel Layers before leveling off on the Tonto Plateau. But relief is short-lived, since the trail suddenly begins another set of steep switchbacks leading down to the Colorado River. The Kaibab Suspension Bridge (aka Black Bridge), built in 1928, takes you across the river, and another 0.5 mile brings you to the Bright Angel Campground, which has designated campsites, drinking water, and a bathroom with running water. Phantom Ranch, where mule riders stay, is located just north of the campground. There is also a Hikers Dorm for those hikers who don't want to camp out. Hot and cold drinks are available at Phantom Ranch.

To get out of this big hole in the ground, hike from the campground area toward the river. Instead of returning to the Black Bridge, cross the wooden Bright Angel Creek bridge and follow the trail to the Silver Bridge, built in the late 1960s to support the pipeline carrying water from Roaring Springs to the South Rim. On the far side of this bridge, turn right and follow the River Trail for 1.5 miles to its junction with the Bright Angel Trail and the River House stone shelter. From here it's only 7.8 miles and 4,400 vertical feet to the South Rim.

At Indian Gardens, 4.5 miles from the South Rim, are toilets, drinking water, a picnic area, and a campground. During the warmer months there is drinking water available at 3 miles and 1.5 miles from the rim.

The trail passes through a short tunnel just below the rim. Before entering the tunnel, look up to your right. There under an overhang are some red pictographs, presumably painted by ancient Indians. Once you reach the South Rim and the Bright Angel trailhead, you will find yourself near the historic Kolb Studio at the west end of Grand Canyon Village.

Miles and Directions

0.0   Start at the South Kaibab trailhead.

1.3   Reach Cedar Ridge. (**FYI:** There is a toilet available at Cedar Ridge.) (**Option:** This is a good turnaround spot for day hikers.)

5.5   Cross the Colorado River on the suspension bridge.

6.0   Arrive at Bright Angel Campground. (**FYI:** The campground has designated sites, drinking water, and a bathroom with running water.)

8.3   Pass the River House stone shelter.

11.6 Reach Indian Gardens. (**FYI:** There are toilets, drinking water, a picnic area, and a campground here.)

16.1 Arrive at Bright Angel trailhead and pick up the shuttle.

9 Clear Creek

This is a multiday backpack trip to a perennial stream located in a dramatic canyon complex below the North Rim of Grand Canyon.

See map on page 48.
Distance: 29.4 miles out and back
Hiking time: About 4 days
Difficulty: Strenuous
Trail surface: Dirt trails
Best season: Fall through spring
Water: Bright Angel Campground, Clear Creek
Other trail users: Mule pack trains on the South Kaibab Trail
Canine compatibility: Dogs prohibited on trails in Grand Canyon National Park

Land status: Grand Canyon National Park
Nearest town: Grand Canyon Village
Fees and permits: Entrance fee; permit and fee required for backcountry camping
Schedule: Open all year
Maps: USGS Phantom Ranch
Trail contacts: Grand Canyon National Park, PO Box 129, Grand Canyon, AZ 86023; (928) 638-7888; www.nps.gov/grca

---

Finding the trailhead: Access to the trail is via the park shuttle bus to the South Kaibab trailhead. GPS: N36 3.19'/W112 5.02'

The Hike

The hike starts at the South Kaibab trailhead near Yaki Point. Descend the South Kaibab Trail to the junction with the River Trail just above the Colorado River. Stay right and cross the Kaibab Suspension Bridge (aka Black Bridge) onto the North Kaibab Trail. The trail follows the east bank of Bright Angel Creek past Bright Angel Campground, then passes through Phantom Ranch. An easy stroll up Bright Angel Canyon on the North Kaibab Trail brings you to the start of the Clear Creek Trail, where you'll turn right to start the ascent out of Bright Angel Canyon.

Several switchbacks later you begin to have great views up and down Bright Angel Canyon and beyond. The Civilian Conservation Corps built this well-constructed trail in 1933. At one switchback corner there is a stone bench—a good place to take off the pack and enjoy the scenery.

The trail eventually rounds a bend. The Colorado River, entrenched in the Inner Gorge, is directly below you. Across the way you can see the South Kaibab Trail making its steep descent into the gorge. Notice the near canyon wall. Here is the contact between the very ancient foliated and shiny (due to mica) Precambrian schist and the coarse, dark-brown Cambrian Tapeats sandstone. The contact represents a gap in geologic time of about 1 billion years—known to geologists as the Great Unconformity.

Once gaining the Tonto Plateau, which is essentially the top of the Tapeats Sandstone Formation, the Clear Creek Trail meanders eastward around Sumner Butte

Along the South Kaibab Trail near O'Neill Butte

and Bradley and Demaray Points. On a hot day with a heavy backpack, the trail can become tedious. But remember that you are slowly climbing in elevation almost all the way to Clear Creek, so the return trip is slightly downhill and therefore faster. Plus your pack should be lighter by then and your body more fit.

The trail must travel north into Clear Creek Canyon quite a ways before making its final descent to the creek and Clear Creek Campground, the backcountry campsite.

Miles and Directions

0.0 Start at South Kaibab trailhead.

1.3 Reach Cedar Ridge.

5.3 Pass junction with River Trail; stay right on the South Kaibab Trail.

5.5 Cross the Colorado River on the Kaibab Suspension Bridge and take the North Kaibab Trail.

6.0 Arrive at Bright Angel Campground.

6.2 Turn right at the junction with the Clear Creek Trail.

8.6 Reach top of Tonto Plateau.

14.4 Begin descent into Clear Creek.

14.7 Reach Clear Creek Campground, your turnaround point.

29.4 Arrive back at the trailhead.

Options

Option 1: From the Clear Creek Campground, there are several options for day hikes. Going downstream from the campground, the Colorado River is about 4 miles distant. A small waterfall near the river is known as the Sideways Waterfall because a scallop in the polished schist usually deflects a jet of water sideways. Getting past this obstacle requires a scramble down along its right side, which can be difficult during high water when the rock may be wet. Your reward for the long walk down the creek is a fine section of Granite Gorge where the Colorado River flows quietly through impressively narrow walls. In the 1880s the river rose more than 80 feet here during spring runoff. More than 300,000 cubic feet per second poured past the mouth of Clear Creek, as evidenced by driftwood found high up on the cliffs. This volume of water is more than twice that recorded since, and far more than the normal average of 20,000 cubic feet per second.

Option 2: Many springtime hikers walk upstream from Clear Creek Campground about 4 miles in hopes of getting a glimpse of Cheyava Falls, one of the tallest waterfalls in the Grand Canyon when it is flowing. Its flow depends on the amount of rain and snow the North Rim receives.

However, going upstream can be problematic. In some years the stream flow is so high and vegetation so thick that upstream progress may be impossible or at least very dangerous. In other years flash floods may have scoured out the vegetation and the stream may be low. In those years, walking along the creek is no problem, but the falls may be no more than a damp stain on the canyon wall. When you pick up your hiking permit, ask the ranger for the latest information.

10 Horseshoe Mesa

This hike features a historic mining district on Horseshoe Mesa in Grand Canyon National Park. Most of the trails in the Grand Canyon were built by miners and prospectors. Some, like the Grandview, were improved to serve the increasing number of tourists coming to the area at the end of the nineteenth century.

Distance: 4.0 miles out and back
Hiking time: About 4 hours
Difficulty: Strenuous
Trail surface: Dirt trails
Best season: Fall through spring
Water: No water available
Other trail users: None
Canine compatibility: Dogs prohibited on trails in Grand Canyon National Park

Land status: Grand Canyon National Park
Nearest town: Grand Canyon Village
Fees and permits: None for day hikes
Schedule: Open all year
Maps: USGS Grandview Point and Cape Royal
Trail contacts: Grand Canyon National Park, PO Box 129, Grand Canyon, AZ 86023; (928) 638-7888; www.nps.gov/grca

Finding the trailhead: From Grand Canyon Village drive south on the main park road, then turn east onto Desert View Drive. Eleven miles from the village, turn left (north) onto the signed Grandview Point Road. Park in the signed Grandview trailhead parking area. GPS: N35 59.87' / W112 59.26'

The Hike

Although this a strenuous hike, it should be no problem for experienced hikers. Keep in mind that the short distance is deceiving. The trail descends 2,400 feet, and you will have to climb this distance on the way out. The Grandview Trail is well named—it features an expansive view right from its start at the east side of the stone wall at the viewpoint. A series of switchbacks leads through the cliffs of the Kaibab limestone and out onto the steep slopes of the Toroweap Formation. Clever trail construction is used in sections through the Coconino sandstone. Parts of the trail are paved with blocks of sandstone fitted on edge, and in other places the trail is built up with log

HISTORY OF THE TRAIL

Pete Berry established the old copper mine before the turn of the twentieth century, and the Grandview Trail was constructed to service the mine. The stone cookhouse still stands several hundred yards north of the campground. A vertical shaft on the mesa provided air to one of the mines, but the main access was via a horizontal shaft just below the rim to the southeast. Another shaft is located near the base of the redwall limestone farther to the east. Water was obtained from either Page Spring or a spring in Cottonwood Creek.

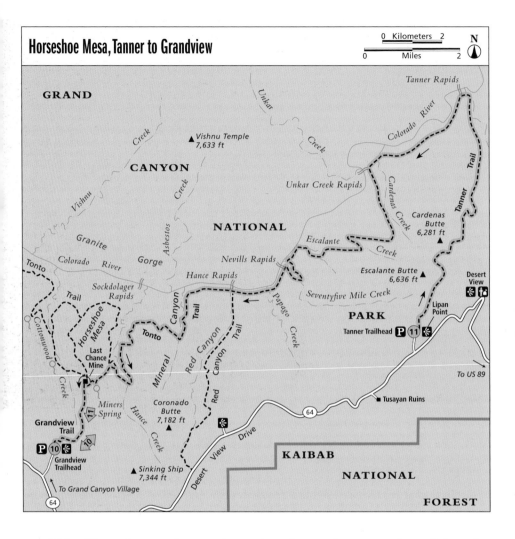

Horseshoe Mesa, Tanner to Grandview

0 Kilometers 2

0 Miles 2

N

GRAND

Tanner Rapids

CANYON

Unkar Creek

Colorado River

Vishnu Temple
7,633 ft

Unkar Creek Rapids

Cardenas Creek

Tanner Trail

Vishnu Creek

Asbestos Creek

NATIONAL

Escalante

Cardenas
Butte
6,281 ft

Escalante Creek

Escalante Butte
6,636 ft

Desert
View

Granite

Colorado River

Gorge

Nevills Rapids

Hance Rapids

Seventyfive Mile Creek

Lipan
Point

Tonto

Sockdolager
Rapids

Trail

Red Canyon Trail

Canyon Trail

Papago Creek

PARK

Tanner Trailhead P 11

Cottonwood Creek

Horseshoe Mesa

Tonto

Mineral Canyon

Red Canyon

To US 89

Last
Chance
Mine

Miners
Spring

Coronado
Butte
7,182 ft

Hance Creek

Desert View Drive

64

Tusayan Ruins

Grandview
Trail

P 10

10

Grandview
Trailhead

Sinking Ship
7,344 ft

KAIBAB

NATIONAL

To Grand Canyon Village

64

FOREST

cribbing. These places can become interesting when a winter storm leaves 2 feet of snow on the trail. After reaching the red slopes of the Hermit shale, the trail descends east and then north around the head of Cottonwood Creek and finally comes out onto Horseshoe Mesa.

When you reach the top of the redwall limestone, it appears that you should be on the same level as Horseshoe Mesa, which is formed on the upper surface of the redwall. However, you'll still descend another 200 feet onto the mesa. This difference is caused by the displacement along the Grandview Fault, which you cross as you descend onto Horseshoe Mesa. The Park Service campground is near the abandoned Last Chance Mine, which is interesting to explore. (**Caution:** Do not enter the old mine shafts—they are very dangerous.)

Descending the Grandview Trail

Miles and Directions

0.0 Start at the Grandview trailhead on Grandview Point Road.

2.0 Reach the Last Chance Mine on Horseshoe Mesa, your turnaround point.

4.0 Arrive back at the trailhead.

11 Tanner to Grandview

Using two of the most scenic trails in Grand Canyon, this hike features some of the canyon's most interesting geology.

See map on page 56.
Distance: 24.8-mile one-way with shuttle
Hiking time: About 4 days
Difficulty: Strenuous
Trail surface: Dirt trails
Best season: Fall through spring
Water: Colorado River, Hance Creek, Page Spring (shown as Miners Spring on the USGS map)
Other trail users: None
Canine compatibility: Dogs prohibited on trails in Grand Canyon National Park

Land status: Grand Canyon National Park
Nearest town: Grand Canyon Village
Schedule: Open all year
Fees and permits: Entrance fee; permit and fee required for backcountry camping
Maps: USGS Desert View, Cape Royal, and Grandview Point
Trail contacts: Grand Canyon National Park, PO Box 129, Grand Canyon, AZ 86023; (928) 638-7888; www.nps.gov/grca

Finding the trailhead: This one-way hike requires a car shuttle. To reach the end of the hike from Grand Canyon Village, drive south on the main park road, then turn east onto Desert View Drive. Eleven miles from the village, turn left (north) onto the signed Grandview Point Road; park in the signed trailhead parking area. GPS: N35 59.87' / W112 59.26'

To reach the start of the hike from Grandview Point, turn left (east) onto Desert View Drive. Go about 11 miles to Lipan Point, and turn left into the parking area. GPS: N36 1.95' / W111 51.13'

The Hike

The Tanner trailhead is signed and starts on the east side of the parking lot to the south of the viewpoint. A steep series of switchbacks descend rapidly through the rim formations to the saddle at the head of Seventyfive Mile Creek. After the confinement of the upper section of the trail, the sudden view to the west is startling. The trail now contours around Escalante and Cardenas Buttes on the gentle slopes of the red Supai sandstone. At the north end of Cardenas Butte, the trail descends abruptly through the redwall limestone in a series of switchbacks, then works its way through the greenish Muav limestone and greenish-purple Bright Angel shale slopes.

There are a few small campsites scattered around the mouth of Tanner Canyon at the Colorado River. Tanner Canyon is normally dry, but water can be obtained from the river. The route now turns south and follows the bench just above the river. Although there has never been a formal trail between Tanner and Red Canyons, enough hikers have traveled the route to create a trail. Tanner Rapids, visible below, is shallow and rocky and creates more of a problem for riverboats than some of the larger rapids. After skirting a narrow section where the river presses against its left bank, the trail moves inland and follows the foot of the shale slopes to the mouth of

Backpacking the Tanner Trail

Cardenas Creek. Campsites are more plentiful here than back at the mouth of Tanner Canyon.

The trail crosses Cardenas Creek but dead-ends with a view of Unkar Creek Rapids, which makes it a worthwhile side trip of about a mile round-trip. Your route goes up the dry bed of Cardenas Creek about 0.2 mile and then climbs onto the ridge above the river. Walk to the west edge for a spectacular view of Unkar Creek Rapids, 200 feet straight down. Now turn south and climb the gentle red-shale ridge directly toward Escalante Butte. Stay on the crest of the ridge to pick up the trail again as the ridge narrows. The trail turns west and heads the nameless canyon west of Cardenas Creek at about the 3,800-foot level. After rounding the west end of the point, the trail turns back to the east to descend into Escalante Creek. Walk down the bed of Escalante Creek, and then leave the bed at about the 3,200-foot level (there is an impassable fall farther downstream) and climb through a low saddle to the south. Descend into the unnamed south fork of Escalante Creek and follow it to the

CHANGE IN TOPOGRAPHY

As the Tanner Trail comes out on the ridge below the redwall limestone, it winds through massive fallen blocks of Tapeats sandstone. These outcrops and broken remnants mark the level of the rim of Granite Gorge to the west, but here in the eastern Grand Canyon, the floor of the canyon is more open and valley-like, filled with gently rolling hills. As the Tanner Trail descends the long ridge west of Tanner Canyon, the reason for the change in the canyon's topography is apparent. Farther west in the Grand Canyon, the hard Vishnu schist is found at this level, and the resistant rock forms cliffs. Here the softer shales of the Grand Canyon series replace the Vishnu schist and erode into relatively gentle slopes and valleys.

Colorado River (a barrier fall has an obvious bypass on the left). Nevills Rapids is a minor one, but as the river enters Granite Gorge ahead, it crashes through some of the hardest rapids in the canyon.

Turn left along the river's left bank. Notice how a rising ramp of hard rock forms a cliff right into the river and forces our route to climb. The bench is Shinumo quartzite, a layer of resistant rock near the bottom of the Grand Canyon series. As the river rolls downstream through this section, the rocks at river level become harder and the gorge becomes steeper-walled and deeper. The contrast between this section and the river valley at the foot of the Tanner Trail is already impressive, but the narrowest section is still downstream. After about 0.5 mile the route reaches the rim of Seventyfive Mile Canyon and turns east along the edge of the narrow, impassable gorge. About 0.4 mile up this side canyon, the route drops into the bed and follows it back to the river, passing almost directly underneath the trail 200 feet above. At the river turn left (downstream) again, and walk about 0.6 mile along the easy beach to the mouth of Papago Creek. There are several good campsites here for small groups.

Just downstream of Papago Creek, a cliff falls directly into the river and appears to block the route. Go up Papago Creek a few yards and climb up a steep gully, which will require some scrambling. Work your way up easier ledges above to a point about 300 feet above the river, and then traverse east. If you are on the correct level, you will be able to reach the head of a steep gully that can be used to descend back to river level. The usual error is to traverse too low. If this happens, retrace your steps until you can climb to a higher level. Once you reach the river, a good trail follows the bank to the mouth of Red Canyon.

There is limited, sandy camping at Red Canyon. The Red Canyon Trail goes up the bed here and could be used for an early exit if necessary, but it is steeper and harder to follow than the Grandview Trail. At this point, start on the Tonto Trail, which climbs the slopes to the west. The view of mile-long Hance Rapids is great. Hance is one of the hardest Grand Canyon rapids to navigate due to the numerous rocks. As you continue to climb above the river on the Tonto Trail, note the trail climbing the slope on the opposite side of the river. This trail goes to Asbestos Canyon and was used to reach the asbestos mines on the north side of the river.

About a mile from Red Canyon, the Tonto Trail turns south. After crossing dry Mineral Canyon, the trail turns west again and climbs a bit more to reach the greenish-gray shale slopes below Ayer Point. This terrace is called the Tonto Plateau and forms a prominent shelf about 1,200 feet above the Colorado River. The rim of the Tonto Plateau is formed from the hard Tapeats sandstone and overlooks dark, narrow Granite Gorge, already impressive in this area. The Tonto Trail follows the Tonto Plateau for about 60 miles. After Ayer Point the Tonto Trail turns south into Hance Canyon along the Tapeats sandstone rim. Hance Creek may be dry where the trail crosses, but there is always water a short distance downstream. There is also camping downstream, below the impressive Tapeats narrows.

After crossing Hance Creek the Tonto Trail continues northwest about 0.5 mile to a side canyon coming from the east side of Horseshoe Mesa. Turn west here onto the East Grandview Trail. Page Spring (shown as Miners Spring on the USGS map) is reliable. It is reached from a spur trail about a mile from the Tonto Trail junction. The final section of the trail climbs the high redwall limestone cliff at the canyon head to reach Horseshoe Mesa and the junction with the main Grandview Trail. There is a Park Service campground on Horseshoe Mesa, but water will have to be carried from Hance Creek or Page Spring.

Turn left onto the Grandview Trail and climb 2 miles to the rim at Grandview Point.

Miles and Directions

0.0 Start at the Tanner trailhead at Lipan Point.

1.2 Reach the head of Seventyfive Mile Creek.

3.4 Begin the redwall descent.

4.3 Start down the ridge above Tanner Canyon.

6.5 Reach the Colorado River at Tanner Canyon. (*FYI:* A few small campsites are scattered around the mouth of the canyon.)

8.9 Reach and cross Cardenas Creek. (*FYI:* Campsites are available.)

10.7 Begin the traverse into Escalante Creek.

12.8 Descend to Escalante Creek.

14.6 Pass Nevills Rapids.

15.3 Reach the mouth of Papago Creek. (*FYI:* Campsites for small groups are available.)

16.1 Reach the mouth of Red Canyon. (*FYI:* Limited, sandy camping is available.)

18.3 Cross Mineral Canyon.

21.5 Cross Hance Creek.

22.8 Pass side canyon coming from the east side of Horseshoe Mesa and turn west onto East Grandview Trail.

24.8 Reach the Grandview trailhead and your shuttle.

Northeast Plateaus

This part of the Colorado Plateau is Navajo and Hopi country, occupied by the tribes' two vast reservations. Hiking and exploring this portion of the Colorado Plateau requires that you respect the native cultural resources as well as backcountry residences. The scenery is spectacular and the cultural experience unrivaled.

Rainbow Bridge and the snow-covered slopes of Navajo Mountain

12 Rainbow Bridge Trail

This is a challenging backpack into some spectacular canyon country to the largest natural bridge in the country.

Distance: 23.6 miles out and back
Hiking time: About 2 or 3 days
Difficulty: Strenuous
Trail surface: Unmaintained dirt trails
Best seasons: Spring and fall
Water: Cliff Canyon, Bridge Canyon
Other trail users: None
Canine compatibility: Dogs prohibited in Rainbow Bridge National Monument

Land status: Navajo Indian Reservation, Rainbow Bridge National Monument
Nearest town: Page
Fees and permits: Permit required from Navajo Nation but may be difficult to obtain
Schedule: Open all year
Maps: USGS Chaiyahi Flat and Rainbow Bridge
Trail contacts: Navajo Nation Parks and Recreation, PO Box 2520, Window Rock, AZ 86515; (928) 871-6647; http://navajonationparks.org

Finding the trailhead: Getting to the trailhead can be an adventure in itself. From Page take Highway 98 about 56 miles southeast to Indian Route 16 (the Inscription House / Navajo Mountain Road). Turn left (north) and drive about 32 miles to a major fork. The right takes you to the old Navajo Mountain Trading Post and Rainbow City, a government housing area. Take the left fork. In about 4 miles you will see a large dome of naked sandstone, Haystack Rock, looming ahead. Take the road to the right of the rock. Pass a Navajo home; shortly you will see a well. Park here unless you have a four-wheel-drive vehicle. The last mile of the road is sometimes so badly washed out that it's difficult for ordinary cars to make it to the trailhead at the ruins of the old Rainbow Lodge, once owned by the late Senator Barry Goldwater. GPS: N36 59.74' / W110 53.55'

The Hike

Rock cairns mark the trailhead on the west side of the parking area. At first the trail is an old road, but it quickly becomes a narrow path. In about a 0.5 mile the trail descends and crosses First Canyon. It crosses Horse Canyon in another 1.5 miles. At both crossings you may notice several paths. They all pretty much do the same thing and eventually rejoin. The trail continues to skirt the rugged slopes around the base of Navajo Mountain until reaching a pass near the head of Cliff Canyon. The trail rapidly descends a steep talus slope to the floor of the canyon.

A seasonal spring may be found a mile or so farther downcanyon. A sign usually marks where to turn right into Redbud Pass—a narrow, spectacular crack in the Navajo sandstone walls—but it won't hurt to refer to your map often. Redbud Pass is rugged and partially blocked by rockslides. In one place you probably will have to take off your pack, lower it, and then scramble down.

Once over the pass, the trail meets Redbud Creek, which may be dry, but shortly joins the permanent Rainbow Bridge Creek. The Old Rainbow Bridge Trail comes

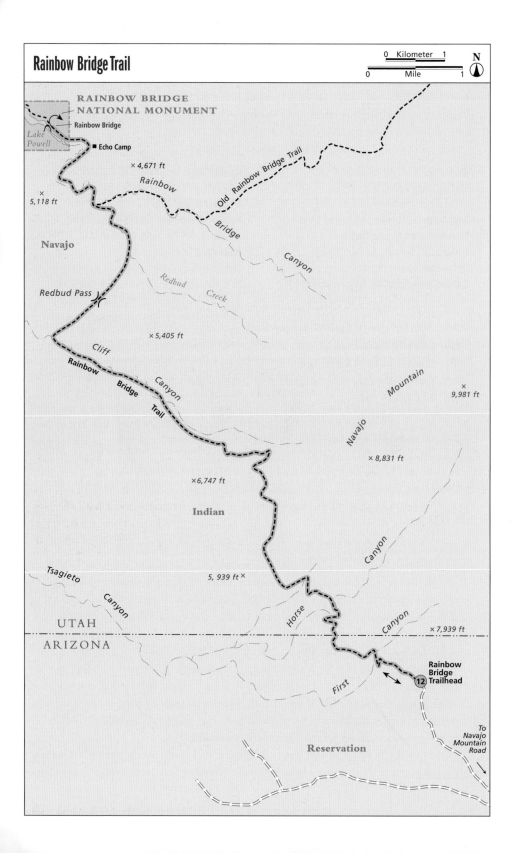

Rainbow Bridge Trail

0   Kilometer   1
0   Mile   1

N

**RAINBOW BRIDGE
NATIONAL MONUMENT**

Rainbow Bridge

■ Echo Camp

*Lake
Powell*

× 4,671 ft

Rainbow

Old Rainbow Bridge Trail

×
5,118 ft

Navajo

Bridge

Canyon

Redbud Pass

Redbud

Creek

× 5,405 ft

Cliff

Rainbow

Canyon

Bridge

Trail

Mountain

×
9,981 ft

×6,747 ft

Navajo

× 8,831 ft

Indian

Canyon

Tsagieto

5, 939 ft ×

Canyon

UTAH

Horse

Canyon

× 7,939 ft

ARIZONA

**Rainbow
Bridge
Trailhead**

12

First

Canyon

*To
Navajo
Mountain
Road*

Reservation

down Rainbow Bridge Creek. (This was the original route into Rainbow Bridge, but it is little used today.) There are some excellent campsites along Rainbow Bridge Creek. From here down to Rainbow Bridge, the canyon walls grow higher and higher and the scenery more and more amazing. About 0.5 mile before the bridge, the trail passes a huge cave called Echo Camp, where horse pack trips would camp in the days before Lake Powell.

▶ **Rainbow Bridge is sacred to the Navajo Nation, and the tribe requests that hikers respect the bridge by not walking underneath it.**

Although Rainbow Bridge is one of the largest natural bridges in the world—290 feet high and 275 feet wide—in some ways, reaching the bridge is anticlimactic. The surrounding cliffs dwarf the bridge, and there may be a lot of tourists here who arrived by boat. Yet the hike in is worth every step.

Miles and Directions

0.0 Start at the Rainbow Bridge trailhead at Rainbow Lodge.

0.6 Following a descent, cross First Canyon.

2.0 Cross Horse Canyon.

4.6 Traverse the rim of Cliff Canyon.

6.3 Following a rapid descent, reach the floor of Cliff Canyon.

7.6 Turn right into Redbud Pass.

9.6 Reach Rainbow Bridge Canyon and the Old Rainbow Bridge Trail.

11.8 Arrive at Rainbow Bridge, your turnaround point.

23.6 Arrive back at the trailhead.

Option

The topo map shows another, longer trail skirting the north slopes of Navajo Mountain. This is the route used by the 1909 Rainbow Bridge Discovery Expedition. It is much less used than the Rainbow Bridge Trail but does offer access to the labyrinth of canyons flanking the mountain.

13 Keet Seel Trail

This overnight backpack trip features one of the largest and best-preserved cliff houses in Arizona.

Distance: 14.0 miles out and back
Hiking time: About 8 hours or 2 days
Difficulty: Strenuous
Trail surface: Dirt trails plus slickrock and sand
Best season: Memorial Day to Labor Day
Water: Seasonal in creek
Other trail users: Horses
Canine compatibility: Dogs prohibited in Navajo National Monument
Land status: Navajo Indian Reservation, Navajo National Monument
Nearest town: Kayenta
Fees and permits: Permit required; reservations can be made up to 60 days in advance.

Visits to Keet Seel are closely regulated to preserve the ruin and prevent vandalism.
Schedule: Open Memorial Day to Labor Day
Maps: USGS Betatakin Ruin, Keet Seel Ruin, and Marsh Pass
Trail contacts: Navajo National Monument, PO Box 7717, Shonto, AZ 86045; (928) 672-2700; www.nps.gov/nava/index.htm
Special considerations: The Park Service will give you directions to the trailhead when you pick up your hiking permit at the visitor center. Before receiving your permit, you must attend a trail orientation meeting either at 4 p.m. the day before your hike or at 8:15 a.m. the day of your hike. You must be on the trail no later than 9:15 a.m.

Finding the trailhead: From Kayenta drive about 20 miles southwest on US 160. Turn right (north) onto Highway 564 and drive another 10 miles to Navajo National Monument. GPS: N36 40.67'/W110 32.445'

The Hike

This trail takes you to one of the largest and most spectacular prehistoric cliff houses in Arizona—the 160-room Keet Seel, tucked under a huge overhang in a remote canyon. People of the Anasazi culture lived for more than a thousand years in the Four Corners region—the area where Utah, Colorado, New Mexico, and Arizona join at a common point.

The trail begins with a short but steep sandy descent to Laguna Creek in Tsegi Canyon. The trail then crosses the creek and heads up Keet Seel Canyon, passing the mouth of Dowozhiebito Canyon, which enters from the right. Most of the route traverses reservation land, and it's not uncommon to encounter Navajos on horseback or foot tending flocks of sheep or goats. Remember that the Park Service permit does not give you permission to deviate from the trail onto other Navajo land.

Keet Seel is an especially well-preserved Anasazi cliff dwelling.

The route up Keet Seel Canyon is between towering walls of Navajo sandstone stained with long, dark stripes of desert varnish. The ledge-forming Kayenta Formation underlies the Navajo. Rainwater easily soaks into the porous sandstone and is pulled downward by gravity. When this groundwater encounters the shales and clay beds in the Kayenta, its downward journey is interrupted. The water then begins to migrate horizontally and, if it comes to a cliff face, emerges as a seep or spring. Look for these seeps at the contact between the Navajo and Kayenta Formations. Remember, too, to treat all water before drinking.

About 0.5 mile from Keet Seel, there is a primitive campground but no purified water. You may enter the cliff house only with the ranger on duty.

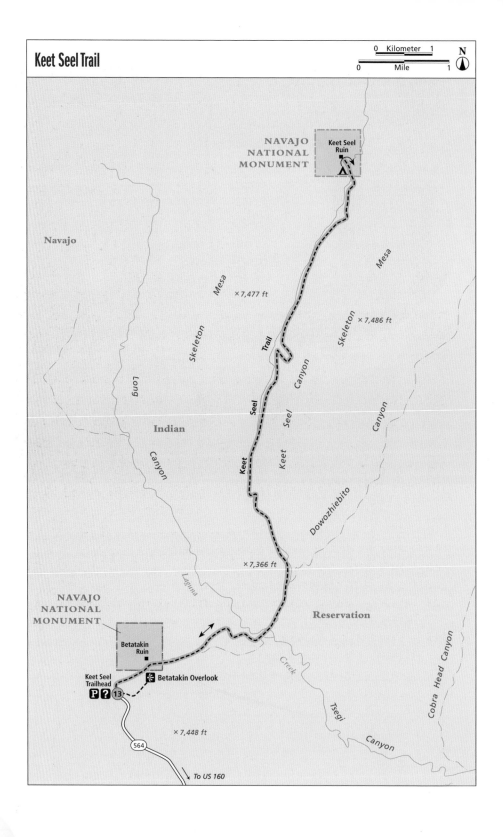

Keet Seel Trail

0 Kilometer 1
0 Mile 1
N

NAVAJO
NATIONAL
MONUMENT

Keet Seel
Ruin

Navajo

Mesa
× 7,477 ft

Skeleton

Mesa

Skeleton
× 7,486 ft

Trail

Long

Canyon

Indian

Seel

Seel

Canyon

Canyon

Keet

Keet

Dowozhiebito

× 7,366 ft

NAVAJO
NATIONAL
MONUMENT

Reservation

Laguna

Betatakin
Ruin

Cobra Head Canyon

Keet Seel
Trailhead
P ? 13

Betatakin Overlook

Creek

Tsegi

Canyon

× 7,448 ft

564

To US 160

LOOK BUT DON'T TOUCH

Along the trail grow high desert plants typical of the Colorado Plateau country—four-wing saltbush, big sage, virgin's bower, Mormon tea, rabbitbrush, snakeweed, skunkbush, juniper, and piñon. You may be lucky and spot a rock squirrel or chipmunk-like antelope squirrel, although most of the canyon country's mammals tend to be nocturnal. Common ravens, turkey vultures, scrub jays, canyon wrens, rock wrens, red-tailed hawks, and other birds may be seen or heard.

Keet Seel is a Navajo phrase meaning "broken pottery," and along the trail you may see pottery shards and other artifacts eroding out of the sand. Admire and photograph them, but please return them to exactly where you found them. Visitors sometimes pile artifacts on a rock for a picture and then leave them there. These "museum rocks" do not reveal as much information to archaeologists as leaving artifacts where they are discovered. All prehistoric artifacts are protected by federal, state, and tribal laws and should not be collected. Besides, the canyon spirits will haunt you.

From the mid-tenth century to the late thirteenth, several hundred Anasazi people occupied Tsegi Canyon and its tributary, Keet Seel. Here they grew corn and several kinds of beans and squash, tended turkeys, and created exquisite pottery painted with geometric and animal designs. Then in the late 1200s, the Anasazi began to abandon the area. The exact cause is uncertain but is likely a combination of drought, disease, warfare, overpopulation, and the attraction of an emerging new religion at the time over in New Mexico.

Miles and Directions

0.0 Start at the trailhead by the visitor center and begin to descend.

0.9 Reach and then cross Laguna Creek.

1.3 Pass the mouth of Dowozhiebito Canyon on the right.

7.0 Arrive at Keet Seel ruin, your turnaround point. (*FYI:* There is a primitive campground about 0.5 mile from the ruin.)

14.0 Arrive back at the visitor center.

14 White House Ruin Trail

This is the only hike you can do in Canyon de Chelly National Monument without a guide. Fortunately, it is a pleasant, easy, and spectacular day hike to one of the Southwest's best-preserved cliff houses.

Distance: 2.5 miles out and back
Hiking time: About 3 hours
Difficulty: Easy
Trail surface: Dirt trail, slickrock and sand
Best seasons: Spring and fall
Water: No water available
Other trail users: None
Canine compatibility: Dogs prohibited on trails in Canyon de Chelly National Monument

Land status: Canyon de Chelly National Monument
Nearest town: Chinle
Fees and permits: None
Schedule: Open all year
Maps: USGS Del Muerto
Trail contacts: Canyon de Chelly National Monument, PO Box 588, Chinle, AZ 86503-0588; (928) 674-5500; www.nps.gov/cach

Finding the trailhead: From the Canyon de Chelly National Monument Visitor Center in Chinle, drive 6.4 miles on South Rim Drive. Turn left onto the road to White House Ruin Overlook. Park in the lot, and walk down the paved path toward the overlook. About 50 yards from the parking lot, a sign marks the trail on your right. GPS: N36 7.82' / W111 28.67'

The Hike

The trail at first crosses slickrock, paralleling the rim for another 100 yards or so before turning sharply to drop off the rim. Rock cairns and painted symbols on the sandstone mark the trail.

Off the rim the trail descends nearly 600 vertical feet in a series of sweeping, not too steep switchbacks. Wonderful close-up views of the distinctly cross-bedded De Chelly sandstone are possible. Try to imagine this rock as golden sand dunes piled up by strong desert winds some 270 million years ago. Later, over an almost unimaginable amount of time, these dunes were buried under other sediments and the sand grains became cemented together into sandstone. As more time passed, the region was uplifted and erosion eventually exposed this layer. Relatively recently, Chinle Creek and its tributaries sliced down through this layer to create the intricate Canyon de Chelly complex.

NO GUIDE REQUIRED

This is the *only* trail that visitors can use in Canyon de Chelly National Monument without a local guide. The monument is unique in that most of the land is Navajo Reservation, with locals still living in the canyon. Guides are necessary in most parts of the national monument to protect the privacy of the residents.

White House Ruin, Canyon de Chelly

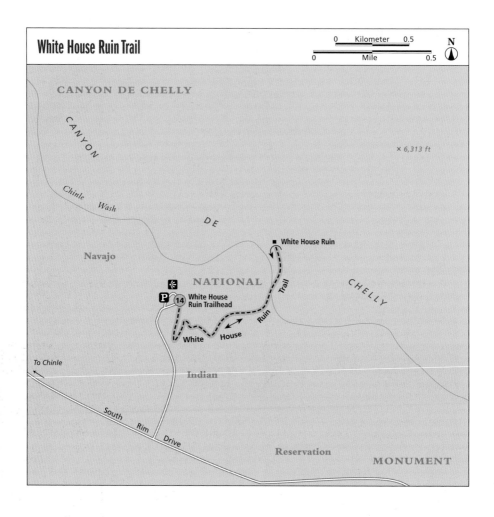

At the canyon bottom the trail passes a Navajo camp (the term for a traditional home-site), crosses Chinle Creek, and delivers you at the base of a tremendous overhanging cliff. Partway up this face, White House Ruin—named for its white-plastered walls—is tucked into a cave. Below White House, at the base of the cliff, is another masonry pueblo. Ladders allowed access to the cave from the rooftops of the lower pueblo. Perhaps fifty or more people lived in this village between AD 1040 and 1275. They planted corn, beans, and squash along Chinle Creek, much like the Navajo people do today.

Miles and Directions

0.0 Start at the White House trailhead, about 50 yards from the parking lot.

1.25 Reach the White House Ruin. Retrace your steps.

2.5 Arrive back at the trailhead.

15 Wupatki Ruin

This is a short walk around an extensive, well-preserved pre-Columbian ruin from the Sinagua culture.

Distance: 0.5-mile loop with a short cherry stem

Hiking time: About 1 hour

Difficulty: Easy

Trail surface: Paved

Best season: Year-round

Water: Visitor center

Other trail users: None

Canine compatibility: Dogs prohibited on trails in Wupatki National Monument

Land status: Wupatki National Monument

Nearest town: Flagstaff

Fees and permits: Entrance fee

Schedule: Open all year

Maps: USGS Wupatki SE

Trail contacts: Wupatki National Monument, 6400 North Highway 89, Flagstaff, AZ 86004; (928) 679-2365; www.nps.gov/wupa

Finding the trailhead: From Flagstaff drive north about 30 miles on US 89, then turn right (east) at the signed Wupatki National Monument turnoff. Follow this paved road east 14 miles, and park at the visitor center. GPS: N35 31.20' / W111 22.28'

Wupatki Ruin

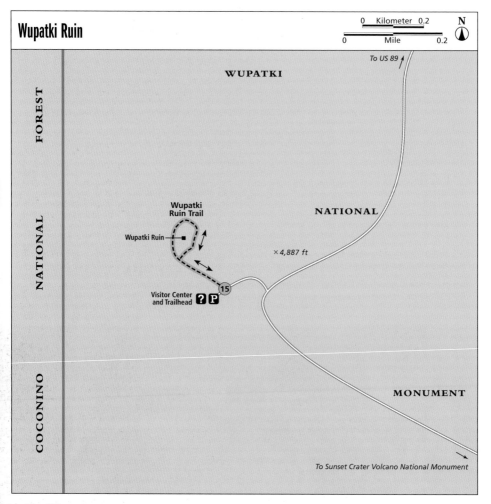

The Hike

The paved trail may be reached either by walking through the visitor center or by walking around the right (north) side of the building. The trail first passes an overlook with a good view of the ruin and its setting, then descends slightly to the ruin itself. The trail forms a loop around the hilltop, and there is a spur trail to an amphitheater. You can walk the loop in either direction.

Miles and Directions

0.0 Start at the visitor center.

0.2 Start the loop around the ruin.

0.5 Arrive back at visitor center.

▶ Spend time in the visitor center to learn about the Sinagua Indians who built Wupatki and many other structures in the area.

San Francisco Peaks

At 12,633 feet, the San Francisco Peaks are the highest mountains in Arizona. They, along with about 800 neighboring cinder cones, stratovolcanoes, and shield volcanoes, make up an interesting and varied region of mountains and alpine meadows. Glaciers once graced the upper slopes of the San Francisco Peaks, leaving behind the southernmost glacially carved terrain in North America. The volcanoes range in age from more than 2 million years to under a thousand. At Sunset Crater, which erupted in AD 1066, volcanic cinder cones and lava flows look as if they happened yesterday—which they did, on the geologic time scale. Native Americans left behind rock art and ruins of their dwellings throughout the area, most notably at Walnut Canyon and Wupatki National Monuments. Most of the rest of the land is part of Kaibab and Coconino National Forests and features a complex network of trails ranging from easy to strenuous. Most of these additional hikes are on various volcanic peaks at elevations of 7,000 to over 10,000 feet.

Solo camp on Kendrick Mountain before the wildfire in 2000

16 Bill Williams Mountain Trail

This popular trail climbs through cool alpine forest to the summit of Bill Williams Mountain—a fine choice for a hot summer day.

Distance: 6.8 miles out and back
Hiking time: About 5 hours
Difficulty: Strenuous
Trail surface: Dirt trails
Best season: Late spring through late fall
Water: No water available
Other trail users: Mountain bikes and horses
Canine compatibility: Controlled dogs allowed
Land status: Kaibab National Forest

Nearest town: Williams
Fees and permits: None
Schedule: Open all year
Maps: USGS Williams South; Kaibab National Forest (Williams and Tusayan Ranger Districts)
Trail contacts: Kaibab National Forest, 800 S. Sixth St., Williams, AZ 86046; (928) 635-8200; www.fs.usda.gov/kaibab

Finding the trailhead: From Williams drive west on Bill Williams Avenue (Business Interstate 40). Just before the I-40 interchange west of town, turn left at the turnoff for the Forest Service Ranger Station. Turn left again at the next signed turnoff for the ranger station; follow the signs to the Bill Williams trailhead, next to the ranger station. GPS: N35 14.23'/W112 12.78'

The Hike

Follow the signed Bill Williams Mountain Trail south from the parking area and across a meadow. Shortly the trail begins to climb moderately in a series of switchbacks. The forest is especially fine in this area, with an interesting mixture of the ever-present ponderosa pine, Gambel oaks, alligator junipers, and even a few white firs.

After the switchbacks end and the Bill Williams Mountain Trail levels out a bit, you'll pass the Clover Spring Trail junction. The Bill Williams Mountain Trail continues south, climbing gradually. As the trail nears the steep north slopes of the

FIR VS. FIR

White fir is much less common than Douglas fir and seems to favor cool drainage bottoms. Usually they can be distinguished from the Douglas fir by their blue-green color. When white fir is growing next to Douglas fir, the color difference is obvious; otherwise, you may have to look more closely. White fir cones grow upward from the branches, as do all true firs; Douglas fir cones hang down. Some people also confuse white fir with blue spruce, but if you attempt to roll a few needles in your fingers, you'll discover that white fir needles are flat. Spruce needles are square in cross section and easily roll in your fingers.

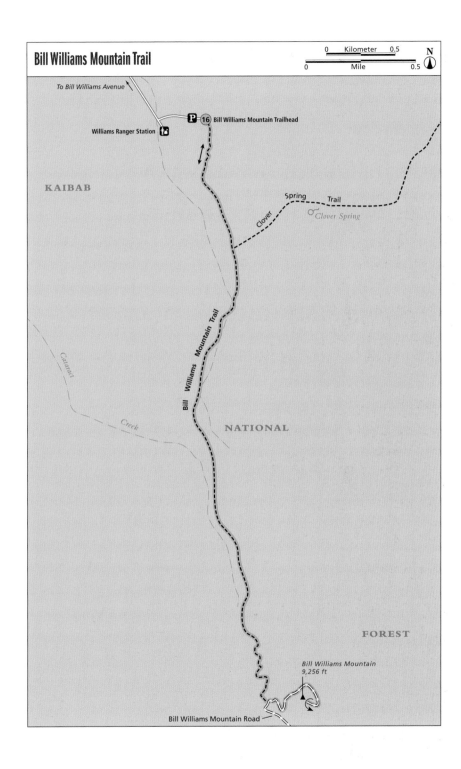

Bill Williams Mountain Trail

0 Kilometer 0.5

0 Mile 0.5

N

To Bill Williams Avenue

P 16 Bill Williams Mountain Trailhead

Williams Ranger Station

KAIBAB

Clover Spring Trail

Clover Spring

Bill Williams Mountain Trail

Cataract

Creek

NATIONAL

FOREST

Bill Williams Mountain
9,256 ft

Bill Williams Mountain Road

mountain, it heads into a north-facing canyon and starts to climb more steeply. The forest changes from open ponderosa pine stands to denser Douglas fir with a scattering of aspen. A series of switchbacks leads up to the trail's end at Bill Williams Mountain Road. To reach the summit, turn left and walk 0.5 mile to the end of the road.

Miles and Directions

0.0   Start at Bill Williams Mountain trailhead.

0.6   Pass junction with the Clover Spring Trail. Continue south on Bill Williams Mountain Trail.

2.9   Reach Bill Williams Mountain Road; turn left.

3.4   Reach the summit of Bill Williams Mountain. Retrace your steps.

6.8   Arrive back at the trailhead.

17 Bull Basin–Pumpkin Trails

This is a rugged hike on less-used trails through sections of beautiful alpine forest with excellent views of the Kendrick Peak Wilderness and the surrounding Coconino Plateau.

Distance: 10.6-mile loop with a cherry stem
Hiking time: About 7 hours
Difficulty: Strenuous
Trail surface: Dirt trails
Best season: Late spring through late fall
Water: No water available
Other trail users: Horses
Canine compatibility: Controlled dogs allowed
Land status: Kendrick Mountain Wilderness, Kaibab National Forest

Nearest town: Flagstaff
Fees and permits: None
Schedule: Open all year
Maps: USGS Kendrick Peak, Moritz Ridge; Kaibab National Forest (Williams and Tusayan Ranger Districts)
Trail contacts: Kaibab National Forest, 800 S. Sixth St., Williams, AZ 86046; (928) 635-8200; www.fs.usda.gov/kaibab

Finding the trailhead: From Flagstaff drive north 17 miles on US 180, then turn left (west) onto a maintained dirt road (FR 193). Continue 3.2 miles, then turn right (northwest) onto another maintained dirt road (FR 171). Drive 7.8 miles to the Pumpkin trailhead, which is on the right. GPS: N35 25.44' / W111 54.66'

The Hike

This is a strenuous hike on steep trails. There is no water, so hikers planning an overnight trip will have to carry water or do the hike in late spring, when there are still snowdrifts near the summit. The rewards are worth the effort. None of the trails are shown on the topographic maps, except for the short segment of the Kendrick Peak Trail used by this loop. Much of Kendrick Mountain was burned in the lightning-caused wildfire of June 2000. Although much of the pine and fir forest was lost, quaking aspen trees are rapidly covering the north and east slopes, in a vivid demonstration of forest recovery and succession.

The Pumpkin Trail heads east through the ponderosa pine forest and almost immediately starts climbing toward the west ridge of Kendrick Peak. After 1.6 miles the trail climbs into a saddle and meets the Connector Trail. Turn left (east) here and continue as the Connector Trail contours the north slopes of the mountain along the wilderness boundary. The Forest Service has logged right up to the boundary, but this section is soon left behind. After about a mile the trail passes through another saddle and crosses into Bull Basin. The Connector Trail ends at the junction with the Bull Basin Trail.

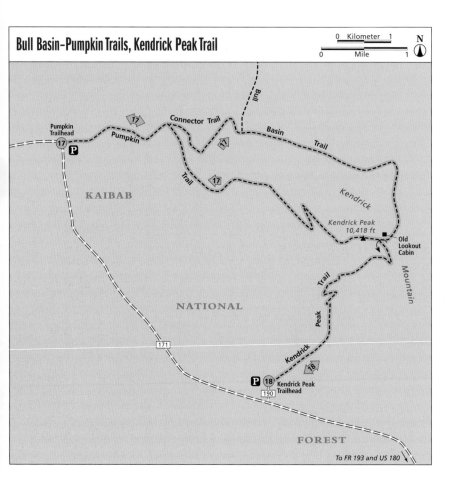

Bull Basin–Pumpkin Trails, Kendrick Peak Trail

0   Kilometer   1

0   Mile   1

N

Pumpkin
Trailhead

17

Pumpkin

Connector Trail

Bull

Basin

Trail

17

Trail

17

KAIBAB

Kendrick

Kendrick Peak
10,418 ft

Old
Lookout
Cabin

Mountain

Trail

NATIONAL

Peak

171

Kendrick

18

P 18 Kendrick Peak
190 Trailhead

FOREST

To FR 193 and US 180

Turn right (southeast) onto the Bull Basin Trail. The trail contours across the head of Bull Basin, then climbs through a beautiful forest as it heads toward the north ridge of Kendrick Peak. The dense forest gives way to a series of alpine meadows just before the trail reaches the ridge crest at a saddle. Here the trail turns south and climbs steeply to the 10,000-foot east shoulder of the mountain. Now the trail climbs more gradually, ending near the old lookout cabin at the junction with the Kendrick Peak Trail.

There are campsites along the tree line at the north edge of the meadow. In early summer or late spring, lingering snowdrifts make it possible to camp without carrying water. The alpine meadow and splendid sunset and sunrise views south are worth the effort of carrying overnight gear up here. Campfires are not recommended. Trees grow very slowly in the Arctic-like environment and should not be burned. Carry a backpacking stove to melt snow and cook meals.

Turn right (west) onto the Kendrick Peak Trail, and follow it as it climbs to the summit. Look on the west side of the lookout building for the beginning of the Pumpkin Trail, which begins descending immediately. The views are excellent from the upper part of the trail as it switchbacks through several meadows. As the trail enters denser forest, it tends to follow the broad west ridge of the mountain. Watch for the junction with the Connector Trail as the forest becomes nearly pure ponderosa pine once again. This closes the loop; continue on the Pumpkin Trail to the trailhead.

Miles and Directions

0.0 Start at the Pumpkin trailhead on FR 171.

1.6 Reach junction with Connector Trail; go left.

2.4 Turn right onto the Bull Basin Trail.

4.6 Reach the ridge crest of Kendrick Peak at a saddle.

5.6 Come to an old lookout cabin; turn right onto Kendrick Peak Trail. (**FYI:** There are campsites along the tree line at the north end of the meadow.)

5.9 Reach Kendrick Lookout. Continue on Pumpkin Trail, which begins on the west side of the lookout building.

9.0 Come to junction with the Connector Trail; turn left.

10.6 Arrive back at the trailhead.

18 Kendrick Peak Trail

This hike follows a well-graded trail to the summit of the fourth-highest mountain in Arizona. The summit features a lookout used by US Forest Service personnel to watch for wildfires during the summer fire season, as well as a historic cabin once occupied by the lookout.

See map on page 80.
Distance: 8.0 miles out and back
Hiking time: About 6 hours
Difficulty: Strenuous
Trail surface: Dirt trails
Best season: Late spring through late fall
Water: No water available
Other trail users: Horses
Canine compatibility: Controlled dogs allowed

Land status: Kendrick Mountain Wilderness, Kaibab National Forest
Nearest town: Flagstaff
Fees and permits: None
Schedule: Open all year
Maps: USGS Kendrick Peak; Kaibab National Forest (Williams and Tusayan Ranger District)
Trail contacts: Kaibab National Forest, 800 S. Sixth St., Williams, AZ 86046; (928) 635-8200; www.fs.usda.gov/kaibab

Finding the trailhead: From Flagstaff drive north about 17 miles on US 180; turn left (west) onto a maintained dirt road (FR 193). Continue 3.2 miles, then turn right (northwest) onto another maintained dirt road (FR 171). Drive 2 miles; turn right onto FR 190 and continue 0.4 mile to the signed trailhead on the right side of the road. GPS: N35 23.06'/W111 52.11'

The Hike

The Kendrick Peak Trail is the easiest of the three trails to the summit of Kendrick Peak. Originally built for access to and maintenance of the Forest Service fire lookout, it climbs the south side of the mountain in gradual switchbacks.

The Kendrick trail climbs the slope to the northeast through ponderosa pine stands to join the original trail just above the old trailhead. This next section of trail was used as a road during a forest fire many years ago, and it is noticeably wider than the remainder of the trail. At first the trail follows the left side of a drainage, then it begins to switchback. Notice that Douglas fir appears as the trail climbs this section.

AMAZING SCENERY

The San Francisco Peaks to the east dominate the scenery. You can also see many of the hundreds of old volcanoes and cinder cones that dot the plateau. The beautiful pine forest stretches in all directions, scarred here and there by old forest fire burns. To the north the cliffs of the Grand Canyon's North Rim are visible 50 miles away.

Kendrick Mountain fire lookout, staffed during the summer fire season

Soon the trail reaches a saddle and becomes narrower again. The trail climbs a short distance up the ridge to the northeast, then starts to ascend the south-facing slope in a series of switchbacks. Limber pine and Arizona corkbark fir appear, as do quaking aspen. Occasional open meadows offer extensive views of the forested Coconino Plateau to the south. Eventually the trail makes a major switchback to the northwest, and there are glimpses of the summit and the squat lookout building. The trail enters a meadow on the east ridge of the peak and meets the Bull Basin Trail near an old cabin.

The cabin was built in the early part of the twentieth century by the fire lookout, who lived in the cabin and rode his horse to the summit each day to watch for fires. The lookout obtained water from a spring to the north, which is unreliable today. In the early days of the Forest Service, fire lookouts often sat on the bare mountaintop to watch for fires. Amenities such as lookout buildings and towers were constructed gradually as the need for permanent fire watches developed.

Continue on the Kendrick Peak Trail about 0.3 mile to the summit. The lookout welcomes visitors unless he or she is busy; ask permission before climbing the stairs. From either the catwalk or the ground, the views are stunning.

Miles and Directions

0.0 Start at the Kendrick trailhead on FR 190.

0.7 Join the old trail.

1.5 Come to a saddle; the trail narrows.

3.7 Reach an old lookout cabin and junction with the Bull Basin Trail. Continue on the Kendrick Peak Trail.

4.0 Reach Kendrick Lookout and the Pumpkin Trail junction. Retrace your steps on the Kendrick Trail.

8.0 Arrive back at the trailhead.

19 Walker Lake

This easy, short hike leads to an unusual lake within a volcanic crater. Although the San Francisco Peaks and the surrounding Coconino Plateau have very little permanent surface water—no lakes or creeks, and relatively few springs, due to the porous surface rocks—there are three cinder cones that collect enough spring snowmelt to sometimes have small, shallow lakes in their craters. Walker Lake is the largest of the three.

Distance: 1.0 mile out and back
Hiking time: About 1 hour
Difficulty: Easy
Trail surface: Dirt trails
Best season: Spring through fall
Water: No water available
Other trail users: Mountain bikes and horses
Canine compatibility: Controlled dogs allowed
Land status: Coconino National Forest

Nearest town: Flagstaff
Fees and permits: None
Schedule: Open all year
Maps: USGS White Horse Hills; Coconino National Forest
Trail contacts: Coconino National Forest, 1824 S. Thompson St., Flagstaff, AZ 86001; (928) 527-3600; www.fs.usda.gov/coconino

Finding the trailhead: From Flagstaff drive north 18 miles on US 180, then turn right (east) onto the north end of Hart Prairie Road (FR 151). Continue on this maintained dirt road 1.5 miles, then turn left (east) onto another maintained road (FR 418). Drive 0.2 mile; turn left again (north) on an unmaintained road. Park at the end of the road, in another 0.2 mile. GPS: N35 23.19' / W111 44.07'

The Hike

The trail follows the old road, closed now, up the southwest slope of the cinder cone. It passes through a broad saddle after 0.3 mile and drops gently into the volcanic crater. Walker Lake is fullest in late spring after a snowy winter. In late summer it is little more than a marsh. Considering how porous this volcanic area is, it's surprising that the runoff from the small watershed formed by the crater is enough to form even a small pond. It is worthwhile to walk around the lake. A human-caused forest fire burned the now-barren north slope of the crater. The fire started near the lake, and high winds swept it up over the rim, where it traveled another 5 miles before being contained by firefighters. A much larger fire in 1996 burned much of the area again. The views of Humphreys Peak, the highest of the San Francisco Peaks, are great from the northwest side of the lake—even better if you climb up the slope through the old burn.

Walker Lake, a seasonal lake in the crater of a cinder cone ▶

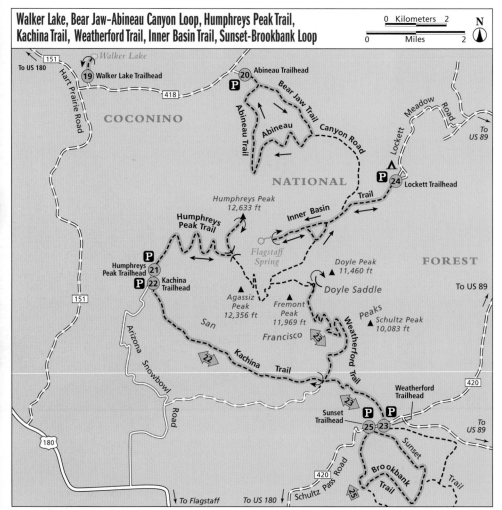

Walker Lake, Bear Jaw-Abineau Canyon Loop, Humphreys Peak Trail, Kachina Trail, Weatherford Trail, Inner Basin Trail, Sunset-Brookbank Loop

0 Kilometers 2

0 Miles 2

N

To US 180

151

Walker Lake

19 Walker Lake Trailhead

Hart Prairie Road

418

COCONINO

20 Abineau Trailhead

Bear Jaw Trail

Abineau Trail

Abineau

Canyon Road

Meadow Road

To US 89

Lockett

NATIONAL

24 Lockett Trailhead

Humphreys Peak
12,633 ft

Inner Basin

Trail

Humphreys
Peak Trail

Flagstaff
Spring

Doyle Peak
▲ 11,460 ft

FOREST

Humphreys
Peak Trailhead 21

22 Kachina
Trailhead

151

San

Arizona

Snowbowl

Road

22

Agassiz
Peak
12,356 ft

▲

Fremont
Peak
11,969 ft

Doyle Saddle

Peaks

▲ Schultz Peak
10,083 ft

Francisco

23

Kachina

Trail

To US 89

Weatherford Trail

Weatherford
Trailhead

420

23

Sunset
Trailhead

25 23

P P

To
US 89

180

420 Road

Sunset

Brookbank

Trail

Trail

To Flagstaff

To US 180

Schultz Pass

25

Miles and Directions

0.0 Start at Walker Lake trailhead at the end of an unmaintained road.

0.3 Pass through a saddle on the crater rim.

0.5 Reach Walker Lake, your turnaround point. (*FYI:* Enjoy views of Humphreys Peak from the northwest side of the lake.)

1.0 Arrive back at the trailhead.

20 Bear Jaw–Abineau Canyon Loop

This cool hike in the Kachina Peaks Wilderness leads to a glacial canyon on the north side of the San Francisco Peaks and is also great for fall color during October.

See map on page 86.
Distance: 7.4-mile loop
Hiking time: About 5 hours
Difficulty: Moderate
Trail surface: Dirt trails
Best seasons: Spring and fall
Water: No water available
Other trail users: Horses
Canine compatibility: Controlled dogs allowed

Land status: Kachina Peaks Wilderness, Coconino National Forest
Nearest town: Flagstaff
Fees and permits: None
Schedule: Open all year
Maps: USGS White Horse Hills and Humphreys Peak; Coconino National Forest
Trail contacts: Coconino National Forest, 1824 S. Thompson St., Flagstaff, AZ 86001; (928) 527-3600; www.fs.usda.gov/coconino

Finding the trailhead: From Flagstaff drive north on US 180 for about 18 miles, then turn right onto the north end of Hart Prairie Road (FR 151), a maintained dirt road. Continue 1.6 miles, then turn left onto the Hostetter Tank Road (FR 418), also maintained dirt. Drive 3.1 miles to the signed Abineau Trail turnoff; turn right and go 0.3 mile to the trailhead. GPS: N35 23.37'/W111 40.73'

The Hike

Start off on the Abineau Trail, which heads southeast and soon drops into the shallow lower portion of Abineau Canyon. A short distance up the canyon, turn left onto the Bear Jaw Trail, which traverses east through open ponderosa pine forest to cross Reese Canyon. Now you'll start to climb as the trail ascends the north slopes of the mountain. The pure pine forest gradually gives way to a pleasing mix of pine, quaking aspen, Douglas fir, and white fir. After the trail crosses Bear Jaw Canyon, it's only a short climb to the Abineau Canyon Road, where you'll turn right.

WHERE ARE ALL THE TREES?

The lack of trees in upper Abineau Canyon is due to numerous snow avalanches that roar down the northeast slopes of Humphreys Peak during winter and spring. Some of these slides reach the bottom of the canyon with such power that they continue below the road, crossing back and forth several times before the snow finally loses its momentum. Such a large avalanche will destroy any small trees attempting to grow in its path. Occasionally a large avalanche will knock down mature, 200-year-old trees. Such destruction occurred during the record snows of 2004–2005.

The road, part of the Flagstaff watershed project, was built in an attempt to tap a spring in Abineau Canyon. Parts of the abandoned pipeline can still be seen in the roadbed. Although the road is in a narrow, nonwilderness corridor, it is open only to official vehicles and rarely used. It makes a pleasant, easy hike along the north side of the mountain. Shortly you'll cross Bear Jaw Canyon; the road then swings around into Reese Canyon, climbing gradually. The fir-aspen forest is a riot of color during the fall, and the road is often paved with golden aspen leaves for a couple of weeks.

The view opens up as you reach Abineau Canyon. Just after emerging from the forest into the open valley, turn right onto the Abineau Trail, which descends Abineau Canyon. After a bit over 2 miles, you'll pass the Bear Jaw Trail turnoff; continue left on the Abineau Trail to return to the trailhead.

Miles and Directions

0.0 Start at Abineau trailhead on the Abineau Trail turnoff.

0.5 Reach junction with Bear Jaw Trail; turn left.

0.9 Cross Reese Canyon.

2.1 Cross Bear Jaw Canyon.

2.5 Turn right onto Abineau Canyon Road.

2.8 Cross Bear Jaw Canyon.

3.7 Cross Reese Canyon.

4.7 Turn right onto Abineau Trail.

6.9 Reach junction with Bear Jaw Trail; stay left.

7.4 Arrive back at the trailhead.

Hiking in Abineau Canyon

21 Humphreys Peak Trail

Although this is an extremely popular hike that sometimes seems like nothing more than a treadmill for the trail-running set, the hike to the highest summit in Arizona is still very much worthwhile. On a clear day the views cover a large portion of the state. Early weekday mornings are the best times to avoid the crowds.

See map on page 86.
Distance: 8.8 miles out and back
Hiking time: About 7 hours
Difficulty: Strenuous
Trail surface: Dirt trails
Best season: Summer through fall
Water: No water available
Other trail users: None
Canine compatibility: Controlled dogs allowed
Land status: Kachina Peaks Wilderness, Coconino National Forest
Nearest town: Flagstaff

Fees and permits: None
Schedule: Open all year
Maps: USGS Humphreys Peak; Coconino National Forest
Trail contacts: Coconino National Forest, 1824 S. Thompson St., Flagstaff, AZ 86001; (928) 527-3600; www.fs.usda.gov/coconino
Other: Cross-country hiking prohibited above 11,400 feet (the approximate level of timberline); camping prohibited in the Interior Valley above Lockett Meadow

Finding the trailhead: From Flagstaff drive 7 miles north on US 180, then turn right (north) onto Arizona Snowbowl Road. Continue 6.5 miles to the ski-area lodge, and turn left into the parking lot below the lodge. Park at the north end, where you will see the signed trailhead. GPS: N35 19.88'/W111 42.65'

The Hike

Note that cross-country hiking is prohibited by the USDA Forest Service above 11,400 feet on the San Francisco Peaks. Above timberline you must stay on the trail. The purpose of this regulation is to protect the San Francisco Peaks groundsel, a plant that grows nowhere else in the world. The trail was completed in 1985 and is not shown on the USGS topographic map.

The trail starts near the base of a chairlift in upper Hart Prairie and then crosses into the forest on the north side of the meadow. The trail ascends in a series of long but well-graded switchbacks through the dense forest. At first the forest is a mixture of ponderosa pine, Douglas fir, and quaking aspen trees associated with the Canadian life zone. These give way to limber pine and Engelmann spruce in the higher sections of the forest. Near timberline, the forest is mostly subalpine fir, Arizona corkbark fir, and bristlecone pine, which represent the classic subalpine life zone. Near timberline the trail crosses the west-facing ridge and climbs up to Agassiz Saddle at 11,800 feet. The few trees in this area show the effect of the harsh Arctic-like climate. They grow in low mats to conserve heat and protect themselves from wind. In winter, snow collects

Humphreys Peak from upper Hart Prairie

around the dense foliage, forming drifts that further protect the trees. The climate in this Arctic life zone is similar to that in the far northern regions of Canada and Alaska.

From Agassiz Saddle the Weatherford Trail branches south along the ridge. The Humphreys Peak Trail turns north and skirts the west side of the ridge. The next mile of the trail is above timberline with no shelter and should not be attempted if thunderstorms, high wind, or snowstorms threaten. After about 0.2 mile the last struggling trees are left behind as the trail continues to climb along the ridge toward the invisible summit. You'll pass several false summits, each one appearing to be the final one. There are choice views of the Interior Valley to the east along the way, a good excuse to stop to catch your breath in the thin air.

A low stone wall marks the summit. A large portion of northern Arizona is visible from this lofty perch. If the air is clear, you can see Utah's 10,300-foot Navajo Mountain to the north-northeast and the 11,400-foot White Mountains in east-central Arizona near the New Mexico border. The Mogollon Rim and some of its canyons can be seen to the south, as well as the rugged mountain ranges of central Arizona.

Miles and Directions

0.0 Start at the Humphreys Peak trailhead at the north end of the ski lodge parking lot.

3.4 Reach Agassiz Saddle.

4.4 Arrive at the summit of Humphreys Peak, marked by a low stone wall. Retrace your steps.

8.8 Arrive back at the trailhead.

22 Kachina Trail

This trail traverses the southwest slopes of the San Francisco Peaks, offering a well-graded trail through beautiful mixed-alpine forest of pine, fir, and aspen and gorgeous meadows with 100-mile views.

See map on page 86.
Distance: 10.6 miles out and back
Hiking time: About 6 hours
Difficulty: Moderate
Trail surface: Dirt trails
Best season: Summer through fall
Water: No water available
Other trail users: Horses
Canine compatibility: Controlled dogs allowed
Land status: Kachina Peaks Wilderness, Coconino National Forest
Nearest town: Flagstaff

Fees and permits: None
Schedule: Open all year
Maps: USGS Humphreys Peak; Coconino National Forest
Trail contacts: Coconino National Forest, 1824 S. Thompson St., Flagstaff, AZ 86001; (928) 527-3600; www.fs.usda.gov/coconino
Other: Cross-country hiking is prohibited above 11,400 feet (the approximate level of timberline); camping is prohibited in the Interior Valley above Lockett Meadow

Finding the trailhead: From Flagstaff drive north on US 180 about 7 miles, then turn right (north) onto the paved and signed Arizona Snowbowl Road. Continue 6.5 miles to the ski-area lodge, and turn right into the first parking lot. Drive to the far end of the parking lot and park at the signed trailhead for the Kachina Trail. GPS: N35 19.53'/W111 42.64'

The Hike

The Kachina Trail is one of several trails built during the mid-1980s as part of a recreational trail system on the San Francisco Peaks, and it is not shown on the USGS topographic map. After a short distance on the Kachina Trail, you'll cross under a power line and enter Kachina Peaks Wilderness. The trail winds in and out of small canyons and through meadows as it traverses the southwest slopes of Agassiz Peak. The forest is an attractive mixture of quaking aspen, Douglas fir, and limber pine. In fall the aspen change to beautiful shades of yellow, orange, and red. This is a good hike for viewing those colors. After about a mile you'll cross a rocky canyon; the trail beyond this point crosses a steeper, more rugged slope.

After crossing several small draws, the trail crosses the deeper canyon coming down from Fremont Saddle, then traverses into Freidlein Prairie, an alpine meadow on the southwest slopes of Fremont Peak. The junction with the Freidlein Prairie Trail is in this meadow. The meadow is much larger than depicted on the topographic map, extending all the way down to the Freidlein Prairie Road. Now the trail descends gradually eastward across the slopes of Fremont Peak, traversing several

Hiking the Kachina Trail

beautiful, aspen-lined meadows. Watch for elk; at times there are more elk tracks than human tracks on the trail. The trail ends at the wilderness boundary and the junction with the Weatherford Trail, which is the turnaround point for the hike.

Miles and Directions

0.0 Start at the signed trailhead at the far end of the first ski lodge parking lot.

2.7 Reach Freidlein Prairie. (*FYI:* The junction with the Freidlein Prairie Trail is in this meadow.)

5.3 Reach the wilderness boundary and junction with the Weatherford Trail, your turnaround point.

10.6 Arrive back at the trailhead.

23 Weatherford Trail

This is one of the most alpine trails in Arizona, and it follows the route of a historic road that was intended to be a scenic toll road to the top of Humphreys Peak. Now a well-graded trail, it winds around Fremont and Agassiz Peaks to end at the 11,800-foot saddle between Humphreys and Agassiz Peaks.

See map on page 86.
Distance: 14.8 miles out and back
Hiking time: About 8 hours
Difficulty: Strenuous
Trail surface: Dirt trails
Best season: Summer through fall
Water: No water available
Other trail users: None
Canine compatibility: Controlled dogs allowed
Land status: Kachina Peaks Wilderness, Coconino National Forest
Nearest town: Flagstaff

Fees and permits: None
Schedule: Open all year
Maps: USGS Humphreys Peak; Coconino National Forest
Trail contacts: Coconino National Forest, 1824 S. Thompson St., Flagstaff, AZ 86001; (928) 527-3600; www.fs.usda.gov/coconino
Other: Cross-country hiking is prohibited above 11,400 feet (the approximate level of timberline); camping is prohibited in the Interior Valley above Lockett Meadow

Finding the trailhead: From Flagstaff drive northwest about 3 miles on US 180, then turn right (north) onto Schultz Pass Road (FR 420). Continue past the end of the pavement on a maintained dirt road to the signed Weatherford Trail just beyond Schultz Pass, about 5.5 miles from US 180. Park on the right (south) at the Weatherford trailhead. GPS: N35 17.17'/W111 37.59'

The Hike

The walk begins across the road from the east end of the parking area and follows the Weatherford Trail, an old road. The trail crosses a cleared pipeline corridor and continues to climb gradually north on a ponderosa pine–covered slope. When the trail emerges into a large meadow at the foot of Fremont Peak, it starts to switchback. You'll pass the Kachina Trail turnoff after one of these switchbacks, and then the trail crosses the meadow and enters the forest. The slope steepens as the trail swings around a small meadow. A series of broad switchbacks takes you up the southeast slopes of Fremont Peak. The old road crosses several large avalanche paths, and a final switchback leads into Doyle Saddle, the goal for the hike. The view from this saddle is especially fine, overlooking the Interior Valley, with its surrounding alpine peaks, and the lower Mount Elden–Dry Lake Hills complex to the south.

▶ The Weatherford Road was built in the 1920s as a scenic toll road, but it was not a success and was soon abandoned. Rockslides and snow avalanche activity have reduced the old road to trail width in many places.

Aspens above Weatherford Canyon

Miles and Directions

0.0   Start at the trailhead at Schultz Tank.

0.2   Cross a cleared pipeline corridor.

1.7   Pass the Kachina Trail turnoff; stay on the Weatherford Trail.

7.4   Reach Doyle Saddle, your goal and turnaround point.

14.8   Arrive back at the trailhead.

Option

The Weatherford Trail continues around Fremont Peak, through Fremont Saddle, and around the east slopes of Agassiz Peak, and ends at the Humphreys–Agassiz Saddle. If you continue to the end, you'll add 1,000 feet of elevation gain and 4.2 round-trip miles to the hike.

24 Inner Basin Trail

This hike follows the path of an ancient glacier through very scenic alpine forests and meadows to the dramatic southeast face of Humphreys Peak.

See map on page 86.

Distance: 6.7-mile loop with a cherry stem
Hiking time: About 5 hours
Difficulty: Moderate
Trail surface: Dirt trails and roads (roads are closed to the public)
Best season: Summer through fall
Water: Watershed cabins during summer only
Other trail users: Mountain bikes
Canine compatibility: Controlled dogs allowed
Land status: Coconino National Forest
Nearest town: Flagstaff

Fees and permits: None
Schedule: Open all year
Maps: USGS Sunset Crater West and Humphreys Peak; Coconino National Forest
Trail contacts: Coconino National Forest, 1824 S. Thompson St., Flagstaff, AZ 86001; (928) 527-3600; www.fs.usda.gov/coconino
Other: Cross-country hiking is prohibited above 11,400 feet (the approximate level of timberline); camping is prohibited in the Interior Valley above Lockett Meadow

Finding the trailhead: From Flagstaff drive north on US 89, the main street through town, and continue about 17 miles to Schultz Pass Road (FR 420); turn left (west). This maintained dirt road is opposite the Sunset Crater National Monument turnoff. Drive 0.4 mile, then turn right at a T intersection. Continue 0.8 mile to another T intersection, and then turn left. About 0.6 mile farther, just before a locked gate at a cinder pit, turn right onto Lockett Meadow Road. Continue 2.8 miles to the Lockett trailhead at the southwest corner of the loop road around Lockett Meadow. GPS: N35 21.46'/W111 37.28'

The Hike

Start on Inner Basin Trail, and hike southwest up the Interior Valley to the watershed cabins. There is untreated springwater at a tap near the largest cabin.

From the cabins take Inner Basin Trail, the road that continues west–southwest up the Interior Valley. (This road is not open to the public and is used only by occasional official vehicles.) One hundred yards beyond the cabins, the road forks. Take the right fork, which goes to Bear Paw and Flagstaff Spring. The road climbs steadily through the dense alpine forest, which sometimes opens up for glimpses of the high peaks. Along the way you will see old signs of construction dating from the beginnings of the watershed project.

About 0.8 mile from the watershed cabins, a road forks left. This will be the return loop. For now continue on the main road (right), which ends in another 0.8 mile below Flagstaff Spring. The most notable feature here is the incredible swath of destruction in the 200-year-old fir and spruce. The winter of 1972–73 was the

Agassiz Peak, Inner Basin, San Francisco Peaks

snowiest winter on record, and sometime during that winter a large avalanche came down the southeast face of Humphreys Peak and destroyed the trees.

To continue on the main hike, retrace your steps east down the road 0.8 mile to the junction mentioned above, and then turn right. This road goes south 0.5 mile to the south branch of the Interior Valley, passing through some fine aspen stands before reaching a broad open meadow just west of one of the city well sites, with its noisy diesel pump. This meadow has the best views in the Interior Valley. From left to right the summits are Doyle, Fremont, Agassiz, and Humphreys Peaks. From this vantage point Fremont Peak is the most striking, with its pyramidal northeast face.

Turn left at the road junction in the meadow, and descend to the east-northeast, following the road back to the watershed cabins. Return to the trailhead via Inner Basin Trail, the way you came.

FLAGSTAFF'S WATER PROBLEM

Flagstaff has outgrown its water supply repeatedly over the years. In the early part of the twentieth century, only a couple of decades after the city's founding, someone had an idea: Tap the springs in the Interior Valley of the San Francisco Peaks. In an area with very few springs, this water was worth considerable effort to reach. A pipeline was built up Schultz Creek, west of the Dry Lake Hills, to Schultz Pass, then around the east slopes of Doyle Peak and into the Interior Valley. From the present site of the watershed cabins, branch pipelines were built to all the springs in the valley. An attempt was even made to tap a spring in Abineau Canyon on the northeast side of Humphreys Peak.

In the 1950s, in an effort to find more water, the city drilled a number of exploratory wells in the Interior Valley. A few were successful and diesel-powered pumps were installed. Most of the old roads dating from the exploration period are overgrown now, but the valley still lacks a truly wild feeling. Until the mid-1970s, the entire watershed was closed to all public access, including hiking and cross-country skiing. Increasing public interest in outdoor activities finally caused the Forest Service to open the area to day hiking, skiing, and snowshoeing. Locked steel covers protect the springs, so there are no water sources in the Interior Valley except for the seasonal tap at the watershed cabins.

Miles and Directions

0.0 Start at the Lockett trailhead, at the southwest corner of the Lockett Meadow loop road.

1.5 Pass the watershed cabins; continue straight on the Inner Basin Trail.

1.6 Go right at the fork onto the Flagstaff Spring road.

2.3 The road forks again; stay right. (*FYI:* The left fork will be your return loop.)

3.1 Reach Flagstaff Spring. Retrace your steps to the loop you passed earlier.

3.9 Turn right at the loop fork.

4.4 Turn left onto Inner Basin Trail.

5.2 Pass the watershed cabins.

6.7 Arrive back at the Lockett trailhead.

Options

From Flagstaff Spring continue cross-country up the forested slope, proceeding southwest from the spring, to reach the rim of Humphreys Cirque at 11,200 feet. You are near timberline, and there are excellent views of the stark alpine ridges above. (The mountain is closed to cross-country hiking above 11,400 feet.) Return to Flagstaff Spring the way you came.

25 Sunset-Brookbank Loop

This hike features relatively easy access and cool, alpine forest and meadows in the Dry Lake Hills, the prominent volcanic mountain just north of Flagstaff.

See map on page 86.
Distance: 5.4-mile loop
Hiking time: About 4 hours
Difficulty: Moderate
Best season: Spring through fall
Trail surface: Dirt trails
Water: No water available
Other trail users: Mountain bikes and horses
Canine compatibility: Controlled dogs allowed

Land status: Coconino National Forest
Nearest town: Flagstaff
Fees and permits: None
Schedule: Open all year
Maps: USGS Humphreys Peak and Sunset Crater West; Coconino National Forest
Trail contacts: Coconino National Forest, 1824 S. Thompson St., Flagstaff, AZ 86001; (928) 527-3600; www.fs.usda.gov/coconino

Finding the trailhead: From Flagstaff drive northwest about 3 miles on US 180; turn right (north) onto the road to Schultz Pass (FR 420). Continue past the end of the pavement on the maintained dirt road to the Sunset trailhead at Schultz Pass, 5.3 miles from the highway. GPS: N35 17.121'/W111 37.923'

The Hike

None of the trails on this hike are shown on the USGS topographic maps. From the trailhead the Sunset Trail first crosses the gentle slope above Schultz Tank through beautiful ponderosa pine and aspen forest. The Little Elden Trail goes left; continue straight ahead. The trail now enters a small drainage and turns uphill. Climbing steadily but at a moderate grade, the trail stays on the right side of the drainage for more than a mile. It then crosses a road, veers out of the drainage to the left, and enters a more open forest. The openness is due to the fact that the area was once logged. The trail reaches the crest of the Dry Lake Hills, where there are good views of the San Francisco Peaks to the north, then descends west on the south side of the ridge to meet the Brookbank Trail.

From this junction continue straight ahead on the Brookbank Trail as it contours the slope westward. Here the forest is a pleasing mixture of ponderosa pine, Douglas fir, and aspen. Soon the trail crosses over a broad saddle and turns north. It descends through a small meadow then descends northwest via several switchbacks through dense fir forest. The trail passes through another saddle and meadow and then contours around a hill to the north. The forest is so dense here that there are very few views. Continuing around the hill, the trail heads south, then meets a T intersection. Turn right, uphill, on the unsigned trail. After a hundred yards the trail levels out into a large meadow with a seasonal lake, the largest in the Dry Lake Hills. (***Note:*** The next section of trail crosses private land. It is open to hikers at present. Please respect private property and all posted signs.)

San Francisco Peaks from the Sunset-Brookbank Loop

The trail turns into an old road as it crosses the meadow. Watch for a good trail branching right (north) before the road crosses the meadow. Take this trail directly toward the San Francisco Peaks, skirting a small stock tank on the east, and then join an old road just north of the stock tank. Follow the road downhill to the north. At the junction with Schultz Loop Trail, turn right and continue to Sunset trailhead.

Miles and Directions

- **0.0** Start at the Sunset trailhead at Schultz Pass.
- **0.2** Stay right at Little Elden Trail junction.
- **1.7** Cross the crest of the Dry Lake Hills.
- **2.0** Go straight ahead onto the Brookbank Trail.
- **3.8** Turn right, uphill, onto an unsigned trail.
- **4.2** Join an old road below the stock tank; turn right, downhill.
- **4.9** Go right at the junction with Schultz Loop Trail.
- **5.4** Arrive back at the trailhead.

26 Walnut Canyon Rim

This scenic hike follows a section of the Arizona Trail along the north rim of Walnut Canyon.

Distance: 13.6 miles out and back
Hiking time: About 7 hours
Difficulty: Moderate
Trail surface: Dirt trails
Best season: Spring through fall
Water: No water available
Other trail users: Mountain bikes and horses
Canine compatibility: Controlled dogs allowed
Land status: Coconino National Forest

Nearest town: Flagstaff
Fees and permits: None
Schedule: Open all year
Maps: USGS Flagstaff East; Coconino National Forest
Trail contacts: Coconino National Forest, 1824 S. Thompson St., Flagstaff, AZ 86001; (928) 527-3600; www.fs.usda.gov/coconino

Finding the trailhead: From Flagstaff at the junction of I-40 and US 89, drive 4 miles east on I-40 to the Walnut Canyon National Monument exit. Go right (south), and continue 2.5 miles. Just before entering the monument, turn right onto Old Walnut Canyon Road (FR 303). Continue 1.8 miles to the Arizona Trail parking area. GPS: N35 10.75'/W111 31.79'

The Hike

This hike follows a section of the Arizona Trail. Parts of the trail follow old roads; other sections are single track trail. Pay close attention to the trail markers. The trail starts off heading southwest through open ponderosa pine–Gambel oak forest, climbing gradually. It turns south and then joins an old road for a short distance. Singletrack trail takes you across a side canyon. On the far side you'll join another old road. Watch for a spur trail on the left. It goes to a viewpoint overlooking Walnut Canyon. After the viewpoint the trail follows old roads for more than a mile and wanders away from the rim. After the trail leaves the road again, it soon hits the north rim of Walnut Canyon and follows it closely all the way to Fisher Point. This viewpoint, reached by a few yards of spur trail, overlooks the point where the canyon makes an abrupt 90-degree change in direction. It makes an ideal goal for a hike on this portion of the Arizona Trail.

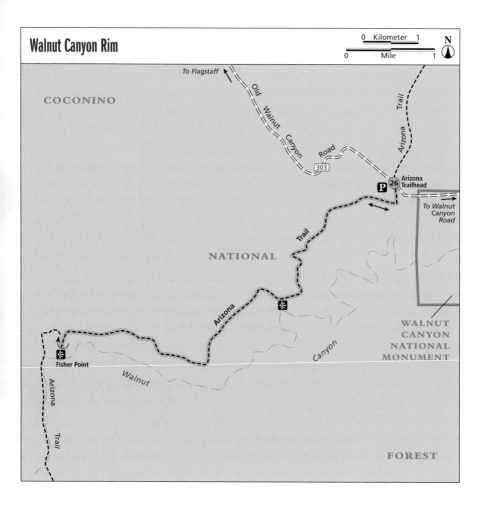

Walnut Canyon Rim

COCONINO

To Flagstaff

Old Walnut Canyon Road

303

Arizona Trail

Arizona Trailhead

P 26

To Walnut Canyon Road

Trail

NATIONAL

Arizona

Canyon

Fisher Point

Walnut

Arizona Trail

WALNUT CANYON NATIONAL MONUMENT

FOREST

0   Kilometer   1

0   Mile   1

N

Miles and Directions

0.0 Start at the trailhead at the Arizona Trail parking area on FR 303.

1.9 Cross a side canyon.

2.4 Reach the first Walnut Canyon viewpoint.

5.5 The trail reaches the Walnut Canyon rim again.

6.8 Reach Fisher Point. Retrace your steps.

13.6 Arrive back at the trailhead.

27 Mormon Lake

Enjoy a hike along the shore of Mormon Lake, Arizona's largest natural lake. This is a great place to view wildlife.

Distance: 6.4 miles out and back
Hiking time: About 3 hours
Difficulty: Easy
Trail surface: Dirt trails, old road
Best season: Spring through fall
Water: No water available
Other trail users: Mountain bikes and horses
Canine compatibility: Controlled dogs allowed
Land status: Coconino National Forest

Nearest town: Flagstaff
Fees and permits: None
Schedule: Open all year
Maps: USGS Mormon Lake; Coconino National Forest
Trail contacts: Coconino National Forest, 1824 S. Thompson St., Flagstaff, AZ 86001; (928) 527-3600; www.fs.usda.gov/coconino

Finding the trailhead: From Flagstaff drive 27 miles southeast on Lake Mary Road (CR 3). The highway skirts the east side of Mormon Lake, then descends through a cut. Watch for the turnoff to Kinnikinick Lake on the left. Drive 0.4 mile farther on CR 3 and turn right (east) onto an unmarked, unmaintained dirt road that descends toward the lake and then turns right. Go through the gate (low-clearance cars should be parked here), and drive a short distance to a fork. Turn right, uphill, and drive a few yards to a second gate and park. This gate is normally locked to protect the area's wildlife. GPS: N35 55.20'/W111 25.97'

The Hike

The walk follows the old road along the shore of the lake. (The USGS topographic map shows this old road but not the present highway, which is to the east, above the lakeside cliffs.) The old road is nearly level and is about 20 feet higher than the lake, so there is a good view. This hike is best done at sunrise or sunset, which are also good times for wildlife viewing. The old road can be followed more than 3 miles along the

HISTORY OF THE LAKE

Most of the year Mormon Lake is more a marsh than a lake. When full—after the spring snow-melt in a wet year—it is the largest "natural" lake in Arizona. Although there is no dam (in contrast with Upper and Lower Lake Mary), man has still influenced the lake. The area was first settled by Mormons who started dairy farming here. In the pioneer days the lake area was never more than a marsh, so the settlers ran cattle on the rich forage. Eventually the hooves of the cattle compacted the soil and made it less porous so that the marsh flooded and became a lake in wet years. Today the lake and its marshes are important havens for wildlife.

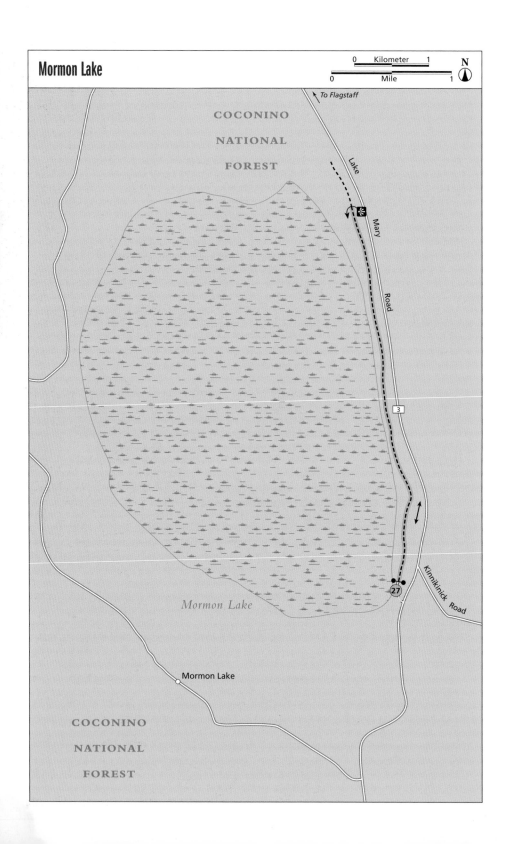

Mormon Lake

0 Kilometer 1

0 Mile 1

N

To Flagstaff

COCONINO

NATIONAL

FOREST

Lake

Mary

Road

3

Kinnikinick Road

27

Mormon Lake

Mormon Lake

COCONINO

NATIONAL

FOREST

At Mormon Lake the trail follows the right bank.

eastern shore to a point just past the viewpoint on the new highway. Cottonwood and aspen trees grow here in an unusual association, and there are fine views of the distant San Francisco Peaks.

Miles and Directions

0.0 Start at the trailhead by the second gate on the unmaintained dirt road.

3.2 Reach the north end of old highway. Retrace your steps.

6.4 Arrive back at the gated trailhead.

Mogollon Rim Country

The thousand-foot-plus escarpment known as the Mogollon (pronounced mug-ee-ON) Rim sweeps across central Arizona, separating the Colorado Plateau from the Central Highlands. Scores of canyons have been eroded into the rim. Many contain perennial streams and lovely riparian habitats that are popular with fishermen and birders.

Upper Sycamore Canyon from the Sycamore Rim Trail

28 Sycamore Rim Trail

This hike is a long and enjoyable walk on a scenic trail along the rim of Sycamore and Big Springs Canyons.

Distance: 9.6-mile loop
Hiking time: About 6 hours
Difficulty: Moderate
Trail surface: Dirt trails
Best season: Spring through fall
Water: No water available
Other trail users: Horses
Canine compatibility: Controlled dogs allowed
Land status: Sycamore Canyon Wilderness, Kaibab National Forest

Nearest town: Williams
Fees and permits: None
Schedule: Open all year
Maps: USGS Davenport Hill and Garland Prairie; Kaibab National Forest (Williams and Tusayan Ranger Districts)
Trail contacts: Kaibab National Forest, 800 S. Sixth St., Williams, AZ 86046; (928) 635-8200; www.fs.usda.gov/kaibab

Finding the trailhead: From Flagstaff drive about 16 miles west on I-40, then turn left (south) at the Parks exit onto the maintained Garland Prairie Road (FR 141). Drive 12 miles and turn left (south) on FR 131, a signed maintained road. Continue about 1.5 miles to the Dow trailhead.

From Williams drive east on I-40 about 4 miles, then turn right (south) at the Garland Prairie Road exit (this is not the same exit for Garland Prairie mentioned above). Drive 8.5 miles on FR 141 to reach FR 131; turn right (south) and continue 1.5 miles to the trailhead. GPS: N35 9.29'/W111 59.03'

The Hike

The Sycamore Rim Trail is only partially shown on the USGS topographic maps. Almost immediately after you leave the parking lot, you'll cross the route of the historic Overland Road. Shortly afterward you meet the Sycamore Rim Trail at a T intersection, where you'll turn right to start the loop. The trail follows the rim of Sycamore Canyon, which is a shallow drainage at this point. A Forest Service sign points out the location of an old lumber mill. Not much is visible now except a few rotting timbers.

The shallow canyon gradually broadens into a meadow, which the trail crosses to meet FR 56. On the west side of the road, the trail starts to climb KA Hill in a series of switchbacks. After crossing the forested summit, the trail drops southwest down the gentle, pine-forested slopes and into a shallow drainage. It crosses a road (FR 13) and then passes Pomeroy Tanks, a series of natural basins in the drainage that sometimes hold water. A spur trail goes southwest to Pomeroy Tanks trailhead on FR 104.

Now the trail follows the drainage, soon crossing back to the east side. The canyon gradually deepens, and the trail meets another spur trail. This one goes to Sycamore

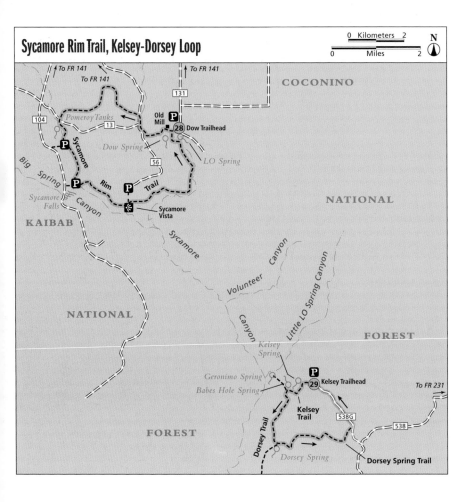

Sycamore Rim Trail, Kelsey-Dorsey Loop

0 Kilometers 2

0 Miles 2

N

To FR 141
To FR 141
To FR 141

COCONINO

131

104

Pomeroy Tanks

13

Old Mill

28 Dow Trailhead

Sycamore

Dow Spring

LO Spring

56

Big Spring

Rim

Trail

NATIONAL

Sycamore
Falls

Canyon

Sycamore
Vista

KAIBAB

Sycamore

NATIONAL

Volunteer Canyon

Canyon

Little LO Spring Canyon

FOREST

Canyon

Kelsey
Spring

Geronimo Spring

Babes Hole Spring

29 Kelsey Trailhead

To FR 231

Kelsey
Trail

538G

538

FOREST

Dorsey Trail

Dorsey Spring

Dorsey Spring Trail

Falls trailhead, also on FR 104. The drainage you've been following is joined by Big Spring Canyon, which soon drops over the falls. The basalt cliffs here are a popular rock-climbing area.

As the canyon deepens, the trail heads southeast along its rim, climbing gradually. At Sycamore Vista you'll have a fine view of Sycamore Canyon Wilderness to the south. Another short spur trail goes to Sycamore Vista trailhead on FR 56. At this point the canyon is more than 500 feet deep. The trail now heads east across the broad point separating Big Spring Canyon from Sycamore Canyon. After it meets the rim of Sycamore Canyon, the trail follows the rim back to the junction near Dow trailhead. Turn right to return to the trailhead.

RAILROAD GRADES

The Overland Road was built in 1858 as part of a route across northern Arizona from east to west. Long abandoned, the Forest Service has now developed some of the route as a recreational trail and marked it with wood posts, brass caps, and rock cairns.

Temporary logging mills and camps, such as the one near the Dow trailhead, were moved to follow the logging operation. The logs were transported on temporary railroad spurs. After the transcontinental railroad reached the area in 1883, railroads were the most economical method of moving cut timber to the mills, as well as men and supplies into the forest. When logging was complete in an area (meaning that all the accessible large trees were cut), the rails would be removed and reused on another spur railroad. The roadbeds were built to the minimum standard necessary for their short-lived purpose. Today these old railroad grades can be traced for miles through the forest; some have been rebuilt into modern dirt roads.

Miles and Directions

0.0 Start at the Dow trailhead on FR 131.
0.1 Meet the Sycamore Rim Trail; turn right.
1.4 Cross FR 56.
2.1 Start to climb KA Hill in a series of switchbacks.
4.2 Cross FR 13.
4.4 Pass Pomeroy Tanks.
5.2 Reach Sycamore Falls.
6.6 Reach Sycamore Vista.
9.6 Arrive back at the trailhead.

Option

From the Dow trailhead you can also hike the route of the Overland Road east into Garland Prairie or west toward Pomeroy Tanks.

29 Kelsey-Dorsey Loop

This scenic, remote hike in Sycamore Canyon features tall pine forest and sandstone canyon views.

See map on page 108.
Distance: 6.4-mile loop
Hiking time: About 4 hours
Difficulty: Moderate
Trail surface: Dirt trails
Best season: Spring through fall
Water: Kelsey, Babes Hole, and Dorsey Springs
Other trail users: Horses
Canine compatibility: Controlled dogs allowed

Land status: Sycamore Canyon Wilderness, Coconino National Forest
Nearest town: Flagstaff
Fees and permits: None
Schedule: Open all year
Maps: USGS Sycamore Point; Coconino National Forest
Trail contacts: Coconino National Forest, 1824 S. Thompson St., Flagstaff, AZ 86001; (928) 527-3600; www.fs.usda.gov/coconino

Finding the trailhead: From Flagstaff drive west on West Route 66 West (Business Interstate 40) about 2 miles, then turn left (south) onto the Woody Mountain Road (FR 231). This road starts out as paved but soon becomes maintained dirt. Continue 13.7 miles and turn right (west) at Phone Booth Tank onto a narrower maintained dirt road (FR 538). Continue on the main road 5.3 miles, and then turn right (northwest) onto an unmaintained road (FR 538G), which is signed for the Kelsey Trail. Go 0.6 mile, turning right at a junction to continue on FR 538G 1.3 miles to the end of the road at the Kelsey trailhead. GPS: N33 4.48'/W111 55.89'

The Hike

The Kelsey Trail drops over the upper rim of Sycamore Canyon and descends steeply for a couple of switchbacks, then reaches gentler terrain as it swings west through the pine-oak forest. In 0.5 mile the trail reaches Kelsey Spring, where it turns sharply left (south) to cross a drainage. The trail follows this drainage to the northwest to Babes Hole Spring. Just past the spring go left on the Dorsey Trail, up the hill, at a junction marked by a huge, ancient ponderosa pine. There are good views as the trail contours along the inner rim of rugged Sycamore Canyon. At Dorsey Spring turn left (east) onto the Dorsey Spring Trail. The trail climbs over a low ridge and drops into a drainage, which it follows nearly to the outer rim before swinging north. The trail goes through a low saddle in the forest before turning east again and climbing gradually to the trailhead.

Continue along the seldom-traveled dirt road for 0.6 mile, and then turn left (northeast) at the junction. In another 0.5 mile you will reach FR 538G. Turn left (north) and walk 1.3 miles to the end of the road and your car. It is possible to do a car shuttle to avoid the hike on the road, but it's not really necessary. There is almost no traffic on these roads, and they form a pleasant loop hike.

Sycamore Canyon near the Kelsey Trail

Miles and Directions

0.0 Start at the Kelsey trailhead on FR 538G.

0.4 Reach Kelsey Spring.

1.0 Reach Babes Hole Spring; turn left onto the Dorsey Trail.

2.5 Pass Dorsey Spring; turn left onto the Dorsey Spring Trail.

4.0 Reach the Dorsey trailhead.

4.6 Turn left at a road junction.

5.1 Turn left onto FR 538G.

6.4 Arrive back at the trailhead.

30 Taylor Cabin Loop

A fine hike through the remote red-rock canyons of the Sycamore Canyon and Red Rock–Secret Mountain Wildernesses. A bonus is the return trail across the top of Casner Mountain, which gives you outstanding views of Sycamore Canyon.

Distance: 18.8-mile loop
Hiking time: About 12 hours or 2 days
Difficulty: Strenuous
Trail surface: Dirt trails
Best seasons: Spring and fall
Water: Seasonal in Sycamore Creek
Other trail users: None
Canine compatibility: Controlled dogs allowed
Land status: Sycamore Canyon Wilderness, Coconino National Forest

Nearest town: Sedona
Fees and permits: None
Schedule: Open all year
Maps: USGS Sycamore Point, Sycamore Basin, and Loy Butte; Coconino National Forest
Trail contacts: Coconino National Forest, 1824 S. Thompson St., Flagstaff, AZ 86001; (928) 527-3600; www.fs.usda.gov/coconino

Finding the trailhead: From Sedona drive about 8 miles south on Highway 89A. Turn right (northwest) onto FR 525, a maintained dirt road. Go 2.2 miles, then turn left (west) onto FR 525C. Continue 8.8 miles to the end of the road at the Sycamore Pass trailhead. The last mile or two frequently washes out and may be very rough, but the rest is passable to ordinary cars. The Casner Mountain Trail, which is the return trail for the loop, meets FR 525C 0.8 mile east of Sycamore Pass trailhead. GPS: N34 55.63' / W111 59.71'

The Hike

There is usually water in Sycamore Creek during spring, but it is dry later in the year. You should carry enough water for a dry camp if the creek is dry. On the other hand, Sycamore Creek may be flooding and impassible during snowmelt or after a major storm. In this case you'll have to make the hike an out-and-back, which you can do in a day.

The start of the Dogie Trail is shown on the Loy Butte USGS quad, but the trail is missing from the Sycamore Basin quad. You'll climb a short distance to cross Sycamore Pass and then descend gradually to the west. The trail turns north and works its way along a sloping terrace through piñon-juniper forest. The inner gorge of Sycamore Canyon is visible to the west, and the cliffs of Casner Mountain rise on the east. Finally the Dogie Trail descends to Sycamore Creek and crosses it to join the Cow Flat and Taylor Cabin Trails on the west bank. There are several campsites for small groups on the bluff just to the south. (In an emergency you may be able to find water in Cedar Creek by hiking upstream.)

Taylor Cabin along Sycamore Creek ▶

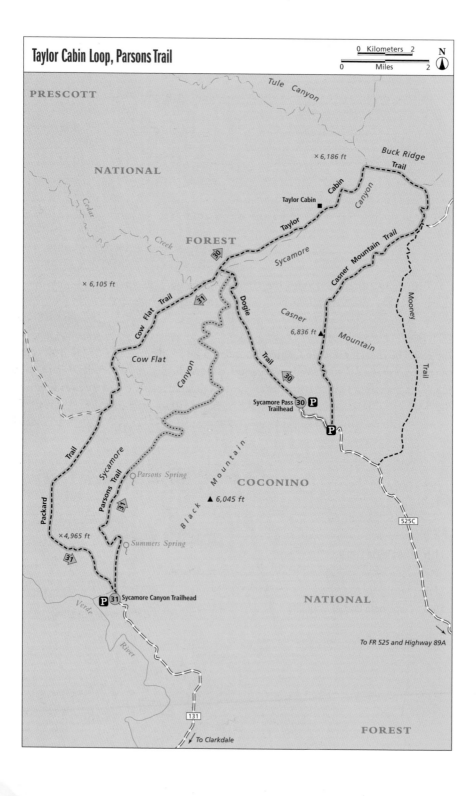

Taylor Cabin Loop, Parsons Trail

0   Kilometers   2

0   Miles   2

N

PRESCOTT

Tule Canyon

× 6,186 ft

Buck Ridge Trail

NATIONAL

Cedar

Creek

Cabin

Taylor Cabin ■

Canyon

Taylor

Casner Mountain Trail

FOREST

30

Sycamore

Mooney

× 6,105 ft

Cow Flat Trail

31

Casner

6,836 ft ▲

Mountain

Trail

Dogie

Cow Flat

Canyon

Trail

30

Sycamore Pass
Trailhead

30 P

P

Trail

Sycamore Trail

Parsons Spring

Black Mountain

COCONINO

525C

Packard

31

▲ 6,045 ft

× 4,965 ft

Summers Spring

31

NATIONAL

Verde

P 31   Sycamore Canyon Trailhead

River

To FR 525 and Highway 89A

131

To Clarkdale

FOREST

Turn right (northeast) on the Taylor Cabin Trail, which stays on the bench to the west of Sycamore Creek. After about 2 miles the trail descends to the creek and becomes harder to find. Watch for Taylor Cabin on the west bank; the trail passes right by this old rancher's line cabin. The trail stays on the west side of the creek after Taylor Cabin. If you lose the trail, boulder-hop directly up the creek bed.

About 1.8 miles from Taylor Cabin, the trail turns right (east) and climbs out of Sycamore Canyon. Watch carefully for the turnoff, which is usually marked with cairns. The USGS topographic maps are essential for finding this trail. Most of the trail follows the major drainage south of Buck Ridge, often staying right in the bed of this very pretty canyon. Near the top the trail turns more to the south and climbs steeply through a fine stand of ponderosa pine and Douglas fir. A single switchback leads to the top of the ridge, where there are excellent views of Sycamore Canyon and the Taylor Basin. The trail reaches a pass and ends at the junction with the Casner Mountain and Mooney Trails.

Turn right (southwest) onto the Casner Mountain Trail, an old road built during power line construction. The road is now closed to vehicles and makes a scenic finish to this loop hike. Follow the trail southwest along the narrow ridge leading to Casner Mountain. There are views of Sycamore Canyon on the west and Mooney Canyon on the east. The trail climbs onto Casner Mountain, a broad plateau capped with dark volcanic rocks. A gradual descent leads to the south edge of the plateau, where the trail descends rapidly in a series of switchbacks. The USGS topographic map shows the trail ending near the bottom of the descent; if you lose the trail, just follow the power line down to FR 525C. Now turn right and walk 0.8 mile up the road back to the Sycamore Pass trailhead.

Miles and Directions

0.0   Start at the Sycamore Pass trailhead on FR 525C, and head out on the Dogie Trail.

0.4   Reach Sycamore Pass.

4.9   Cross Sycamore Creek.

5.0   Turn right onto Taylor Cabin Trail.

7.9   Pass Taylor Cabin.

9.7   Taylor Cabin Trail turns right, up an unnamed side canyon.

12.0   Turn right onto Casner Mountain Trail.

15.6   Climb onto Casner Mountain.

18.0   Reach FR 525C; turn right.

18.8   Arrive back at the trailhead.

31 Parsons Trail

This is a challenging trail and cross–country hike through the remote red-rock country in Sycamore Canyon Wilderness.

See map on page 114.
Distance: 21.4-mile loop
Hiking time: About 2 days
Difficulty: Strenuous
Trail surface: Dirt trails, cross-country along dry washes on sand and boulders
Best seasons: Spring and fall
Water: Sycamore Creek downstream from Parsons Spring; seasonal pools upstream
Other trail users: None
Canine compatibility: Controlled dogs allowed

Land status: Sycamore Canyon Wilderness, Coconino National Forest
Nearest town: Cottonwood
Fees and permits: None
Schedule: Open all year
Maps: USGS Clarkdale and Sycamore Basin; Coconino and Prescott National Forests
Trail contacts: Coconino National Forest, 1824 S. Thompson St., Flagstaff, AZ 86001; (928) 527-3600; www.fs.usda.gov/coconino

Finding the trailhead: From Cottonwood drive to the north end of town on Highway 89A and into the town of Clarkdale, then turn right (east) onto the road to Tuzigoot National Monument. After 0.2 mile, just after crossing the Verde River bridge, turn left (north) onto CR 139 (it becomes FR 131), a maintained dirt road. Drive 10 miles to the end of the road at the Sycamore Canyon trailhead. GPS: N34 51.81'/W112 4.20'

The Hike

Sycamore Creek is normally dry above Parsons Spring. In the spring, seasonal pools above this point make it possible to do this loop without carrying water. During summer and fall, though, you'll have to pick up enough water at Parsons Spring for your camp farther up the canyon. The catch is that during early spring, Sycamore Creek may be flooding from snowmelt in the high country, making this loop trip impossible. If the creek is running muddy at the trailhead, content yourself with a short day hike to Summers or Parsons Spring. Do not attempt to cross the creek when it is flooding. In summer this loop is recommended only for hikers experienced at dry camping in hot weather.

From the trailhead follow the good trail 0.2 mile north into Sycamore Creek. On the left the Packard Trail crosses the creek; this is our return trail. (**Note:** Sycamore Canyon is closed to camping between the trailhead and Parsons Spring.) Continue following Sycamore Creek on the broad, easy trail along the east bank. Sycamore Creek flows year-round and supports a rich variety of riparian trees, including the Arizona sycamore for which the canyon is named. About 1.5 miles from the trailhead, the canyon swings sharply left, then right. During the winters of 1993 and 1994, massive flooding completely rearranged the creek bed. Evidence of the flooding is everywhere: saplings leaning downstream, piles of driftwood and even huge logs far above

Sycamore Creek along the Parsons Trail

normal stream level, and collapsed stream banks. But flooding is a normal occurrence in these deep canyons. The streamside trees and vegetation are well adapted to the environment and recover with amazing rapidity.

Above Parsons Spring, the source for Sycamore Creek, the creek bed dries up. Continue up Sycamore Creek by boulder-hopping along the broad, dry wash. You may see seasonal pools of water in the bends of the creek. Watch for petroglyphs along the rock walls of the canyon. Although strenuous, progress up the creek bed is relatively fast because the periodic floods keep the bed clear of brush. The gorge becomes shallower after about 6 miles. The Dogie Trail crosses Sycamore Creek 7.6 miles above Parsons Spring. Turn left (west) onto the Dogie Trail, which joins the Taylor Cabin and Cow Flat Trails above the west bank. Now turn left (south) onto the Cow Flat Trail. There are several good campsites for small groups on the bluffs overlooking the creek to the west. There is no water except for possible seasonal pools in Sycamore Creek.

After the confines of Sycamore Creek and the rugged boulder-hopping, it is a pleasure to walk the easy Cow Flat Trail southwest through the open piñon-juniper forest. Shortly the trail crosses Cedar Creek. (This creek is usually dry at the crossing, but water can sometimes be found about a mile upstream.) The trail climbs gradually for another mile and passes through a broad saddle to enter Sycamore Basin. The walking is very easy through this open basin, with fine views of the surrounding red-rock formations. Camping is unlimited—if you carry water for a dry camp. The trail crosses Cow Flat then skirts the head of a side canyon. It then climbs gradually to another pass. On the far side of the pass, the trail ends at a trailhead at the end of FR 181.

Now go south on the Packard Trail. Packard Mesa forms the west rim of lower Sycamore Canyon, and the trail generally stays near the crest of the mesa as it works its way south through open piñon pine and juniper stands. About 4 miles from FR 181, the trail turns east and descends into Sycamore Canyon. It crosses the creek and meets the Parsons Trail; turn right to return to the trailhead.

Miles and Directions

0.0 Start at the Sycamore Canyon trailhead at the end of FR 131.

0.2 Reach Sycamore Creek and junction with the Packard Trail; stay right. (**FYI:** The Packard Trail to the left, which crosses the creek, is the return trail.)

1.2 Pass Summers Spring.

3.6 Pass Parsons Spring.

11.2 Turn left onto the Dogie Trail.

11.3 Turn left onto the Cow Flat Trail.

11.7 Cross Cedar Creek.

12.7 Reach pass into Sycamore Basin.

15.8 Climb gradually to a second pass.

19.8 Reach rim of Sycamore Canyon.

21.2 Cross Sycamore Creek and turn right onto Parsons Trail.

21.4 Arrive back at the trailhead.

32 Secret Mountain Trail

This trail wanders out onto Secret Mountain, an isolated mesa featuring a historic cabin and some good views of the red-rock canyons in the Red Rock–Secret Mountain Wilderness.

Distance: 9.8 miles out and back
Hiking time: About 5 hours
Difficulty: Moderate
Trail surface: Dirt trails
Best seasons: Spring and fall
Water: No water available
Other trail users: Horses
Canine compatibility: Controlled dogs allowed
Land status: Red Rock–Secret Mountain Wilderness, Coconino National Forest

Nearest town: Flagstaff
Fees and permits: None
Schedule: Open all year
Maps: USGS Loy Butte and Wilson Mountain; Coconino National Forest
Trail contacts: Coconino National Forest, 1824 S. Thompson St., Flagstaff, AZ 86001; (928) 527-3600; www.fs.usda.gov/coconino

Finding the trailhead: From Flagstaff drive west on West Route 66 (Business Interstate 40) about 2 miles, then turn left (south) onto Woody Mountain Road (FR 231). This road starts out as paved but soon becomes maintained dirt. Continue 13.7 miles, then turn right (west) at Phone Booth Tank onto a narrower maintained dirt road (FR 538). Continue on this road 6.8 miles, passing the turnoff to Turkey Butte Lookout. The road is unmaintained after this point but is passable to low-clearance vehicles with care when it is dry. After a storm or during snowmelt, the mud will be impassable. In another 1.5 miles the road passes just west of a power line, then passes a stock tank. About 8.9 miles from Phone Booth Tank, FR 538 turns left (southeast) at the junction with FR 538B and crosses under the power line. Continue 2.7 miles on FR 538 to the end of the road. GPS: N34 58.81' / W111 54.09'

The Hike

The trailhead is on the edge of the Mogollon Rim, but the view is mostly blocked by the bulk of Secret Mountain, rising to the south. Start by following the Secret Mountain Trail along the ridge to the southeast. It drops down to the saddle between the rim and Secret Mountain, meeting the Loy Canyon Trail, a 9.6-mile out and back through the canyon.

The Secret Mountain Trail climbs about 200 feet onto Secret Mountain, where there is a trail junction. These two side trails lead east to viewpoints overlooking Secret Canyon. The main trail continues south across the pine and oak–forested plateau to the ruins of Secret Cabin. Most likely, ranchers built the cabin as a line cabin for use during roundups. Water can sometimes be found in the drainage east of the ruin.

Secret Mountain Trail, Loy Canyon Trail, Secret Canyon, Bear Sign Canyon

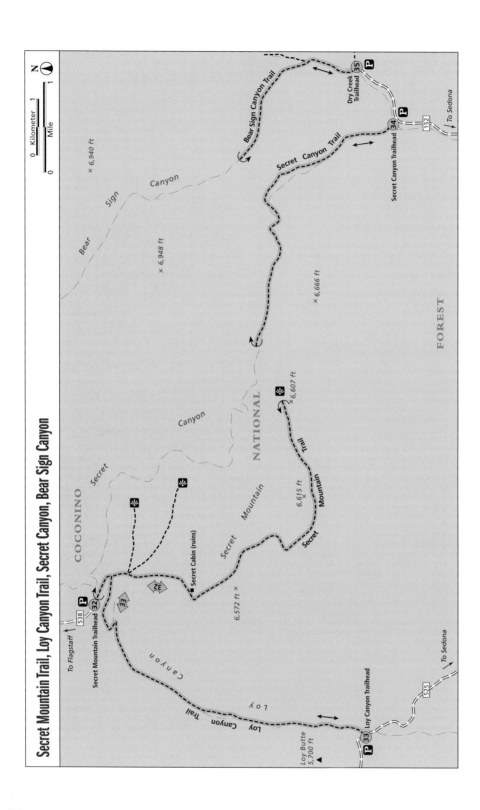

From the cabin continue south. Soon the trail reaches a point on the west rim of Secret Mountain, with views to the southwest toward the Verde Valley and Mingus Mountain. After this point the trail heads generally southeast and skirts the southwest rim of Secret Mountain. A large fire burned much of this area in 1996. The trail finally turns east and ends at the eastern tip of Secret Mountain. You're looking down Long Canyon and at the mass of Maroon Mountain, which divides Long and Secret Canyons.

There is unlimited camping along the trail, so it makes a pleasant, easy overnight backpack trip if you're willing to carry water for a dry camp.

Miles and Directions

0.0 Start at Secret Mountain trailhead at the end of FR 538.

0.4 Meet Loy Canyon Trail at saddle; stay left on Secret Mountain Trail.

0.6 Pass two side trails. (**FYI:** These side trails lead east to Secret Canyon viewpoints.)

1.4 Arrive at Secret Cabin ruins.

4.9 Reach viewpoint at the eastern tip of Secret Mountain. Retrace your steps.

9.8 Arrive back at the trailhead.

33 Loy Canyon Trail

This scenic hike up a red-rock canyon takes you to the top of the Mogollon Rim.

See map on page 120.
Distance: 9.6 miles out and back
Elevation change: 1,900 feet
Hiking time: About 6 hours
Difficulty: Strenuous
Trail surface: Dirt trails
Best season: Fall through spring
Water: No water available
Other trail users: Horses
Canine compatibility: Controlled dogs allowed

Land status: Red Rock–Secret Mountain Wilderness, Coconino National Forest
Nearest town: Sedona
Fees and permits: None
Schedule: Open all year
Maps: USGS Loy Butte; Coconino National Forest
Trail contacts: Coconino National Forest, 1824 S. Thompson St., Flagstaff, AZ 86001; (928) 527-3600; www.fs.usda.gov/coconino

Finding the trailhead: From Sedona drive to the west end of town on Highway 89A; turn right at a traffic light onto Dry Creek Road. Drive 2.8 miles and turn left onto Boynton Canyon Road. Continue 1.6 miles and turn left onto FR 152C, a maintained dirt road. After 3 miles turn right onto FR 525. Continue 3.7 miles to the Loy Canyon trailhead. (If you see Hancock Ranch to the right, you have gone too far.) GPS: N34 56.10'/W111 55.63'

The Hike

Initially the trail skirts the Hancock Ranch along the ranch's east boundary. It then joins the dry creek bed, which it follows northward through the open piñon pine, juniper, and Arizona cypress forest. Conical Loy Butte looms to the west, and the cliffs of Secret Mountain tower over Loy Canyon on the east. After 2.1 miles the canyon becomes narrower, and the trail turns slightly toward the northeast. In another mile the trail turns toward the east as the canyon opens up a bit. The buff-colored Coconino sandstone cliffs of the Mogollon Rim loom above the trail to the north; matching cliffs form the north end of Secret Mountain. Watch carefully for the point where the trail leaves the canyon bottom and begins climbing the north side of the canyon in a series of switchbacks. Although it is a steep climb, the reward is an expanding view of Loy Canyon. Notice the contrast between the brushy vegetation on this dry south-facing slope and the cool, moist pine-and-fir forest across the canyon to the south.

The Loy Canyon Trail ends where it joins the Secret Mountain Trail in the saddle between Secret Mountain and the Mogollon Rim. Turn left here and climb the short distance to the rim and the Secret Mountain trailhead. Views are limited here, but if you walk a few hundred yards along the road, there is a great view down Loy Canyon.

Miles and Directions

0.0 Start at the Loy Canyon trailhead on FR 525.

2.1 Begin red-rock narrows.

3.0 Reach end of narrows.

4.4 Turn left onto the Secret Mountain Trail.

4.8 Reach Secret Mountain trailhead, your turnaround point.

9.6 Arrive back at the trailhead.

Options

Combine the Loy Canyon and Secret Mountain Trails for a longer hike. (See the Secret Mountain Trail description for information.)

34 Secret Canyon

This is an exceptionally fine hike up the longest canyon in the Red Rock–Secret Mountain Wilderness. Its length keeps the crowds away.

See map on page 120.
Distance: 7.8 miles out and back
Hiking time: About 5 hours
Difficulty: Moderate
Trail surface: Dirt trails
Best season: Fall through spring
Water: Upper Secret Canyon
Other trail users: None
Canine compatibility: Controlled dogs allowed

Land status: Red Rock–Secret Mountain Wilderness, Coconino National Forest
Nearest town: Sedona
Fees and permits: None
Schedule: Open all year
Maps: USGS Wilson Mountain; Coconino National Forest
Trail contacts: Coconino National Forest, 1824 S. Thompson St., Flagstaff, AZ 86001; (928) 527-3600; www.fs.usda.gov/coconino

Finding the trailhead: From Sedona drive to the west end of town on Highway 89A. Turn right at a traffic light onto Dry Creek Road. After 2 miles turn right onto dirt FR 152 (also called Dry Creek Road). Although this road is maintained, it receives a lot of traffic, and its condition varies. Drive 3.2 miles to the Secret Canyon trailhead on the left side of the road. The parking area is small, but there are other parking spots nearby. GPS: N34 55.781' / W111 48.39'

The Hike

Secret Canyon, the longest and most remote canyon in the Dry Creek Basin, is nearly as long as its more famous neighbor, Oak Creek. It also has a perennial stream in the upper section, a rarity in the red-rock area.

The Secret Canyon Trail crosses Dry Creek and enters the Red Rock–Secret Mountain Wilderness only a few yards from the road. You'll cross Secret Canyon wash several times; if either it or Dry Creek is flooding, this hike will be impossible. Normally, however, lower Secret Canyon is dry and the hike is easy through the piñon-juniper-cypress forest. About 0.5 mile from the trailhead, the HS Canyon Trail branches left. The old jeep trail ends at a small clearing, giving you good views into upper Secret Canyon. Now the trail contours along the north side of the drainage for a short distance before dropping back into the bed. The canyon walls become narrower here and are formed by the Mogollon Rim on the north and Maroon Mountain on the south. There is normally water in this section. Watch for poison ivy, a low-growing plant with shiny leaves that grow in groups of three. Fall colors in this part of the canyon are a beautiful mix of reds, oranges, and violets, with most of the color provided by Arizona bigtooth maple and poison ivy. About 4 miles from the trailhead, the hike ends as the trail fades out. Only those willing to do difficult cross-country hiking should continue above this point.

Upper Secret Canyon

Miles and Directions

0.0 Start at the Secret Canyon trailhead on FR 152 / Dry Creek Road.

1.8 Reach end of old jeep road.

3.9 Reach the end of the trail in Secret Canyon. Retrace your steps.

7.8 Arrive back at the trailhead.

35 Bear Sign Canyon

This is a very easy and scenic hike into a red-rock canyon tucked under the white cliffs of the Mogollon Rim.

See map on page 120.
Distance: 4.4 miles out and back
Hiking time: About 2 hours
Difficulty: Easy
Trail surface: Dirt trails
Best season: Fall through spring
Water: No water available
Other trail users: None
Canine compatibility: Controlled dogs allowed

Land status: Red Rock–Secret Mountain Wilderness, Coconino National Forest
Nearest town: Sedona
Fees and permits: None
Schedule: Open all year
Maps: USGS Wilson Mountain; Coconino National Forest
Trail contacts: Coconino National Forest, 1824 S. Thompson St., Flagstaff, AZ 86001; (928) 527-3600; www.fs.usda.gov/coconino

Finding the trailhead: From Sedona drive to the west end of town on Highway 89A, then turn right at a traffic light onto Dry Creek Road. After 2 miles turn right onto dirt FR 152 (also called Dry Creek Road). Although this road is maintained, it receives a lot of traffic, and its condition varies. Drive 4 miles to the end of the road at the Dry Creek trailhead. GPS: N34 56.22'/W111 47.70'

The Hike

Start out on the Dry Creek Trail. (Two trails begin at this trailhead. The Dry Creek Trail goes north; the Vultee Arch Trail goes east.) Hike 0.6 mile north, then turn left (northwest) at Bear Sign Canyon, the first side canyon on the left. The trail continues about 1.6 miles up Bear Sign Canyon before fading out. It is possible to go farther, but the canyon becomes much rougher. There are great views of the cliffs of the Mogollon Rim, and after wet periods the creek will be running. The vegetation is the usual, but still delightful, mix of Arizona cypress, piñon pine, juniper, and chaparral brush.

Miles and Directions

0.0 Start at the Dry Creek trailhead at the end of FR 152 / Dry Creek Road.
0.6 Turn left onto Bear Sign Canyon Trail.
2.2 Reach the end of the hike as the trail fades out. Retrace your steps.
4.4 Arrive back at the trailhead.

Lunch stop above Bear Sign Canyon ▶

36 Thomas Point Trail

This hike is a great alternative to the crowded West Fork Trail and is located right across the highway. There are excellent views of the West Fork of Oak Creek and Oak Creek Canyon itself.

Distance: 2.0 miles out and back
Hiking time: About 2 hours
Difficulty: Easy
Trail surface: Dirt trails
Best season: Spring through fall
Water: No water available
Other trail users: None
Canine compatibility: Controlled dogs allowed
Land status: Coconino National Forest
Nearest town: Sedona

Fees and permits: Red Rock Pass required for parking at the trailhead, plus an additional parking lot fee
Schedule: Open all year
Maps: USGS Munds Park; Coconino National Forest
Trail contacts: Coconino National Forest, 1824 S. Thompson St., Flagstaff, AZ 86001; (928) 527-3600; www.fs.usda.gov/coconino

Finding the trailhead: From Sedona drive about 11 miles north on Highway 89A. Turn left into the West Fork parking area and trailhead. GPS: N34 59.29'/W111 44.70'

The Hike

Like most of the trails in Oak Creek Canyon, this trail is not shown on the USGS topographic map. From the parking area follow the trail south through an old orchard for about 100 yards, then cross the highway to a trail sign. The trail climbs south through shady ponderosa pine–Gambel oak forest and then turns a corner onto a much drier, south-facing slope. Here, because of the increased temperature and evaporation, the chaparral plants dominate: scrub oak, mountain mahogany, and manzanita. There are fine views down the canyon to the flat-topped mesa of Wilson Mountain.

A switchback leads to a point overlooking the mouth of the West Fork, and then the trail turns east again and climbs into a pine saddle. The trail finishes by following the ridge east 100 yards to the rim, where views are limited because of the thick forest. You'll find a better viewpoint by walking about 100 yards west from the saddle onto a rock outcrop. Here you're looking directly west into the West Fork of Oak Creek.

Miles and Directions

0.0 Start at the West Fork trailhead.
0.4 The trail emerges onto the south-facing slope.
1.0 Reach the east rim of Oak Creek Canyon, your turnaround point.
2.0 Arrive back at the trailhead.

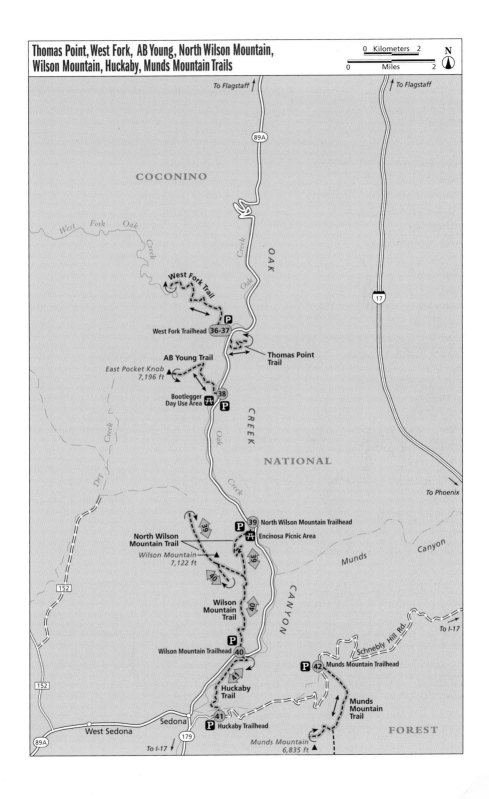

37 West Fork Trail

This is an easy and very popular hike along the spectacular West Fork of Oak Creek, the wilderness fork of Oak Creek Canyon. A fine forest of tall ponderosa pine and Douglas fir as well as a perennial stream grace the canyon floor, while red-rock formations and towering buttresses of white Coconino sandstone form the canyon walls.

See map on page 129.
Distance: 6.0 miles out and back
Hiking time: About 3 hours
Difficulty: Easy
Trail surface: Dirt trails
Best season: Year-round
Water: West Fork of Oak Creek
Other trail users: None
Canine compatibility: Controlled dogs allowed
Land status: Red Rock–Secret Mountain Wilderness, Coconino National Forest
Nearest town: Sedona

Fees and permits: Red Rock Pass required for parking at the trailhead, plus an additional fee for the parking lot
Schedule: Open all year
Maps: USGS Dutton Hill, Wilson Mountain, and Munds Park; Coconino National Forest
Trail contacts: Coconino National Forest, 1824 S. Thompson St., Flagstaff, AZ 86001; (928) 527-3600; www.fs.usda.gov/coconino
Other: Lower 6 miles of the West Fork is closed to camping

Finding the trailhead: From Sedona drive about 11 miles north on Highway 89A. Turn left into the West Fork trailhead parking area. GPS: N34 59.29' / W111 44.70'

The Hike

The West Fork is an easy but extremely popular hike. It is not the place to go to escape crowds, especially on weekends. For solitude try the Thomas Point Trail on the opposite side of Oak Creek. Note that the Forest Service prohibits camping in the lower West Fork due to heavy use. Stay on the trail and do not pick flowers or otherwise disturb this fragile environment. Watch for poison ivy, which is common along the trail.

Follow the trail, which is not shown on the USGS topographic map, over the bridge across Oak Creek. The trail now goes south along the creek and then turns right (west) into the West Fork. Soon you'll leave the sounds of the busy highway behind and be able to hear the pleasant murmur of the creek and the whisper of the wind in the trees. Buttresses of Coconino sandstone tower on the left, while the canyon floor is filled with a tall ponderosa pine and Douglas fir forest. The trail crosses the creek several times and ends about 3 miles up the canyon. Walking is very easy to this point, which is the end of the hike.

Miles and Directions

0.0   Start at the West Fork trailhead.

0.4   Reach the mouth of the West Fork.

3.0   The trail ends. Retrace your steps.

6.0   Arrive back at the trailhead.

Options

Experienced canyon hikers can continue up the West Fork to its head near FR 231. This hike requires wading in the creek and occasional swimming to cross deep pools. There is a serious danger of flash flooding. Do not continue unless you have a stable weather forecast and are prepared to handle the deep, often cold, pools.

Another possible hike for the adventurous, experienced canyon hiker is to climb to the south rim of the canyon and then hike to East Pocket Knob and use the AB Young Trail to descend back into Oak Creek Canyon. There is a route up the nameless canyon that is just west of West Buzzard Point.

West Fork Trail in the fall

38 AB Young Trail

This is a good trail to the west rim of Oak Creek Canyon. It offers the best views of Oak Creek Canyon of all the rim trails.

See map on page 129.
Distance: 4.4 miles out and back
Hiking time: About 4 hours
Difficulty: Moderate
Trail surface: Dirt trails; boulder hopping across Oak Creek at the beginning of the hike
Best season: Year-round
Water: No water available
Other trail users: None
Canine compatibility: Controlled dogs allowed

Land status: Red Rock–Secret Mountain Wilderness, Coconino National Forest
Nearest town: Sedona
Fees and permits: None
Schedule: Open all year
Maps: USGS Munds Park and Wilson Mountain; Coconino National Forest
Trail contacts: Coconino National Forest, 1824 S. Thompson St., Flagstaff, AZ 86001; (928) 527-3600; www.fs.usda.gov/coconino

Finding the trailhead: From Sedona drive about 9 miles north on Highway 89A to the Bootlegger Day Use Area. Do not block the entrance; park in the highway pullout just to the north. GPS: N34 58.21'/W111 45.03'

The Hike

Walk through the campground and cross Oak Creek. Turn right (north) onto the trail, which parallels the creek, and watch for the signed junction with the AB Young Trail. You'll turn left onto this good, maintained trail, which then turns sharply right and starts climbing to the northwest. The broad-leafed trees in the riparian habitat along the creek are soon left behind as the trail climbs through ponderosa pine forest. After a short distance the trail begins switchbacking directly up the steep slope. The dry southwest exposure supports dense chaparral brush, and the view opens up as you climb. Just below the rim the trail veers north in a long final switchback. At the rim the trail enters pine forest again. Turn southwest and follow the cairned trail, which is fainter, along the pine-forested rim to the crest of an east–west ridge. Here the trail turns west and follows the flat-topped ridge to East Pocket Knob and the end of the trail at the USDA Forest Service fire tower. Get permission from the lookout before climbing the tower for a panoramic view of the Mogollon Rim and Oak Creek Canyon.

▶ The AB Young Trail was originally built to move cattle to and from the rim country and was improved by the Civilian Conservation Corps in the 1930s. The CCC, along with several other conservation agencies, built thousands of miles of trails in the national forests and parks during this period.

Oak Creek Canyon from the AB Young Trail

Miles and Directions

0.0 Start at the trailhead at Bootlegger Campground. Cross Oak Creek and turn right onto the trail.

0.3 Turn left onto the AB Young Trail. Turn sharply right and then begin to climb.

1.4 Reach the west rim of Oak Creek Canyon.

1.8 The trail leaves the rim.

2.2 Reach the East Pocket Lookout. (**FYI:** Ask permission from the lookout before climbing the tower.) Retrace your steps.

4.4 Arrive back at the trailhead.

39 North Wilson Mountain Trail

This is a good hike on a hot day—much of the trail is in a north-facing, shady canyon in the Red Rock–Secret Mountain Wilderness. You'll have excellent views of Oak Creek Canyon, the Dry Creek basin, and the Mogollon Rim.

See map on page 129.
Distance: 7.6 miles out and back
Hiking time: About 5 hours
Difficulty: Strenuous
Trail surface: Dirt trails
Best season: Year-round
Water: No water available
Other trail users: None
Canine compatibility: Controlled dogs allowed

Land status: Red Rock–Secret Mountain Wilderness, Coconino National Forest
Nearest town: Sedona
Fees and permits: None
Schedule: Open all year
Maps: USGS Munds Park and Wilson Mountain; Coconino National Forest
Trail contacts: Coconino National Forest, 1824 S. Thompson St., Flagstaff, AZ 86001; (928) 527-3600; www.fs.usda.gov/coconino

Finding the trailhead: From Sedona drive about 5 miles north on Highway 89A to the Encinosa Picnic Area. Park in the trailhead parking area at the entrance to the picnic area. GPS: N34 55.55'/W111 44.13'

The Hike

The trailhead is signed, although the North Wilson Mountain Trail is not shown on the USGS topographic map. The trail starts climbing immediately through mixed chaparral, ponderosa pine, and oak forest. When the trail reaches the ridge above the picnic area, it turns to the south and follows the ridge a short distance, giving you good views of Oak Creek Canyon. After leaving the ridge the trail climbs southwest up a wooded drainage. The shade of the large ponderosa pines is a welcome relief on hot days. As the trail nears the base of the massive, buff-colored Coconino sandstone cliffs, it crosses the drainage and begins to switchback up the slope to the east. There are more fine views when the trail reaches the ridge at the top of this slope. Now the trail turns to the south again and follows the ridge onto the First Bench of Wilson Mountain, a gently sloping volcanic plateau level with the east rim of Oak Creek Canyon.

Aerial view of Wilson Mountain from above Bear Wallow Canyon ▶

Near the south end of the bench, the North Wilson Mountain Trail meets the Wilson Mountain Trail at a signed junction. The Wilson Mountain Trail is shown on the USGS topographic map. Turn right (west) here and follow the Wilson Mountain Trail as it climbs Wilson Mountain itself. Several short switchbacks lead through the basalt cliffs near the rim. The trail swings left into a drainage, which it follows to reach a gentle saddle on the wooded summit plateau. The actual summit is a small knob just to the north of this saddle.

There is a signed trail junction in the saddle. Continue straight ahead and follow the trail northwest about 1.4 miles to the north end of Wilson Mountain. The USGS topographic map shows the trail ending just west of the point marked 7,076 on the map, but actually it continues to the rim. Here you are overlooking Sterling Pass, upper Dry Creek, Oak Creek, the Mogollon Rim, and the San Francisco Peaks. The view of the maze of red, buff, and gray cliffs is well worth the long hike.

Miles and Directions

0.0   Start at the North Wilson Mountain trailhead at the entrance to Encinosa Picnic Area.

1.4   Reach First Bench of Wilson Mountain.

1.8   Turn right onto the Wilson Mountain Trail.

2.4   Continue straight (northwest) at the signed summit trail junction.

3.8   Reach the north rim of Wilson Mountain. Retrace your steps.

7.6   Arrive back at the trailhead.

Options

The actual summit, a small knob with limited views, is located 0.2 mile north of the summit trail junction. A better option is to walk 0.4 mile to the south rim of the mountain. See the Wilson Mountain Trail description for information.

40 Wilson Mountain Trail

This popular trail climbs the south slopes of Wilson Mountain in the Red Rock–Secret Mountain Wilderness. Your reward for the effort is one of the best views of the Sedona area.

See map on page 129.
Distance: 6.4 miles out and back
Hiking time: About 5 hours
Difficulty: Strenuous
Trail surface: Dirt trails
Best season: Fall through spring
Water: No water available
Other trail users: None
Canine compatibility: Controlled dogs allowed

Land status: Red Rock–Secret Mountain Wilderness, Coconino National Forest
Nearest town: Sedona
Fees and permits: None
Schedule: Open all year
Maps: USGS Wilson Mountain and Munds Park; Coconino National Forest
Trail contacts: Coconino National Forest, 1824 S. Thompson St., Flagstaff, AZ 86001; (928) 527-3600; www.fs.usda.gov/coconino

Finding the trailhead: From Sedona drive 1.6 miles north on Highway 89A. Cross Midgely Bridge, then turn left into the Wilson Mountain trailhead and viewpoint. GPS: N34 53.14' / W111 44.49'

The Hike

The Wilson Mountain Trail starts climbing immediately, but then the climb moderates for a bit as the trail goes north through open piñon-juniper forest. The climb starts in earnest as the trail starts switchbacking up the steep, south-facing slopes. The view opens out as the chaparral brush that favors this sunbaked slope replaces the pygmy forest. The trail reaches the First Bench of Wilson Mountain then continues north past the junction with the North Wilson Mountain Trail. Stay left here, and continue as the trail swings west and climbs onto the summit plateau. At a trail junction in a saddle, turn left and walk 0.4 mile to the south rim of Wilson Mountain. This great spot affords a sweeping view of the Sedona area.

Miles and Directions

0.0   Start at the Wilson Mountain trailhead and viewpoint.

2.2   Reach First Bench of Wilson Mountain.

2.8   Turn left at saddle trail junction.

3.2   Reach south rim of Wilson Mountain. Retrace your steps.

6.4   Arrive back at trailhead.

Options

The actual summit, a small knob with limited views, is located 0.2 mile north of the summit trail junction. A better option is to hike 1.4 miles to the north rim of the mountain. (See the North Wilson Mountain Trail description for information.)

41 Huckaby Trail

A fine day hike on one of the few trails along Oak Creek itself. It also features stunning views of Steamboat and Wilson Mountains.

See map on page 129.
Distance: 5.0 miles out and back
Hiking time: About 3 hours
Difficulty: Moderate
Trail surface: Dirt trails
Best season: Fall through spring
Water: Oak Creek
Other trail users: Mountain bikes and horses
Canine compatibility: Controlled dogs allowed

Land status: Coconino National Forest
Nearest town: Sedona
Fees and permits: None
Schedule: Open all year
Maps: USGS Munds Park, Munds Mountain, and Sedona; Coconino National Forest
Trail contacts: Coconino National Forest, 1824 S. Thompson St., Flagstaff, AZ 86001; (928) 527-3600; www.fs.usda.gov/coconino

Finding the trailhead: From the junction of Highways 89A and 179 in Sedona, go south 0.4 mile on Highway 179. Cross Oak Creek Bridge; turn left onto Schnebly Hill Road and drive 1.9 miles. Turn left into the Margs Draw / Huckaby trailhead. GPS: N34 51.98' / W111 44.99'

The Hike

From the Margs Draw / Huckaby trailhead, the trail goes west and then turns right at the Margs Draw Trail junction. The Huckaby Trail now follows an old road down into Bear Wallow Canyon, the major canyon north of the trailhead. Follow the old road across normally dry Bear Wallow Canyon and out the north side. Here the foot trail leaves the old road and contours northeast above the canyon. Soon a switchback takes you to the north as the trail begins to work its way toward Oak Creek. This is a delightful traverse through piñon-juniper forest, although it would be hot on a summer afternoon.

Soon you'll start to descend to Oak Creek via a few switchbacks. For about 0.5 mile, the trail stays on the east side of the creek, then it crosses to the west side below Midgely Bridge, the impressive structure spanning Mormon Canyon on Highway 89A. Now it follows an old wagon road that climbs steeply out of the canyon and switchbacks up to the north end of the bridge. Follow the trail past the viewpoint, under the bridge, and up to the Wilson Mountain trailhead.

Wilson Mountain from the Huckaby Trail

Miles and Directions

0.0 Start at the Margs Draw / Huckaby trailhead.

0.1 After junction with Margs Draw Trail, turn right onto the Huckaby Trail.

0.3 Head down into Bear Wallow Canyon.

1.5 Reach Oak Creek, staying on the east side of the creek.

2.1 Cross Oak Creek.

2.5 Reach the Wilson Mountain trailhead, your turnaround point.

5.0 Arrive back at the trailhead.

Options

This hike can be done one-way with a car shuttle. You can also hike farther on the Wilson Mountain Trail.

42 Munds Mountain Trail

This hike takes you up a historic road and offers excellent views of Mitten Ridge, Bear Wallow Canyon, Munds Mountain, and Sedona.

See map on page 129.
Distance: 4.2 miles out and back
Hiking time: About 3 hours
Difficulty: Moderate
Trail surface: Dirt trails and roads
Best season: Spring through fall
Water: No water available
Other trail users: None
Canine compatibility: Controlled dogs allowed

Land status: Munds Mountain Wilderness, Coconino National Forest
Nearest town: Sedona
Fees and permits: None
Schedule: Open all year
Maps: USGS Munds Park and Munds Mountain; Coconino National Forest
Trail contacts: Coconino National Forest, 1824 S. Thompson St., Flagstaff, AZ 86001; (928) 527-3600; www.fs.usda.gov/coconino

Finding the trailhead: From the junction of Highways 89A and 179 in Sedona, go south 0.4 mile on Highway 179. Cross Oak Creek Bridge, and turn left onto Schnebly Hill Road. This road gets heavy use and little maintenance, and can be rough. Drive 4.3 miles and park at the unsigned trailhead where the road passes through a saddle between the red buttes to the west and the brushy slope on the right. GPS: N34 52.94' / W111 42.66'

The Hike

From the parking area look across the road and up. You will see an old road descending the slopes from the left (southeast). It comes nearly down to the present road, then does a switchback to the right and parallels the road just above it. Walk south down the main road about 100 yards until you can climb up to reach the old road. Follow the old road back to the left (north), around the switchback, and then southward. The trail reaches the Mogollon Rim after 0.9 mile, and the old road turns sharply north.

Take the foot trail, which continues south along the rim through tall ponderosa pines, climbing gradually. About 0.7 mile from the old road, the trail reaches a high point along the rim and crosses a grassy section with scattered juniper trees where the view opens out to the southeast. The long ridge of Munds Mountain dominates the view ahead to the southwest. The trail drops down a short ridge to a saddle, where there is a signed junction with the Hot Loop Trail to the left. Continue straight ahead about 50 yards to another saddle, where there is a signed junction with the Jacks Canyon Trail.

Stay right and follow the Munds Mountain Trail as it climbs steeply up the northeast slopes. Several switchbacks lead to a ridge, where the grade moderates. This section is interesting for the extreme contrast in vegetation on the two sides of the ridge. Douglas firs growing on the north slopes meet piñon, juniper, and Arizona cypress

THE OLD ROAD

The first part of the hike follows the old alignment of the Schnebly Hill Road, which was originally built as a wagon road from Sedona to the Mogollon Rim and on to Flagstaff. It is now closed to motorized vehicles and makes a fine hiking trail with a panoramic view. Because of the west-facing slope, the dominant vegetation is chaparral brush. Near the top there is a dense stand of Gambel oak, a small slender deciduous tree about 10 to 20 feet high. Gambel oaks often favor the slopes just below escarpments or rims.

growing on the south slopes. The trail reaches the rim of Munds Mountain about 0.3 mile from the junction at the saddle. According to the map, the actual high point is about 100 yards south along the east edge of the clearing. But it's more rewarding to walk about 200 yards west to the rim for a sweeping view of Sedona and the red-rock country. You can also walk about 100 yards to the north rim for a superb view of lower Oak Creek Canyon and nearly the entire trail you just came up.

Miles and Directions

0.0   Start at the unsigned trailhead.

0.9   Continue south on the foot trail.

1.8   Reach saddle with junction with Jacks Canyon Trail. Stay right on Munds Mountain Trail.

2.1   Reach rim of Munds Mountain. Retrace your steps.

4.2   Arrive back at the trailhead.

43 Tramway Trail

This very enjoyable hike on a short trail provides access to the spectacular upper portions of West Clear Creek.

Distance: 0.8 mile out and back
Hiking time: About 1 hour
Difficulty: Easy
Trail surface: Dirt trails
Best season: Spring through fall
Water: West Clear Creek
Other trail users: None
Canine compatibility: Controlled dogs allowed
Land status: West Clear Creek Wilderness, Coconino National Forest

Nearest town: Flagstaff
Fees and permits: None
Schedule: Open all year
Maps: USGS Calloway Butte; Coconino National Forest
Trail contacts: Coconino National Forest, 1824 S. Thompson St., Flagstaff, AZ 86001; (928) 527-3600; www.fs.usda.gov/coconino

Finding the trailhead: From Flagstaff drive about 50 miles southeast on Lake Mary Road (CR 3), then turn right (west) onto FR 81. Stay on this maintained dirt road for 3 miles, and turn left onto FR 81E. After 3.6 miles turn right onto FR 693. Go 1.2 miles on this unmaintained road; turn left at a fork and continue 0.3 mile to the end of the road. The last 1.5 miles of road may be impassible during wet weather, and a high-clearance vehicle is recommended. GPS: N34 33.50'/W111 25.27'

The Hike

The short but spectacular trail descends into the gorge of West Clear Creek, affording fine views both up and down the canyon. The trail follows the route of an old aerial tramway, ending at the bottom of the canyon.

Miles and Directions

0.0   Start at the trailhead and begin to descend.
0.4   Reach West Clear Creek. Retrace your steps.
0.8   Arrive back at the trailhead.

▶ The Kaibab limestone forms the edge of the Mogollon Rim in this area. This fossil-rich layer was originally deposited in a shallow ocean. Below the Kaibab limestone, the cross-bedded Coconino sandstone appears, with its layers of overlapping petrified sand dunes.

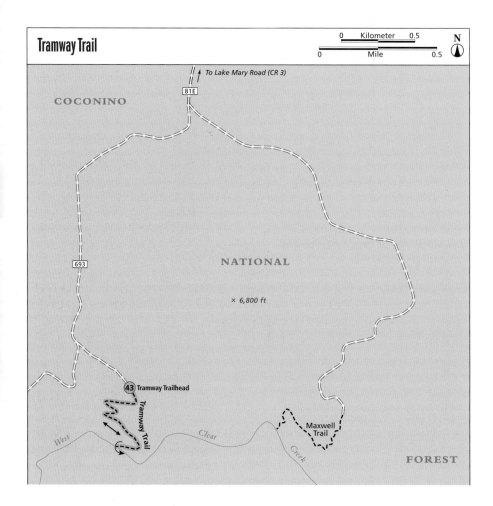

Tramway Trail

To Lake Mary Road (CR 3)

81E

COCONINO

693

NATIONAL

× 6,800 ft

43 Tramway Trailhead

Tramway Trail

West

Clear

Creek

Maxwell Trail

FOREST

Options

Option 1: Hike cross-country 0.8 mile upstream and climb out via the Maxwell Trail.

   Option 2: Hike and swim the entire 25-mile length of West Clear Creek downstream to the Bull Pen Ranch trailhead. This is a difficult, multiday backpack trip that requires swimming and floating your pack across numerous pools. It should be attempted only in warm, stable weather by experienced canyon hikers.

44 Bell Trail

This is a popular summer hike along Wet Beaver Creek, one of Arizona's rare perennial streams. The trail climbs to the Mogollon Rim for some good views.

Distance: 8.4 miles out and back
Hiking time: About 6 hours
Difficulty: Moderate
Trail surface: Dirt trails
Best season: Year-round
Water: Wet Beaver Creek
Other trail users: None
Canine compatibility: Controlled dogs allowed
Land status: Wet Beaver Creek Wilderness, Coconino National Forest

Nearest town: Sedona
Fees and permits: None
Schedule: Open all year
Maps: USGS Casner Butte; Coconino National Forest
Trail contacts: Coconino National Forest, 1824 S. Thompson St., Flagstaff, AZ 86001; (928) 527-3600; www.fs.usda.gov/coconino

Finding the trailhead: From Sedona drive about 14 miles southeast on Highway 179 and go under the I-17 interchange. Continue 2.1 miles on the Beaver Creek Road (FR 618); turn left into the Wet Beaver Creek trailhead. GPS: N34 40.45' / W111 42.87'

The Hike

The trail stays along the north side of Wet Beaver Creek. Stands of Fremont cottonwood and other riparian vegetation crowd the creek, but there are several short side trails down to the water. One of several perennial streams flowing through the canyons below the Mogollon Rim, Wet Beaver Creek is very popular during summer.

At 2.1 miles you'll pass the Apache Maid Trail. Continue east along the canyon on the Bell Trail. There are a number of good swimming holes along the creek, just below the trail. After another mile the trail crosses the creek and climbs up a steep ridge to the Mogollon Rim. Although the trail continues to FR 214, this scenic spot makes a good turnaround point for the hike.

LEFT AND RIGHT

As you walk up the canyon, notice how the slope to the left, which is sunnier and drier, features a nearly pure stand of juniper trees. On the other hand, the slope to the right faces north and is cooler and moister and supports a mixed stand of juniper and piñon. Evidently the piñon pines require just a bit more moisture, and possibly cooler temperatures, than the junipers. Very slight changes in climate can have a dramatic effect on plant and animal communities.

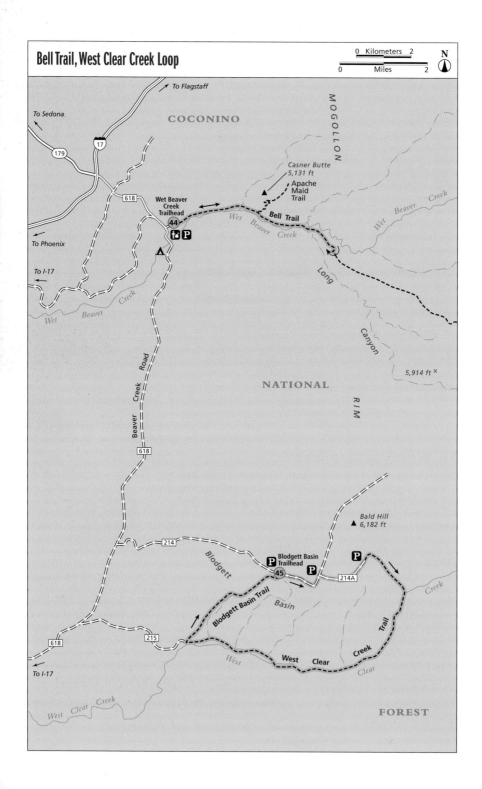

Bell Trail, West Clear Creek Loop

0   Kilometers   2
0   Miles   2

N

To Flagstaff

To Sedona

COCONINO

MOGOLLON

17

179

Casner Butte
5,131 ft

Apache
Maid
Trail

618

Wet Beaver
Creek
Trailhead

Bell Trail

44

Wet Beaver Creek

Wet Beaver Creek

To Phoenix

Long

To I-17

Canyon

Wet Beaver Creek

NATIONAL

RIM

5,914 ft ×

Beaver Creek Road

618

Bald Hill
▲ 6,182 ft

214

Blodgett

Blodgett Basin
Trailhead

45

214A

Creek

618

215

Blodgett Basin Trail

Basin

Trail

West Clear Creek

Creek

West

Clear

To I-17

West Clear Creek

FOREST

Remains of Bull Pen Ranch, West Clear Creek

Miles and Directions

0.0 Start at the Wet Beaver Creek trailhead.

2.1 Pass the Apache Maid Trail; continue east on the Bell Trail.

3.1 Cross Wet Beaver Creek.

4.2 Reach Mogollon Rim, your turnaround point.

8.4 Arrive back at the trailhead.

Options

You can also reach the rim via the Apache Maid Trail, which climbs the north slope of the canyon. The juniper forest is open, and the first section of the trail provides good views down Wet Beaver Creek. A series of switchbacks leads up to the base of Casner Butte, and then the trail crosses the drainage to the north and angles up to the Mogollon Rim. Here the view ranges from the San Francisco Peaks to the north to the Verde Valley to the west and southwest. Originally built for access to the Apache Maid fire tower, the remainder of the trail is faint and difficult to follow, so this is a good place to turn around. This option adds 2.8 miles and 1,050 feet of elevation gain to the main hike.

45 West Clear Creek Loop

This long day hike or overnight backpack drops into West Clear Creek from its north rim, follows the permanent creek downstream, and then returns along the north rim.

See map on page 146.
Distance: 12.9-mile loop
Hiking time: About 8 hours
Difficulty: Strenuous
Trail surface: Dirt trails and roads, stream crossings
Best seasons: Spring and fall
Water: West Clear Creek
Other trail users: Horses
Canine compatibility: Controlled dogs allowed

Land status: West Clear Creek Wilderness, Coconino National Forest
Nearest town: Camp Verde
Fees and permits: None
Schedule: Open all year
Maps: USGS Walker Mountain and Buckhorn Mountain; Coconino National Forest
Trail contacts: Coconino National Forest, 1824 S. Thompson St., Flagstaff, AZ 86001; (928) 527-3600; www.fs.usda.gov/coconino

Finding the trailhead: From I-17 take exit 298 and drive east toward Beaver Creek on FR 618. Cross Beaver Creek at 2.5 miles and continue on FR 618. At about 10 miles from I-17, turn left onto Cedar Flat Road (FR 214). Drive another 4.3 miles and park at the Blodgett Basin trailhead sign. GPS: N34 33.74' / W111 40.18'

The Hike

From the trailhead sign, walk along FR 214 for 1.1 miles. The road will make a fairly sharp left bend; just a little farther a poor vehicle track takes off to the right. Follow this track, FR 214A, which may or may not be signed. There are several forks, but continue on the most obvious road. After about 1.5 miles on FR 214A, the track reaches the signed trailhead for the West Clear Creek Trail. GPS: N34 33.65' / W111 38.25'

West Clear Creek Trail starts in piñon–juniper woodland. In a few hundred yards, the trail begins to descend into an unnamed side canyon to West Clear Creek. Yucca, agave, mountain mahogany, prickly pear cactus, and other hardy shrubs cling to the rocky slopes composed of volcanic tuff and basalt. Other plants along the trail include Mormon tea, snakeweed, and nolina. Look for both white-tailed and mule deer and javelina.

The trail drops quickly to West Clear Creek. Here grow Arizona sycamores, Fremont cottonwoods, and velvet ash trees. During spring and summer, birding can be quite rewarding in this relatively lush riparian habitat. Expect kingbirds, orioles, tanagers, warblers, wrens, and possibly the rare yellow-billed cuckoo or Southwestern willow flycatcher. Anglers try their luck fishing for catfish.

The trail continues downstream 6 miles past the site of the former Bull Pen Ranch to a fence and gate. On the far side of the gate is FR 215. Walk along this road a few yards and look to your right for the Blodgett Basin Trail sign. Take this trail back to the rim and FR 214 and your vehicle.

West Clear Creek

Miles and Directions

0.0 Start at the Blodgett Basin trailhead and continue to walk east along FR 214.

1.1 Turn right onto a vehicle track (FR 214A).

2.0 Reach the West Clear Creek trailhead and begin to follow this trail.

3.6 Reach West Clear Creek and follow the trail downstream.

10.1 Come to Bull Pen Ranch site.

12.9 Arrive back at the trailhead.

46 Fossil Springs Trail

This trail leads to Fossil Springs and a historic diversion dam on Fossil Creek. The dam—and its associated hydropower system—was decommissioned in 2005 and the flow in lower Fossil Creek was restored. This trail takes you to the warm springs that feed the creek and the former dam site. Fossil Creek is once again a major wildlife habitat area.

Distance: 6.8 miles out and back
Hiking time: About 5 hours
Difficulty: Moderate
Trail surface: Dirt trails
Best season: Spring through fall
Water: Fossil Springs
Other trail users: None
Canine compatibility: Controlled dogs allowed
Land status: Fossil Springs Wilderness,
Coconino National Forest
Nearest town: Strawberry
Fees and permits: None
Schedule: Open all year
Maps: USGS Strawberry; Tonto National Forest
Trail contacts: Tonto National Forest, 2324 E. McDowell Rd., Phoenix, AZ 85006; (602) 225-5200; www.fs.usda.gov/tonto

Finding the trailhead: From Strawberry on Highway 87, go west 4.7 miles on the main road through town. This becomes FR 708, a maintained dirt road. Turn right after 4.7 miles and go another 0.4 mile to the Fossil Springs trailhead. GPS: N34 24.53'/W111 34.12'

An aerial view of Fossil Creek

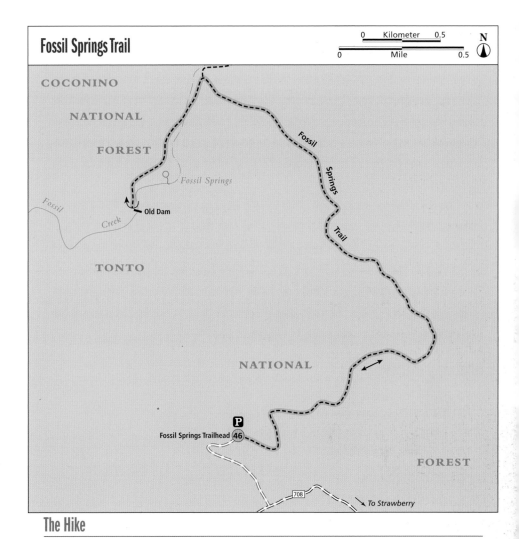

0   Kilometer   0.5

0   Mile   0.5

N

COCONINO

NATIONAL

FOREST

Fossil Springs

Fossil

Creek

Old Dam

Fossil

Springs

Trail

TONTO

NATIONAL

Fossil Springs Trailhead (46)

P

FOREST

708

To Strawberry

The Hike

The trail follows the route of an old jeep road and descends northeast below the rim of the canyon. It soon turns northwest and continues its descent through piñon-juniper woodland to reach Fossil Creek. Now turn left and hike downstream. Although upper Fossil Creek often flows, there's no mistaking the added volume when you reach Fossil Springs. These warm springs gush from the right bank of the creek. A short distance below the springs, you'll leave the wilderness area and reach an old concrete dam, the hike's destination.

WATER DIVERSION

The Fossil Creek Dam was constructed in 1916 and was used to divert water into a flume. Several miles downstream the water spun the turbines at the Irving Power Plant. Another flume and pipeline carried the water to the Childs Power Plant near the mouth of Fossil Creek, on the Verde River, which harnessed the power of Fossil Creek a second time. These facilities, among Arizona's first hydroelectric generating stations, were used to produce power until 2005.

That year Arizona Public Service, the current owner of the Fossil Creek Power System, stopped diverting water from Fossil Creek for the first time in eighty-nine years. The purpose was to restore the creek's natural flow. Prior to the diversion, Fossil Creek provided a rich riparian habitat from Fossil Springs to the Verde River. The heavily mineralized creek is expected to reestablish this habitat as well as re-create the travertine dams and small waterfalls that once graced the creek. After APS removes the dam, flumes, and pipelines, the Irving Power Plant will be maintained as a historical site.

Miles and Directions

0.0 Start at the Fossil Springs trailhead.

2.8 Come to Fossil Creek; turn left and hike downstream.

3.4 Reach the old concrete dam, your turnaround point.

6.8 Arrive back at the trailhead.

Options

Option 1: Hike the access road to the dam, FR 154. Closed to private vehicles, the road is open to hikers to its end at the site of the Irving Power Plant and FR 708.

Option 2: Hike upstream, cross-country, in Fossil Creek, from the point where the trail first reached the canyon bottom. The bulk of the wilderness lies upstream and encompasses two major side canyons, Calf Pen and Sandrock.

47 Kinder Crossing Trail

This short, historic trail provides access to East Clear Creek. You can explore up- or downstream from the foot of the trail. East Clear Creek runs year-round, and the deep, clear pools are a delight during the hot days of summer.

Distance: 1.2 miles out and back
Hiking time: About 1 hour
Difficulty: Easy
Trail surface: Dirt trails
Best season: Spring through fall
Water: East Clear Creek
Other trail users: Mountain bikes and horses
Canine compatibility: Controlled dogs allowed
Land status: Coconino National Forest

Nearest town: Flagstaff
Fees and permits: None
Schedule: Open all year
Maps: USGS Blue Ridge Reservoir; Coconino National Forest
Trail contacts: Coconino National Forest, 1824 S. Thompson St., Flagstaff, AZ 86001; (928) 527-3600; www.fs.usda.gov/coconino

Finding the trailhead: From Flagstaff drive about 55 miles southeast on Lake Mary Road (CR 3) to Clints Well. Turn left onto Highway 87 and drive 9 miles. Turn right onto FR 95. Continue 4.2 miles on this maintained road, and turn left on a signed, unmaintained road to the Kinder Crossing Trail. Continue 0.6 mile to the end of the road. GPS: N34 34.01'/W111 9.44'

Clints Well can also be reached from Camp Verde by driving 30 miles east onto the General Crook Trail (Forest Highway 9), then turning left (north) onto Highway 87 and continuing 11 miles.

The Hike

The Kinder Crossing Trail descends into East Clear Creek by following the ridge to the east, reaching the creek at the confluence of East Clear Creek and Yeager Canyon. There is a large and very inviting swimming hole at the confluence. After cooling off, it is fun to explore the canyon, both up- and downstream.

DIFFICULT CROSSINGS

This trail is one of several historical trails that cross East Clear Creek and other canyons on the forested Mogollon Plateau north of the Mogollon Rim. During the settlement and ranching days, before the present road network was built, the primary access to the area was via pack trails. Canyons such as East Clear Creek created formidable barriers to travel and were crossable by trail at only a few points. Even today, the forest road system is constrained by the crossing points along the deep canyons.

Kinder Crossing Trail, Cabin Loop

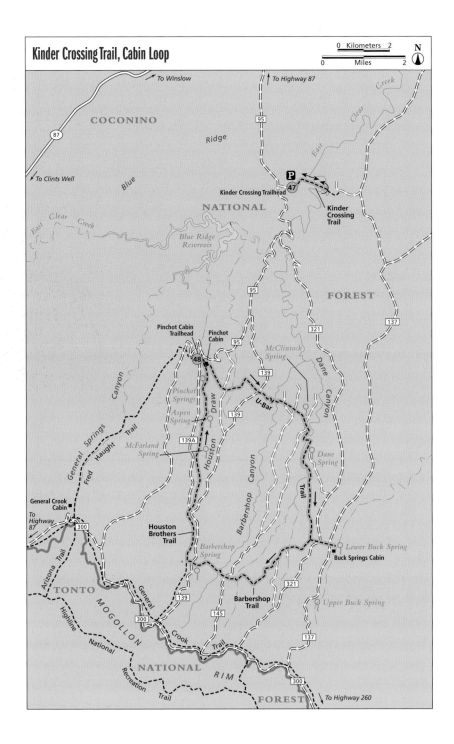

0 Kilometers 2

0 Miles 2

N

To Winslow

To Highway 87

Creek

COCONINO

95

87

Ridge

East

To Clints Well

Blue

Kinder Crossing Trailhead

P

47

Kinder Crossing Trail

NATIONAL

East Clear Creek

Blue Ridge Reservoir

95

FOREST

137

Pinchot Cabin Trailhead

Pinchot Cabin

95

321

McClintock Spring

Dane Canyon

Canyon

48

139

Pinchot Springs

Draw

U-Bar

Aspen Spring

139

General Springs Trail

Fred Haught Trail

McFarland Spring

139A

Houston

Dane Spring

Trail

General Crook Cabin

To Highway 87

300

Houston Brothers Trail

Barbershop Canyon

Lower Buck Spring

Buck Springs Cabin

Arizona Trail

Barbershop Spring

321

TONTO

General

139

Barbershop Trail

Upper Buck Spring

MOGOLLON

Highline

300

Crook

145

137

National

Trail

300

Recreation

NATIONAL

RIM

To Highway 260

Trail

FOREST

East Clear Creek near Kinder Crossing

Miles and Directions

0.0   Start at the Kinder Crossing trailhead.

0.6   Reach East Clear Creek at its confluence with Yaeger Canyon. Enjoy a swim and explore the canyon before retracing your steps.

1.2   Arrive back at the trailhead.

Options

Option 1: Follow the remainder of the Kinder Crossing Trail, which climbs out the west side of the canyon to a spur road from FR 137.

Option 2: With a car shuttle, hike cross-country downstream about 3 miles to Horse Crossing.

48 Cabin Loop

This loop hike on a series of historic trails connects several historic cabins north of the Mogollon Rim. The entire loop makes an enjoyable backpack trip, or you can do shorter segments as day hikes.

See map on page 154.
Distance: 17.8-mile loop
Hiking time: About 2 days
Difficulty: Moderate
Trail surface: Dirt trails
Best seasons: Spring and fall
Water: Seasonally at Barbershop Canyon, Dane Canyon, Dane Spring, Coyote Spring, Barbershop Spring, Houston Draw, and Aspen Spring
Other trail users: Mountain bikes and horses

Canine compatibility: Controlled dogs allowed
Land status: Coconino National Forest
Nearest town: Flagstaff
Fees and permits: None
Schedule: Open all year
Maps: USGS Blue Ridge Reservoir and Dane Canyon; Coconino National Forest
Trail contacts: Coconino National Forest, 1824 S. Thompson St., Flagstaff, AZ 86001; (928) 527-3600; www.fs.usda.gov/coconino

Finding the trailhead: From Flagstaff drive about 55 miles southeast on Lake Mary Road (CR 3) to Clints Well. Turn left onto Highway 87, and go north 9 miles; turn right onto FR 95. Continue 11.1 miles on this maintained road, and then turn left onto FR 139A. Travel just over 0.1 mile, and park at the Pinchot Cabin trailhead, where the Fred Haught Trail crosses the road. GPS: N34 30.56' / W111 11.79'

Clints Well can also be reached from Camp Verde by driving 30 miles east on the General Crook Trail (Forest Highway 9), then turning left onto Highway 87 and continuing 11 miles.

The Hike

This hike is part of the Cabin Loop, a system of trails that connect three historic cabins in the Mogollon Rim country. (None of the trails in this system is shown on the USGS topographic maps.) Sections of the trail are cross-country, but they are well marked with tree blazes.

Walk southeast along the Fred Haught Trail down into Houston Draw to Pinchot Cabin, where a junction marks the start of the Houston Brothers and U-Bar Trails. Turn left to start the U-Bar Trail, which follows an old road past the cabin and up the hill to the east. Note the standard Forest Service tree blazes, which consist of short and long vertical slashes. The entire trail is blazed with the same-style blazes. After less than 1 mile, turn right (south) onto another road (note the blaze and right arrow), and continue a short distance to a third road intersection. The trail crosses the road and continues east into the forest, ignoring both roads. The Cabin Loop trails are getting more and more use, but sections may still be faint. If the trail isn't clear, follow the blazes carefully. The trick is to walk from blaze to blaze, always keeping the last blaze

Ruins of a cabin at Dane Spring

in sight. If you lose the route, return to the last known blaze and locate the next one before continuing.

The route crosses Dick Hart Draw and meets another road. The U-Bar Trail now turns left (north) and follows the road past a large steel water tank. Watch carefully for the place where the trail turns sharply right (east) and leaves the road. Next the trail crosses a maintained dirt road (FR 139), and a sign marks the U-Bar Trail. The trail veers somewhat left as it crosses the road. The U-Bar trail goes to the southeast out onto a point, then descends through a gate.

After the fence the trail becomes obvious as it descends into Barbershop Canyon. Serious trail construction was done on this section. Barbershop Canyon has a fine little perennial stream—a good goal for hikers wanting an easy day. For those on a backpack trip, there is very limited camping in the canyon bottom. It would be better to carry water up to the east rim, where there is unlimited camping.

The trail, still distinct, climbs the east wall of the canyon and crosses a faint road. Where the trail crosses a road at right angles, a sign marks the U-Bar Trail. On the east side of the main road, the U-Bar Trail follows an unmaintained road past a fine little meadow bordered by pines and aspens and containing McClintock Spring. Beyond the meadow the road joins another road; the U-Bar Trail continues across the road and descends into Dane Canyon. There are sections of historic trail construction

THE CABIN LOOP TRAIL SYSTEM

This hike follows the historic U-Bar, Barbershop, and Houston Brothers Trails. These trails are part of the Cabin Loop Trail System, which connects several historic cabins in the Mogollon Rim country. Pinchot Cabin is named for Gifford Pinchot, the first chief of the USDA Forest Service. It was used for many years as a fire guard station. The trail system provided the main transportation routes through this remote country during the early days of ranching and forestry. Most of the trails have been lost during the development of the forest road system, but several, including these three trails, have been relocated and restored. Sections of the trail are cross-country but are well marked by tree blazes.

along this section. Dane Canyon has a perennial stream and offers plentiful campsites in grassy meadows. A lush forest of Douglas fir and ponderosa pine covers the canyon walls, spiced by an occasional aspen, limber pine, or white fir.

After crossing the creek, the U-Bar Trail climbs east out of the canyon, then turns south along the east rim. This is one of the prettiest sections of the trail, staying below the heavily logged ridgetop. You'll soon reach Dane Spring, which is marked by the ruins of a log cabin. This is an excellent goal for a more ambitious day hike.

The U-Bar Trail continues south along the east side of a shallow drainage, then crosses the drainage and climbs to cross a road on a ridgetop. It descends into the next drainage to end at the junction with the Barbershop Trail. Turn right onto the Barbershop Trail, which passes Coyote Spring, follows the drainage west to Bill McClintock Draw, then climbs southwest to cross a low ridge. The next section of the Barbershop Trail crosses several drainages and follows several roads for short distances. Follow the blazes carefully so that you don't miss the places where the trail leaves the roads.

The Barbershop Trail crosses upper Dane Canyon at a sign. The trail climbs up a drainage to the west, crosses a maintained road, then drops into Barbershop Canyon, which usually has flowing water. The trail climbs steeply for a couple hundred yards then contours into a meadow at Barbershop Spring. After the spring the trail goes up the bed of a shallow drainage to the west and then climbs out on the right to cross FR 139. The Barbershop Trail ends just west of the road, at the signed junction with the Houston Brothers Trail.

Turn right and follow the Houston Brothers Trail north along Dick Hart Ridge. Very little of the original trail remains along this section; follow the tree blazes carefully. If you lose the trail, you can always walk east to FR 139, which is never more than 0.25 mile away. Eventually the trail crosses FR 139A and descends into Houston Draw, where it becomes a distinct footpath. The forest at the head of Houston Draw is a delightful mix of Douglas fir, white fir, and ponderosa pine. Soon the trail emerges into a series of fine alpine meadows, bordered with quaking aspen. You'll pass McFarland and then Aspen Springs. There is also an intermittent flow in the creek.

The Houston Brothers Trail ends at Pinchot Cabin, completing the loop. Turn left onto the Fred Haught Trail and walk to the end of the hike at the Pinchot trailhead.

Miles and Directions

0.0 Start at the Pinchot Cabin trailhead and hike southeast on the Fred Haught Trail.

0.4 Reach Pinchot Cabin in a meadow at the junction of the Fred Haught, Houston Brothers, and U-Bar Trails. Turn left onto the U-Bar Trail, which follows an old road northeast of the cabin.

1.2 Turn right onto a road.

1.4 Come to a T intersection; cross the road and follow the blazed trees east.

1.9 The trail turns left (north) along a road.

2.1 Pass a steel water tank; turn sharply right, leave the road, and follow the blazed trail east.

2.6 Cross FR 139, where a sign marks the U-Bar Trail; follow the blazes carefully.

3.2 Cross Barbershop Canyon. (**FYI:** Very limited camping is available in the canyon bottom.) (**Option:** Turn around here for an easy day hike.)

4.2 Pass McClintock Spring.

4.9 Cross the creek in Dane Canyon.

6.2 Reach Dane Spring. (**Option:** This is a good turnaround point for a longer day hike.)

8.2 Turn right onto the Barbershop Trail. (**Option:** Turn left and hike 0.5 mile to the Buck Springs Cabin trailhead.)

8.4 Pass Coyote Spring, which may be dry.

8.6 Cross Bill McClintock Draw.

10.6 Cross Dane Canyon.

11.3 Cross Barbershop Canyon.

11.7 Reach Barbershop Spring.

12.0 Cross FR 139.

12.1 Barbershop Trail ends. Turn right onto the Houston Brothers Trail, which parallels FR 139 just to the west.

13.7 Cross FR 139A, and follow the trail north into the head of Houston Draw.

15.3 Pass McFarland Spring.

16.1 Pass Aspen Spring.

17.4 The Houston Brothers Trail ends at the Pinchot Cabin. Turn left onto the Fred Haught Trail.

17.8 Arrive back at the trailhead.

Options

From the junction of the Barbershop and Houston Brothers Trails, continue south another 1.4 miles on the Houston Brothers Trail to reach FR 300. Cross the road to the edge of the Mogollon Rim. The view of the rim country and the central mountains to the south is a treat, marred only slightly by the carnage wreaked on the forest by the Dude Fire in 1990. This side hike adds 2.8 miles round-trip and 150 feet of elevation gain to the hike.

49 Chevelon Canyon

Enjoy a backpack trip or long day hike into a little-visited canyon with a trout stream coursing through it. Chevelon Canyon is one of several major canyon systems that have their headwaters north of the Mogollon Rim and flow northward to join the Little Colorado River.

Distance: 16.8 miles out and back
Hiking time: About 7 hours
Difficulty: Moderate
Trail surface: Informal trail, numerous stream crossings
Best season: Spring through fall
Water: Chevelon Creek
Other trail users: None
Canine compatibility: Controlled dogs allowed

Land status: Apache-Sitgreaves National Forest
Nearest town: Winslow
Fees and permits: None
Schedule: Open all year
Maps: USGS Chevelon Crossing; USFS Apache-Sitgreaves National Forest
Trail contacts: Apache-Sitgreaves National Forest, PO Box 640, Springerville, AZ 85938; (928) 333-4301; www.fs.usda.gov/asnf

Finding the trailhead: From Winslow drive south 1.3 miles on Highway 87, then turn left on Highway 99. Continue 23.5 miles, then bear left on CR 308. This dirt road is somewhat rough at first but becomes much better when it crosses the Apache-Sitgreaves National Forest boundary and becomes FR 504. Continue 10.4 miles to Chevelon Crossing Campground, and park here. GPS: N34 35.59'/W110 47.30'

The Hike

This backpack is an 8.4-mile hike upstream to Chevelon Canyon Lake, a man-made reservoir. There is no formal trail, but anglers, day hikers, and wildlife have made paths that follow the course of the creek. A few stream crossings are necessary, so this hike would not be possible during periods of high water.

The easy route passes beaver ponds, swimming holes, and grassy campsites amid ponderosa pine, Fremont cottonwood, New Mexican locust, and other riparian species. Be wary of poison ivy. Elk and mule deer are common, and at night it's not unusual to hear a beaver slapping its tail upon the water.

Exploration downstream from Chevelon Crossing is possible but somewhat more challenging. The canyon narrows, and more time is needed to make deepwater crossings. Sometimes swimming is necessary to make progress downstream.

▶ In 1851 Captain Lorenzo Sitgreaves wrote that the stream received its name from a trapper called Chevelon, who died after eating some poisonous root along its banks. Poison hemlock does grow along the creek and may have been the culprit.

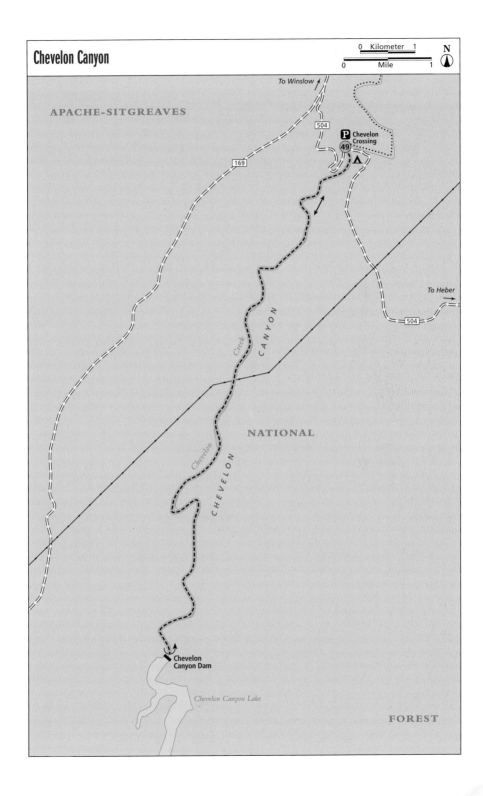

Chevelon Canyon

To Winslow

APACHE-SITGREAVES

504

P Chevelon
Crossing
49

169

Creek

CANYON

To Heber

504

Chevelon

CHEVELON

NATIONAL

Chevelon
Canyon Dam

Chevelon Canyon Lake

FOREST

0   Kilometer   1

0   Mile   1

N

Miles and Directions

0.0 Start at the trailhead in Chevelon Crossing Campground.

3.5 Power lines cross the canyon overhead.

8.4 Reach Chevelon Canyon Dam and Lake. Retrace your steps.

16.8 Arrive back at the trailhead.

50 Tunnel Trail

This is a short and easy day hike off the spectacular Mogollon Rim that connects several historic sites.

Distance: 1.5 miles out and back
Hiking time: About 2 hours
Difficulty: Easy
Best season: Spring through fall
Trail surface: Dirt trails
Water: No water available
Other trail users: Mountain bikes and horses
Canine compatibility: Controlled dogs allowed
Land status: Tonto National Forest

Nearest town: Payson
Fees and permits: None
Schedule: Open all year
Maps: USGS Dane Canyon and Kehl Ridge; USFS Tonto National Forest
Trail contacts: Tonto National Forest, 2324 E. McDowell Rd., Phoenix, AZ 85006; (602) 225-5200; www.fs.usda.gov/tonto

Finding the trailhead: Take Highway 87 about 13 miles north of the tiny community of Strawberry, and turn right onto FR 300 (Rim Road). About 14 miles farther you will come to a historical marker for the Battle of Big Dry Wash on the left (north) side of the road. Park here, at the General Springs trailhead. GPS: N34 27.24' / W111 15.03'

The Hike

To the south, toward the Mogollon Rim, is a sign marking the Arizona Trail. Start south down this trail, descending off the Mogollon Rim. In about 0.5 mile there is a signed turnoff to the left for the Tunnel Trail. This trail winds uphill a short distance to the uncompleted railroad tunnel and the ruins of a building.

Miles and Directions

0.0 Start at the General Springs trailhead.
0.4 Turn left onto the Tunnel Trail.
0.8 Reach the railroad tunnel. Retrace your steps.
1.5 Arrive back at the trailhead.

UNFINISHED BUSINESS

In 1883 developers proposed a trans–Mogollon Rim rail line to connect Flagstaff and the Union Pacific Railroad with the rich mineral district of Morenci. Several years passed before financing became available. Thirty-five miles of track were laid heading southeast out of Flagstaff. At the same time, a tunnel was begun under the Mogollon Rim. However, before the planned 3,100-foot tunnel was completed, the Arizona Mineral Belt Railroad went bankrupt.

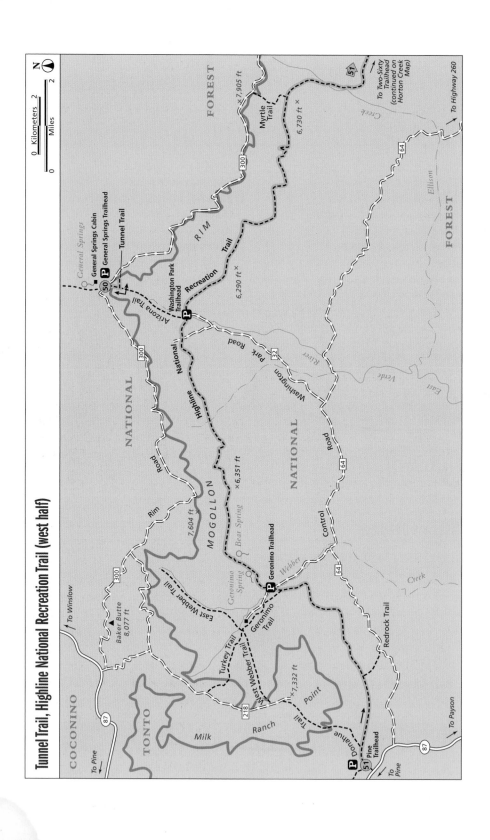

Tunnel Trail, Highline National Recreation Trail (west half)

51 Highline National Recreation Trail

This long, scenic trail wanders along the base of the ramparts of the Mogollon Rim. There are six trailheads, so you can hike the entire trail or pick segments. A number of side trails branch from the Highline Trail, most climbing to the top of the Mogollon Rim.

See map on pages 164 and 171.
Distance: 40.5 miles one-way with a shuttle
Hiking time: About 5 to 7 days
Difficulty: Strenuous
Trail surface: Dirt trails
Best season: Spring through late fall
Water: Weber Creek, East Verde River, Tonto Creek, Horton Spring, and Christopher Creek; seasonal springs and creeks possible after a wet winter
Other trail users: Mountain bikes and horses
Canine compatibility: Controlled dogs allowed

Land status: Tonto National Forest
Nearest town: Payson
Fees and permits: None
Schedule: Open all year
Maps: USGS Pine, Buckhead Mesa, Kehl Ridge, Dane Canyon, Diamond Point, Promontory Butte, Knoll Lake, and Woods Canyon; Tonto National Forest
Trail contacts: Tonto National Forest, 2324 E. McDowell Rd., Phoenix, AZ 85006; (602) 225-5200; www.fs.usda.gov/tonto

Finding the trailheads: *Pine trailhead:* From Payson drive 12.9 miles north on Highway 87. Turn right into the Pine trailhead; this is the western trailhead. GPS: N34 22.07'/W111 25.98'
Two-Sixty trailhead: From Payson drive 26.5 miles east on Highway 260 to the trailhead on the left. (Because of construction on Highway 260, the exact mileage may change.) GPS: N34 18.41'/W111 57.12'

The Hike

The Highline National Recreation Trail (shortened to Highline Trail for the rest of this description) runs along the base of the Mogollon Rim, and it crosses numerous drainages. Because the trail was developed by horsemen in a piecemeal fashion, it tends to climb over ridges rather than contour around, so you can expect constant climbing and descending. Also, even though the trail crosses numerous creeks, as elsewhere in Arizona, the term "creek" usually refers to a seasonal stream—don't expect to find water at every creek crossing.

Vegetation along the trail ranges from tall stands of ponderosa pine to dense thickets of chaparral. Chaparral is common at the elevations and exposures of the Highline Trail and refers to a mixture of scrub oak, mountain mahogany, and manzanita. Several large fires have burned the south slopes of the Mogollon Rim in recent years; the Highline Trail passes through these burns.

From the Pine trailhead the Highline Trail climbs east a short distance before leveling off and passing the Donahue Trail. The Highline Trail now contours east along

General Springs Cabin, near the Tunnel Trail trailhead

the south slopes of Milk Ranch Point. Redrock Trail forks right, and the Highline Trail begins to turn northeast and then north. It passes Geronimo Trail just before reaching the Geronimo trailhead and crossing Webber Creek Road.

Now the Highline Trail climbs northeast past Geronimo Spring to Bear Spring before leveling off and heading east along the base of the Mogollon Rim. It crosses numerous seasonal creeks before crossing Mail Creek and a road. Here the trail skirts the Washington Park summer home area on the north by climbing over a ridge before descending to the East Verde River and Washington Park trailhead on FR 32.

After leaving the East Verde River, the Highline Trail climbs east just a bit before leveling off and heading southeast along the base of the Mogollon Rim. The trail crosses several seasonal creeks before meeting the Myrtle Trail and turning south to descend along Ellison Creek. Near the old Pyle Ranch the Highline Trail again turns eastward and climbs gradually to the base of Myrtle Point. After crossing Big Canyon the trail reaches the Hatchery trailhead.

After crossing Tonto Creek the Highline Trail continues east, crossing under a power line and reaching Horton Creek Trail and Horton Spring. This spring gushes from the base of the rim and creates Horton Creek, one of several beautiful creeks issuing from the rim. After Horton Spring the Highline Trail crosses the East Fork of Horton Creek and climbs through a fine stand of quaking aspen before turning south along Promontory Butte. As the trail begins to turn southeast around Promontory Butte, the Derrick Trail forks southwest. The Highline Trail continues around Promontory Butte and descends to the See Canyon trailhead.

Crossing Christopher Creek, the Highline Trail continues east, climbing to regain the base of the Mogollon Rim. As the trail levels off, the Drew Trail forks left. The final section of the Highline Trail closely parallels the rim and crosses numerous unnamed drainages before ending at the Two-Sixty trailhead.

Miles and Directions

0.0 Start at the Pine trailhead.

0.5 Pass junction with the Donahue Trail.

2.1 Pass Redrock Trail junction.

5.5 Pass Geronimo Trail; stay right.

5.8 Reach Geronimo trailhead.

6.3 Pass Geronimo Spring.

7.6 Pass Bear Spring.

12.8 Cross Washington Park Road (FR 32).

13.4 Pass the Washington Park trailhead.

20.3 Meet junction with Myrtle Trail. Keep south to stay on the Highline Trail.

26.9 Reach the Hatchery trailhead.

29.5 Pass the Horton Creek Trail.

31.7 The Derrick Trail forks right. Keep to the left.

35.2 Pass the See Canyon trailhead.

37.0 The Drew Trail forks left. Keep to the right.

40.5 Arrive at the Two-Sixty trailhead and your shuttle.

Options

Donahue Trail (at 0.5 mile) leaves the Highline Trail east of the Pine trailhead and climbs 2.2 miles northwest onto the Mogollon Rim at Milk Ranch Point, ending at FR 218.

Redrock Trail (at 2.1 miles) leaves the Highline Trail west of the Geronimo trailhead and descends 0.6 mile southeast to end at Control Road (FR 64).

Geronimo Trail (at 5.8 miles) forks north just west of the Geronimo trailhead and runs 1.3 miles past Camp Geronimo to a trail junction in the Webber Creek basin. Three trails leave this junction: The West Webber Trail goes left and climbs 1.9 miles west to Milk Ranch Point and the Mogollon Rim, ending on FR 218. The

HISTORY OF THE HIGHLINE

The Highline Trail and most of its side trails were built in the late 1800s to link several homesteads and ranches located under the Mogollon Rim. Many of the spur trails connected to the General Crook Trail, a wagon road that closely followed the edge of the Mogollon Rim. The Highline Trail was designated a National Recreation Trail in 1979.

Turkey Trail, the center choice, heads 1.8 miles past Turkey Spring; it also climbs to Milk Ranch Point and the Mogollon Rim, ending at FR 218. The East Webber Trail, the right fork, climbs 2.4 miles up Webber Creek before ending under the cliffs of the Mogollon Rim.

Col. Devin Trail (at 13.4 miles) leaves the Highline Trail at the Washington Park trailhead and climbs 2 miles north to end on the Rim Road (FR 300) on the Mogollon Rim. This trail, part of the Arizona Trail, also connects to the Tunnel Trail (see that hike description) and the Fred Haught Trail.

Myrtle Trail (at 20.3 miles) leaves the Highline Trail west of Myrtle Point and climbs 1 mile north to the Mogollon Rim and the Rim Road (FR 300).

Babe Haught Trail (at 26.9 miles) leaves the Highline Trail at the Hatchery trailhead and climbs 1.3 miles north to the Mogollon Rim. The trail ends 1 mile north of the rim at the Rim Road (FR 300).

Horton Creek Trail (at 29.5 miles) meets the Highline Trail at Horton Spring and descends 3.2 miles southwest along beautiful Horton Creek to Upper Tonto Creek Campground on Tonto Creek Road (FR 289).

Derrick Trail (at 31.7 miles) leaves the Highline Trail along the west side of Promontory Butte and descends 2.2 miles west to Upper Tonto Creek Campground on Tonto Creek Road (FR 289). The Derrick Spur Trail forks off to the southwest from Derrick Trail and descends 0.7 mile to Lower Tonto Creek Campground on Tonto Creek Road (FR 289).

See Canyon Trail (at 35.2 miles) leaves the Highline Trail at the See Canyon trailhead and follows Christopher Creek 3 miles north to the Mogollon Rim and the Rim Road (FR 300). A 0.5-mile spur trail (the See Spring Trail) leads to See Spring.

Drew Trail (at 37 miles) leaves the Highline Trail east of Christopher Creek and climbs 1 mile northeast to the Mogollon Rim and the Rim Road (FR 300).

◀ *Highline Trail below the Mogollon Rim*

52 Horton Creek

This is a pleasant day hike along a trout stream under the cliffs of the Mogollon Rim.

Distance: 6.8 miles out and back
Hiking time: About 5 hours
Difficulty: Easy
Trail surface: Dirt trails
Best season: Spring through fall
Water: Horton Creek and Horton Spring
Other trail users: Mountain bikes and horses
Canine compatibility: Controlled dogs allowed
Land status: Tonto National Forest

Nearest town: Payson
Fees and permits: None
Schedule: Open all year
Maps: USGS Promontory Butte; USFS Tonto National Forest
Trail contacts: Tonto National Forest, 2324 E. McDowell Rd., Phoenix, AZ 85006; (602) 225-5200; www.fs.usda.gov/tonto

Finding the trailhead: From Payson drive about 15 miles east on Highway 260. Turn left (north) onto Tonto Creek Road (FR 289). Travel 1 mile to the Horton (Upper Tonto) Campground. Park below the entrance gate to the campground, but do not block the road. The trail begins about 150 feet up the campground road. GPS: N34 20.38'/W111 5.74'

Horton Creek

Highline National Recreation Trail (east half), Horton Creek

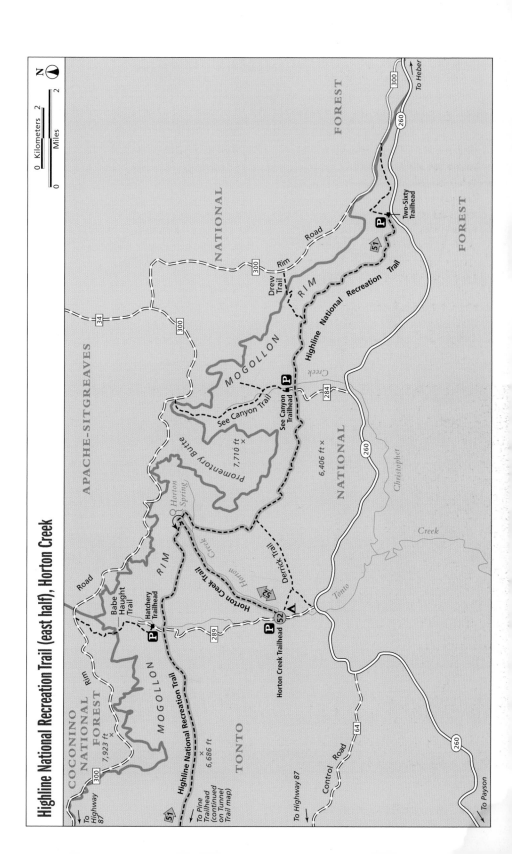

The Hike

The trail follows an old logging road that parallels Horton Creek. The trail is within sight of the creek for the first 1.2 miles and is no more than 300 yards away the rest of the way. After 3 miles this trail joins the Highline Trail. Turn left onto the Highline Trail and go another 0.4 mile to the large, beautiful Horton Spring, which gushes out the side of the mountain.

Miles and Directions

0.0   Start at the Horton Creek trailhead, below the campground entrance gate.

3.0   Turn left at junction with Highline Trail.

3.4   Reach Horton Spring, your turnaround point.

6.8   Arrive back at the trailhead.

53 Hells Gate Trail

This an interesting hike to the confluence of Tonto and Haigler Creeks, a spot noted for its spectacular canyon narrows.

Distance: 16.2 miles out and back
Hiking time: About 10 hours or 2 days
Difficulty: Strenuous
Trail surface: Dirt trails
Best seasons: Spring and fall
Water: Seasonally in Tonto Creek
Other trail users: None
Canine compatibility: Controlled dogs allowed
Land status: Hells Gate Wilderness, Tonto National Forest

Nearest town: Payson
Fees and permits: None; groups limited to 15; pack stock is limited to 15 animals
Schedule: Open all year
Maps: USGS McDonald Mountain, Diamond Butte, Diamond Point, and Promontory Butte; Tonto National Forest
Trail contacts: Tonto National Forest, 2324 E. McDowell Rd., Phoenix, AZ 85006; (602) 225-5200; www.fs.usda.gov/tonto

Finding the trailhead: From Payson drive 11.2 miles east on Highway 260, then turn right into Hells Gate trailhead. GPS: N34 16.78'/W111 8.10'

The Hike

The Hells Gate Trail wanders south over a low pass and climbs up a ravine through ponderosa pine forest. It crosses a flat for a short distance, then turns southeast and descends into the head of Salt Lick Canyon. A short climb leads south over a low saddle, then down and across a tributary of Salt Lick Canyon. After crossing the head of another unnamed tributary of Salt Lick Canyon, the trail climbs south onto Apache Ridge. A foot trail has been constructed that bypasses the old jeep trail. Generally this trail contours around the hilltops instead of going over the tops. Finally the trail starts a steep descent off the east side of the ridge, passes El Grande Tank, and drops steeply into Tonto Creek. It reaches the creek bed a short distance downstream of Hells Gate and ends at the confluence of Tonto and Haigler Creeks. There is seasonal water in both creeks and limited camping at the confluence.

Miles and Directions

0.0 Start at the Hells Gate trailhead.

1.3 Reach the head of Salt Lick Canyon; start to climb.

3.4 Reach high point on ridge.

6.0 Start the steep descent from Apache Ridge.

7.4 Pass El Grande Tank.

8.1 Arrive at Hells Gate. Retrace your steps. (**FYI:** There is limited camping available at the creek confluence.)

16.2 Arrive back at the trailhead.

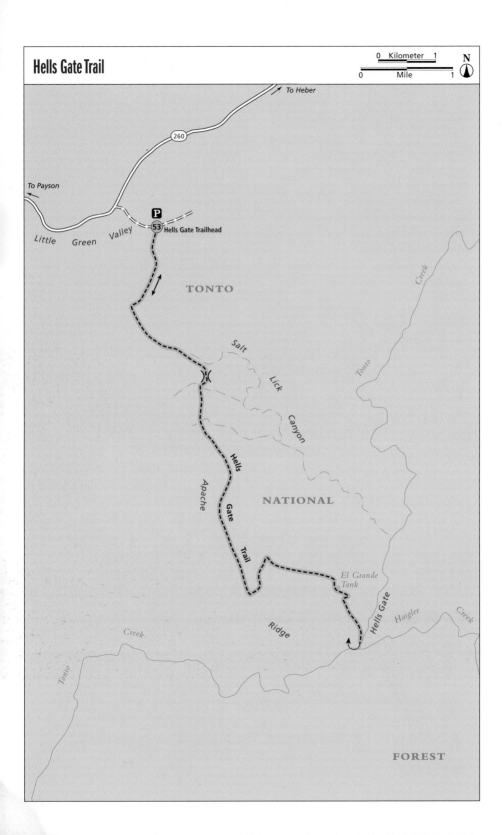

Hells Gate Trail

0 Kilometer 1

0 Mile 1

N

To Heber

260

To Payson

P

53 Hells Gate Trailhead

Little Green Valley

TONTO

Salt Lick Canyon

Creek

Tonto

Hells Gate Trail

Apache

NATIONAL

El Grande Tank

Hells Gate

Haigler

Creek

Ridge

Creek

Tonto

FOREST

Central Highlands

In the transition zone between the layer cake–like geology of the Colorado Plateau and the somewhat regular block-faulted mountains and valleys of the Basin and Range Country, Arizona's "middle" was broken and twisted into very rugged, steep mountains cut by precipitous canyons. The Sierra Prietas, Bradshaws, Sierra Anchas, Mazatzals, and Superstition Mountains offer some of the most challenging hiking in the state.

Stormy weather over the Mazatzal Mountains

54 Yaeger Canyon Loop

This is an enjoyable loop hike on Mingus Mountain with views of Prescott Valley.

Distance: 6.0-mile loop
Hiking time: About 4 hours
Difficulty: Moderate
Trail surface: Dirt trails
Best season: Spring through fall
Water: No water available
Other trail users: Mountain bikes and horses
Canine compatibility: Controlled dogs allowed
Land status: Prescott National Forest

Nearest town: Prescott
Fees and permits: None
Schedule: Open all year
Maps: USGS Hickey Mountain; Prescott National Forest
Trail contacts: Prescott National Forest, 344 S. Cortez St., Prescott, AZ 86303; (928) 443-8000; www.fs.usda.gov/prescott

Finding the trailhead: From Jerome drive 10 miles west on Highway 89A to the unmarked trailhead. The trailhead is 3.2 miles southwest of the Potato Patch Campground turnoff. Turn left onto the dirt road, and park on either side of the normally dry creek. GPS: N34 40.67'/W111 10.46'

The Hike

The hike starts on the Little Yaeger Canyon Trail, which begins from the southeast side of the parking area. Several switchbacks through piñon-juniper forest lead to the top of a gentle ridge, where ponderosa pines begin to take over. The trail climbs more gradually through a small saddle and then ends at FR 105. Turn left and walk down the road 0.2 mile to the Yaeger Cabin Trail (Forest Trail 111), then turn left.

Still in pine-oak forest, the Yaeger Cabin Trail drops slightly as it traverses a side canyon of Little Yaeger Canyon, then begins to work its way up the head of the canyon. There is sometimes water in the bed of the canyon near its head. The trail comes out onto a pine flat on the southwest ridge of Mingus Mountain and closely parallels FR 105 for a short distance. Several spur trails branch right; stay left. Continue 0.1 mile to the end of the Yaeger Cabin Trail at a junction near FR 105.

Turn left (west) and follow the Yaeger Canyon Trail (Trail 28) to the rim, where there is a good view of Little Yaeger Canyon and the rim of Mingus Mountain. The trail descends to the southwest in a series of switchbacks, and the trailhead is visible next to the highway. When the trail reaches the bottom of Yaeger Canyon, it turns left onto the old highway roadbed. It stays on the left (east) side of the creek and doesn't cross the old highway bridge. Continue down the canyon to your vehicle.

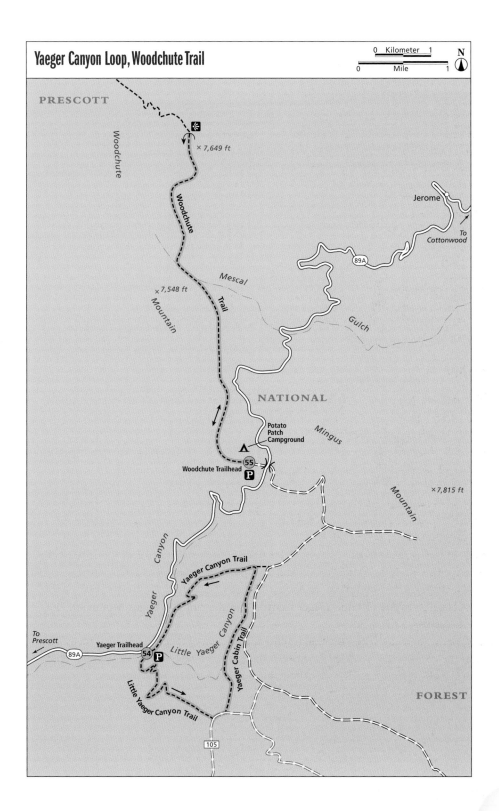

Yaeger Canyon Loop, Woodchute Trail

PRESCOTT

Woodchute

× 7,649 ft

Woodchute

Jerome

To
Cottonwood

Mescal

89A

× 7,548 ft

Mountain

Trail

Gulch

NATIONAL

Mingus

Potato
Patch
Campground

Woodchute Trailhead

55

P

× 7,815 ft

Mountain

Canyon

Yaeger

Yaeger Canyon Trail

Little Yaeger Canyon

Yaeger Cabin Trail

To
Prescott

89A

Yaeger Trailhead

54

P

Little Yaeger Canyon

FOREST

Little Yaeger Canyon Trail

105

0   Kilometer   1

0   Mile   1

N

Miles and Directions

0.0 Start at the Yaeger trailhead.

1.6 Turn left onto FR 105.

1.8 At junction with the Yaeger Cabin Trail (Trail 111), turn left.

3.6 Turn left at an unsigned trail junction.

3.7 Turn left onto the Yaeger Canyon Trail (Trail 28).

5.5 Reach an old highway; turn left.

6.0 Arrive back at the trailhead.

55 Woodchute Trail

This is an easy trail to the north end of Woodchute Mountain. You'll enjoy some panoramic views of the western Mogollon Rim and Sycamore Canyon.

See map on page 177.
Distance: 7.4 miles out and back
Hiking time: About 4 hours
Trail surface: Dirt trails
Difficulty: Easy
Best season: Spring through fall
Water: No water available
Other trail users: Horses
Canine compatibility: Controlled dogs allowed

Land status: Woodchute Wilderness, Prescott National Forest
Nearest town: Jerome
Fees and permits: None
Schedule: Open all year
Maps: USGS Hickey Mountain and Munds Draw; Prescott National Forest
Trail contacts: Prescott National Forest, 344 S. Cortez St., Prescott, AZ 86303; (928) 443-8000; www.fs.usda.gov/prescott

Finding the trailhead: From Jerome drive about 7 miles southwest on Highway 89A. At the highway pass on Mingus Mountain, turn right at Potato Patch Campground. Go about 0.4 mile and turn left into the Woodchute trailhead. GPS: N34 42.44' / W112 9.12'

The Hike

Hike north from the trailhead through ponderosa pine woodland. Notice the large alligator junipers—these are the trees with bark that looks like alligator hide, appropriately enough. The Woodchute Trail then climbs onto the main crest of the ridge. After crossing several dips in the ridge, it contours into the head of Mescal Gulch, then climbs to the south rim of Woodchute Mountain. The trail continues north across the flat summit area and finally reaches the north rim of Woodchute, our destination. (**Note:** The trail continues, descending the north slopes of Woodchute Mountain and ending at FR 318A. This section of the trail is little used.) From here you have a panoramic view of the headwaters of the Verde River, the western Mogollon Rim, and Sycamore Canyon Wilderness.

Miles and Directions

0.0 Start at the Woodchute trailhead.
1.7 Reach a ridgetop.
2.2 Contour into the head of Mescal Gulch.
2.7 Reach the south rim of Woodchute Mountain.
3.7 Reach the north rim of Woodchute Mountain. Retrace your steps to the trailhead.
7.4 Arrive back at the trailhead.

56 Granite Mountain Trail

This popular hike climbs through rugged granite terrain to a viewpoint overlooking Granite Basin and the Sierra Prieta.

Distance: 7.4 miles out and back
Hiking time: About 6 hours
Difficulty: Moderate
Trail surface: Dirt trails
Best season: Spring through fall
Water: No water available
Other trail users: Horses
Canine compatibility: Controlled dogs allowed
Land status: Granite Mountain Wilderness, Prescott National Forest

Nearest town: Prescott
Fees and permits: Fee required for trailhead parking
Schedule: Open all year
Maps: USGS Iron Springs and Jerome Canyon; Prescott National Forest
Trail contacts: Prescott National Forest, 344 S. Cortez St., Prescott, AZ 86303; (928) 443-8000; www.fs.usda.gov/prescott

Finding the trailhead: From Prescott drive northwest about 4.5 miles on Iron Springs Road. Turn right onto paved Granite Basin Road, and continue 4 miles to the Metate trailhead. GPS: N34 36.86'/W112 33.01'

The Hike

The Granite Mountain Trail crosses a wash, then follows a drainage uphill through a forest of juniper, piñon pine, oak, and ponderosa pine. To the right there are occasional views of Granite Mountain, the destination for this hike. At Blair Pass you meet the junction with the Cedar Spring and Little Granite Mountain Trails. Turn right to continue on the Granite Mountain Trail. After following a broad ridge a short distance, the trail begins to ascend the rocky slopes in a series of switchbacks.

WORLD-CLASS CLIMBING

As you start up the switchbacks above Blair Pass, you may see rock climbers taking an unmarked turnoff toward the prominent granite cliff above. Granite Mountain Wall offers world-class technical climbing on excellent granite.

The terrain faces south here, and the increased heat and dryness cause the pines to give way to chaparral and juniper. Chaparral is not a single plant—it is an association of three shrubs that commonly grow together in the upper Sonoran life zone. The red-barked bush is manzanita; the brush with the oaklike prickly leaves is scrub oak; and the plant with longish leaves, curled under at the edges and fuzzy underneath, is mountain mahogany. Chaparral provides vital cover and habitat for wildlife.

Granite Mountain Wilderness after a fall snowstorm

The reward for the steady climb is expanding views. Little Granite Mountain forms a conspicuous landmark to the south; beyond are the pine-forested slopes of the Sierra Prieta. After reaching another pass, the trail turns east and climbs the beautiful west ridge of Granite Mountain, passing through stately groves of ponderosa pines and winding around granite slabs. Some of the slabs look almost glacial in origin. When the trail reaches the summit plateau, it turns south and ends at a viewpoint above Granite Mountain Wall. Granite Basin Lake, Prescott, and the northern Bradshaw Mountains are all visible. Although this is not the true summit of the mountain, the views are still excellent.

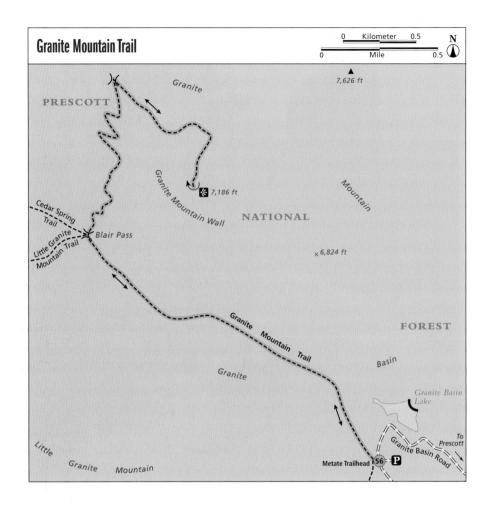

Granite Mountain Trail

Miles and Directions

0.0 Start at the Metate trailhead on Granite Basin Road.

1.8 Reach Blair Pass and the junction with the Cedar Spring and Little Granite Mountain Trails. Turn right to continue on the Granite Mountain Trail.

2.9 Reach another pass.

3.7 Arrive at the viewpoint above the Granite Mountain Wall. Retrace your steps.

7.4 Arrive back at the trailhead.

57 Pine Mountain

This is a most enjoyable loop over the summit of Pine Mountain on the Verde Rim. From the trail along the rim, you'll be treated to sweeping views of the Verde River, Arizona's only Wild and Scenic River, and the rugged Mazatzal Mountains.

Distance: 13.3-mile loop with a cherry stem
Hiking time: About 8 hours
Difficulty: Moderate
Trail surface: Dirt trails
Best season: Spring through fall
Water: Seasonal at Nelson Place; Beehouse, Bishop, Pine, and Willow Springs
Other trail users: Horses
Canine compatibility: Controlled dogs allowed

Land status: Pine Mountain Wilderness, Prescott National Forest
Nearest town: Prescott
Fees and permits: None
Schedule: Open all year
Maps: USGS Tule Mesa; Prescott National Forest
Trail contacts: Prescott National Forest, 344 S. Cortez St., Prescott, AZ 86303; (928) 443-8000; www.fs.usda.gov/prescott

---

Finding the trailhead: From Phoenix drive north about 75 miles on I-17 to the Dugas interchange. Turn east onto CR 171, which becomes FR 68. After 10.9 miles FR 68G continues straight ahead; be sure to turn right here to remain on FR 68. Continue another 6.6 miles to the end of the road and the Pine Mountain trailhead, where there is limited camping available. GPS: N34 19.58' / W111 50.19'

The Hike

Pine Mountain is a small wilderness area astride the Verde Rim offering super views of the Mazatzal Wilderness and the wild Verde River country south of Camp Verde. A power-line corridor is the only nonwilderness feature separating the two wildernesses. This loop hike circumnavigates the higher, western portion of the Pine Mountain Wilderness. Numerous wildfires have burned parts of the wilderness over the years, and you will encounter evidence of these fires on most of the trails. Expect to see downed trees across the trail periodically.

The trail heads southeast and follows Sycamore Creek past Nelson Place Spring. This was the site of an old homestead and ranch—remains of the fruit orchard and building foundations can still be seen. Turn right (south) onto the Beehouse Canyon Trail, which follows its namesake canyon past Beehouse Spring and up to a saddle at Pine Flat. Turn left here onto the Pine Flat Trail, and cross Pine Flat itself, which features a fine stand of ponderosa pines. Now the trail drops into the South Prong of Sycamore Creek, crosses the drainage, and works its way along the east side of the canyon to meet the Verde Rim Trail in a saddle. Turn left here and follow the trail northwest into Bishop Canyon. The Verde Rim Trail passes Bishop Spring in a side canyon and then contours into the main arm of Bishop Creek. Here the Bishop Creek Trail forks left; stay right.

Hiking the Verde Rim Trail, Pine Mountain

After passing through a shallow saddle, the trail finally reaches the Verde Rim itself. As promised, the views of the Verde River and Mazatzal Mountains are expansive. The trail now climbs along the Verde Rim to the northeast, heading toward Pine Mountain. Another trail goes left from a shallow saddle before you reach Pine Mountain. The main trail skirts Pine Mountain on the west, but a short spur trail makes it an easy walk to the summit—the highest point on the Verde Rim.

Continuing north on the Verde Rim Trail, descend steeply into a saddle, and then turn left on the Pine Mountain Trail (the Verde Rim Trail continues straight ahead). This trail descends into the headwaters of Sycamore Creek through another fine stand of ponderosa pine and Gambel oak. There are several possible campsites as the grade levels out, and there is seasonal water at Pine and Willow Springs. After passing Willow Spring, the Bishop Creek Trail joins from the left. Continue down Sycamore Creek past Beehouse Canyon Trail, which completes the loop, and on past Nelson Place Spring to the trailhead.

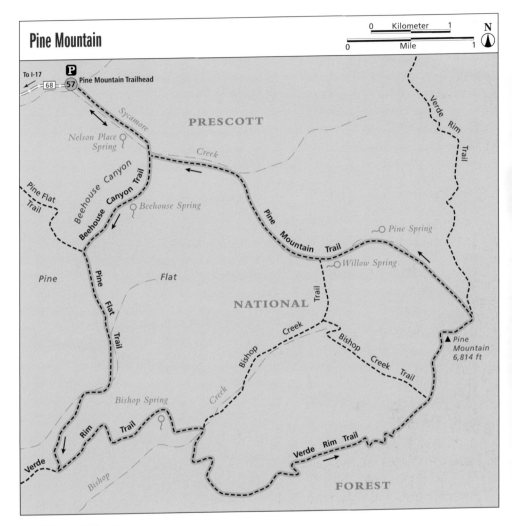

Pine Mountain

Pine Mountain Trailhead

To I-17

68 57

PRESCOTT

Sycamore

Nelson Place Spring

Creek

Beehouse Canyon

Beehouse Canyon Trail

Beehouse Spring

Pine Flat Trail

Pine Mountain Trail

Pine Spring

Willow Spring

Pine

Flat

Pine Flat Trail

NATIONAL

Bishop Creek

Bishop Creek Trail

▲ Pine Mountain 6,814 ft

Bishop Spring

Creek

Rim Trail

Verde Rim Trail

Verde

Bishop

FOREST

Miles and Directions

0.0 Start at the Pine Mountain trailhead on FR 68.

0.8 Turn right onto Beehouse Canyon Trail.

1.8 Reach Pine Flat; turn left onto the Pine Flat Trail.

3.7 Turn left onto the Verde Rim Trail.

8.3 The Bishop Creek Trail joins from the left; stay right.

8.9 Reach Pine Mountain.

9.3 Turn left onto the Pine Mountain Trail.

10.8 The Bishop Creek Trail joins from the left.

12.6 Pass Beehouse Canyon Trail on the left.

13.3 Arrive back at the Pine Mountain trailhead.

58 Y Bar Basin-Barnhardt Canyon Loop

This classic route travels around the range's highest peak and through a remarkable variety of terrain in the Mazatzal Mountains. These trails are better maintained and easier to find than most other trails in the Mazatzal Wilderness.

Distance: 11.6-mile loop
Hiking time: About 8 hours
Difficulty: Strenuous
Trail surface: Dirt trails
Best season: Spring through fall
Water: Seasonal at Y Bar Tanks
Other trail users: Horses
Canine compatibility: Dogs under control allowed
Land status: Mazatzal Wilderness, Tonto National Forest

Nearest town: Payson
Fees and permits: None
Other: Group size limited to 15; 14-day stay limit
Schedule: Open all year
Maps: USGS Mazatzal Peak; USFS Mazatzal Wilderness, Tonto National Forest
Trail contacts: Tonto National Forest, 2324 E. McDowell Rd., Phoenix, AZ 85006; (602) 225-5200; www.fs.usda.gov/tonto

Finding the trailhead: From Mesa drive about 67 miles north on Highway 87, then turn left onto the Barnhardt Road (this turnoff is just south of the Gisela turnoff). Continue 5 miles to the end of the maintained dirt road to the trailhead. GPS: N34 5.56' / W111 25.28'

The Hike

Start on the Barnhardt Trail; just a dozen yards from the trailhead, turn left onto the Y Bar Trail (sometimes called the Shake Tree Trail). The Barnhardt Trail will be your return. The Y Bar Trail climbs up a broad ridge in a series of rocky switchbacks, heading generally southwest through piñon pine and juniper forest. When the trail passes the wilderness boundary, it turns more to the south and climbs along the east slopes of Mazatzal Peak, crossing numerous small canyons. After about a mile of this, the trail crosses into Shake Tree Canyon and climbs along the west slopes. Below to the east, Shake Tree Canyon cuts through a spectacular area of cliffs and rock fins.

The trail continues up Shake Tree Canyon, entering a pine-forested northeast-facing slope, then works its way across the slopes west of the canyon's bed. The climb ends as the trail reaches the saddle between Mazatzal Peak and Cactus Ridge. It's possible to camp here, although the nearest water is at Y Bar Tanks. The Y Bar Trail descends southwest from the saddle, then levels out and contours across a small drainage. A small seep spring here, Y Bar Tanks, often has water. If it doesn't, follow the drainage downstream a hundred yards, where you may find large pools. After the seep the trail contours westward, then turns northwest and climbs to Windsor Saddle. There is limited camping in Windsor Saddle.

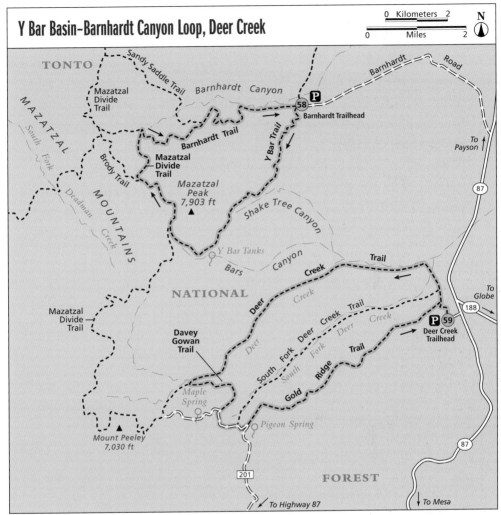

Turn right onto the Mazatzal Divide Trail, which heads north and contours the west slopes of Mazatzal Peak. You'll have fine views of the rocky summit, as well as the head of the South Fork of Deadman Creek to the west. The well-constructed trail (also the route of the Arizona Trail) descends gradually northwest as it works its way around ridges and ravines. You'll pass the junction with Brody Trail (Brody Seep is 0.7 mile northwest and there are several campsites nearby); stay right on the Divide Trail. You'll turn northward again and pass through several small stands of ponderosa pine as the trail contours to the saddle at the head of Barnhardt Canyon.

Turn right here, onto the Barnhardt Trail. This popular trail is well constructed and easy to find. It heads generally east, contouring the south slopes of the broad basin at the head of Barnhardt Canyon. The trail passes through several stands of ponderosa pine, but much of the basin is covered with dense chaparral brush. Stay right at the junction with the Sandy Saddle Trail (Casterson Seep, shown on the maps where

THE WILLOW FIRE

Much of the Mazatzal high country burned in the Willow Fire during the summer of 2004. Ongoing drought combined with trees killed by bark beetles have created conditions for wildfires of unprecedented size in Arizona in recent years, including the Willow Fire, which burned more than 100,000 acres. Large stands of ponderosa pine were burned in the fire, as were large areas of chaparral brush and grasslands. While the brush and grass will quickly grow back, it will be difficult for the pine forests to reestablish themselves at these marginal elevations. On the other hand, fires have always been part of the Arizona forest ecology, and numerous other fires have burned in the Mazatzal Mountains in the past. Pockets of pine trees have survived all these fires and will undoubtedly survive future ones.

the Sandy Saddle Trail crosses Barnhardt Creek, is not reliable). The Barnhardt Trail swings around a ridge, where you can leave the trail momentarily and walk a few yards north to a viewpoint overlooking the impressive gorge of Barnhardt Canyon. The trail swings south after this point and crosses a drainage where there may be seasonal pools a short distance upstream from the trail. In cold weather the waterfall above the upper pool is often graced with a beautiful tapestry of icicles.

Now the trail descends eastward along the south slopes of Barnhardt Canyon, skirting some impressive cliffs. Note the bent and twisted layers of metamorphic rock—mute testimony to the inconceivable forces that created these mountains. The trail turns north and descends a steep ridge in a series of switchbacks until it is close to the canyon bottom, then heads east again and stays just above the bed all the way to the Barnhardt trailhead.

Miles and Directions

0.0 Start at the Barnhardt trailhead on Barnhardt Road. In a few yards turn left onto the Y Bar Trail.

4.2 Reach saddle between Mazatzal Peak and Cactus Ridge.

4.8 Pass Y Bar Tanks. (**FYI:** This small spring often has water.)

5.7 Reach Windsor Saddle; turn right onto the Mazatzal Divide Trail.

6.9 Pass Brody Trail junction; stay right.

8.3 Turn right onto the Barnhardt Trail.

11.6 Arrive back at the trailhead.

59 Deer Creek

This loop hike through several deep canyons in the eastern portion of the Mazatzal Mountains offers options for exploring the several forks of Deer Creek. The hike starts from one of the few Mazatzal Wilderness trailheads located next to a paved highway.

See map on page 187.
Distance: 14.9-mile loop
Hiking time: About 2 days
Difficulty: Strenuous
Trail surface: Dirt trails
Best seasons: Spring and fall
Water: Seasonal in Deer Creek and at Maple and Pigeon Springs
Other trail users: Horses
Canine compatibility: Controlled dogs allowed

Land status: Mazatzal Wilderness, Tonto National Forest
Nearest town: Payson
Fees and permits: None
Other: Group size limited to 15; 14-day stay limit
Schedule: Open all year
Maps: USGS Mazatzal Peak; USFS Mazatzal Wilderness, Tonto National Forest
Trail contacts: Tonto National Forest, 2324 E. McDowell Rd., Phoenix, AZ 85006; (602) 225-5200; www.fs.usda.gov/tonto

Finding the trailhead: From Mesa drive about 63 miles north on Highway 87. Turn left into the Deer Creek trailhead, just south of the junction with Highway 188. GPS: N34 25.28' / W111 25.28'

The Hike

From the trailhead start northwest on the Deer Creek Trail (Forest Trail 45) as it climbs onto a low ridge. Within a short distance, both the Gold Ridge Trail (which will be your return) and the South Fork Deer Creek Trail branch left; stay right at both junctions. The Deer Creek Trail crosses the South Fork of Deer Creek, then swings into Deer Creek just upstream of a ranch located on private land. Now the trail follows the creek west toward the mountains. Although the stream flow is seasonal, depending on recent rain and snow, the canyon bottom is still delightfully shaded by Arizona sycamores and other streamside trees. When Deer Creek starts a turn toward the southwest, Bars Canyon joins from the right. As you continue upstream along Deer Creek, the trail becomes fainter but always stays near the bottom of the canyon. The appearance of the first ponderosa pines along the north-facing slopes signal that you're reaching the head of the canyon. After an unnamed tributary canyon comes in from the northwest, Deer Creek swings to the south briefly before resuming its southwesterly direction. You'll hike through a brushy meadow and then meet the Davey Gowan Trail (Forest Trail 48).

Turn left here and follow the Davey Gowan Trail as it climbs east out of the canyon, then swings south onto a ridge and climbs to meet the Mount Peeley Road (FR 201). This entire section is covered with a fine ponderosa pine and Douglas fir forest. Turn left onto the road, and hike east about 0.9 mile to a spur road branching left and downhill. Follow this road northeast about 0.2 mile to the road closure and the start of the Gold

Ridge Trail (Forest Trail 47). The trail, an old jeep road, drops off the northwest side of the ridge, then swings east to follow the general ridge system. You'll leave the pine forest behind as the trail descends onto lower, drier slopes. Watch for the point where the old jeep road veers north and the Gold Ridge Trail becomes a foot trail, heading east for a short distance before turning northeast again. It descends a ridge, which gives you great views to the northeast, then finally emerges onto gentler slopes covered with high desert grasses. Continue for about 1 mile back to the Deer Creek trailhead.

Miles and Directions

0.0 Start at the Deer Creek trailhead on Highway 87.

0.1 Stay right at junction with the Gold Ridge Trail.

0.3 Stay right again at junction with the South Fork Deer Creek Trail.

1.0 Cross Deer Creek.

7.0 Turn left onto the Davey Gowan Trail.

8.6 Turn left onto the Mount Peeley Road (FR 201).

9.2 Pass the South Fork Deer Creek Trail.

9.5 Turn left onto the old road to the Gold Ridge Trail.

9.7 Pass the road closure and start the descent.

14.8 Turn right to return to the trailhead.

14.9 Arrive back at the Deer Creek trailhead.

Options

Option 1: Instead of leaving Deer Creek on the Davey Gowan Trail, stay right and follow the Deer Creek Trail southwest as it climbs through dense pine-fir forest to the Mount Peeley trailhead. Turn left and walk the Mount Peeley Road 1.4 miles to the Davey Gowan Trail junction (FT 48). Continue 0.9 mile east to the Gold Ridge Trail. This option gets you into the head of Deer Creek, although it involves a little more road walking. It adds 0.7 mile and less than an hour to the loop.

Option 2: From the Mount Peeley Road, return via the South Fork Deer Creek Trail (Forest Trail 46). This little-used trail leaves the road 0.6 mile east of the Davey Gowan Trail and passes Maple Spring before dropping into the South Fork of Deer Creek. This option is 0.2 mile shorter.

Old stone cabin along Deer Creek

60 Browns Peak

This cross-country hike takes you to the top of the highest of the Four Peaks—and the highest in the southern Mazatzal Mountains. Although the craggy peak looks impressive, it's actually easy to climb; you'll need your hands in only a few places.

Distance: 4.6 miles out and back
Hiking time: About 5 hours
Difficulty: Strenuous
Trail surface: Dirt trails, cross-country scrambling
Best season: Spring through fall
Water: No water available
Other trail users: None
Canine compatibility: Controlled dogs allowed
Land status: Four Peaks Wilderness, Tonto National Forest

Nearest town: Mesa
Fees and permits: None
Other: Group size limited to 15; 14-day stay limit
Schedule: Open all year
Maps: USGS Four Peaks; USFS Tonto National Forest
Trail contacts: Tonto National Forest, 2324 E. McDowell Rd., Phoenix, AZ 85006; (602) 225-5200; www.fs.usda.gov/tonto

Finding the trailhead: From Mesa drive northeast on Highway 87. At Shea Boulevard note your mileage and continue 14 miles to FR 143. Turn right onto this maintained dirt road, which becomes unmaintained and much rougher after 6.7 miles. When you are 18.3 miles from the highway, turn right onto FR 648 and continue 1 mile south to the Lone Pine Saddle trailhead at the end of the road. GPS: N33 42.34' / W111 20.28'

THE VIEW FROM HERE

From this lofty vantage point, you can see much of the country covered by this guidebook. Although the bulk of the other three peaks blocks some of the view to the south, you can still see much of the Superstition Mountains. To the west lies the Valley of the Sun, home to Phoenix and its sister cities. The desert plain is dotted with low mountain ranges that seem to recede into the distance. On a clear day you can see the McDowell Mountains and, far to the west, the Harquahala Mountains. To the northwest the bulk of the Bradshaw Mountains looms above the lower-elevation New River Mountains. The Mazatzal Mountains run north-northwest from your perch—the rounded summit of Mount Ord, crowned with radio towers and a fire lookout, is clearly visible. The rugged peaks of the Mazatzal Wilderness form the backdrop for Mount Ord. North and eastward, the clean line of the Mogollon Rim slices across the horizon near Payson. To the east the wide bulk of the Sierra Ancha dominates the skyline. To the southeast you can see Pinal Peak rising above the town of Globe.

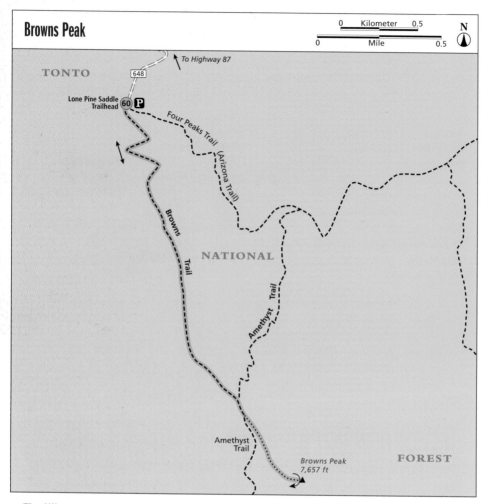

0   Kilometer   0.5

0   Mile   0.5

N

TONTO

To Highway 87

648

Lone Pine Saddle
Trailhead 60 P

Four Peaks Trail

(Arizona Trail)

Browns

Trail

NATIONAL

Amethyst Trail

Amethyst
Trail

Browns Peak
7,657 ft

FOREST

The Hike

The trail climbs south from the trailhead through a fine stand of ponderosa pine and Gambel oak that was nearly untouched by the Lone Fire of 1996. It swings southwest and passes through a broad saddle, then turns southeast, back toward the main ridge, and enters an area where the fire killed nearly 100 percent of the trees. Be alert for falling dead trees, which can topple at any time but are especially likely to fall during windy or wet weather. The view is much better without the trees—or at least it will be until the chaparral brush gets reestablished. After crossing the main ridge, the trail works its way up the northeast slopes, switchbacking occasionally. Finally it meets the Amethyst Trail. Turn right and continue a short distance to Browns Saddle.

Now leave the trail and continue cross-country south up the ridge toward Browns Peak. Note the prominent ravine that splits the north face of the peak. This is your

Four Peaks, with Browns Peak on the left

goal, but you won't be able to see it when you get closer. Although there are several different routes to the summit, the following route is one of the easiest. When you reach the first rock outcrops, turn right and work your way into the main gully that drains the ravine mentioned above. If you stay high, right at the base of the rock, you'll avoid the worst of the brush. Head directly up the ravine; there's one spot in the ravine where you'll need your hands. The ravine tops out on the west shoulder of the peak; then it's just a short scramble to the left (east) to reach the summit.

Miles and Directions

0.0 Start at the Lone Pine Saddle trailhead on FR 648.

1.7 Turn right onto the Amethyst Trail.

1.9 Reach Browns Saddle. Leave the trail and head south cross-country toward Browns Peak.

2.3 Reach Browns Peak. Retrace your steps.

4.6 Arrive back at the trailhead.

61 Hells Hole

This is an overnight backpack into Workman Creek in the Sierra Ancha.

Distance: 9.2 miles out and back
Hiking time: About 7 hours
Difficulty: Strenuous
Trail surface: Dirt trails
Best season: Spring through fall
Water: Workman Creek
Other trail users: Horses
Canine compatibility: Controlled dogs allowed
Land status: Salome Wilderness, Tonto National Forest

Nearest town: Young
Fees and permits: None
Other: Group size limited to 15; 14-day stay limit
Schedule: Open all year
Maps: USGS Aztec Peak, Armor Mountain, and Copper Mountain; USFS Tonto National Forest
Trail contacts: Tonto National Forest, 2324 E. McDowell Rd., Phoenix, AZ 85006; (602) 225-5200; www.fs.usda.gov/tonto

Finding the trailhead: From Globe drive Highway 88, then Highway 288 toward Young. About 20 miles south of Young is the Reynolds Creek Group Campground. There is a turnout to the south just before entering the campground, which is the parking area for this trail. GPS: N33 52.31'/W111 58.51'

The Hike

The trail starts in ponderosa pine forest and climbs southwesterly to the pass between Jack Mountain and an unnamed peak (6,076 feet) to the north. Beyond the pass the trail drops into Workman Creek, which it crosses, and then climbs about 600 vertical feet to the top of the far rim. The trail passes south of a knoll (5,682 feet) and then descends steeply into Hells Hole, a particularly dramatic section of Workman Creek. The trail may be overgrown in places, making route finding challenging.

▶ **The determined angler can try his or her luck at Workman Creek for German brown and rainbow trout. Other wildlife in the area includes mule deer, white-tailed deer, javelinas, mountain lions, coyotes, black bears, and wild turkeys.**

Miles and Directions

0.0 Start at the trailhead just before the Reynolds Creek campground.
0.8 Reach the first pass.
1.6 Cross Workman Creek.
3.0 Reach the far rim.
4.6 Reach Hells Hole. Retrace your steps.
9.2 Arrive back at the trailhead.

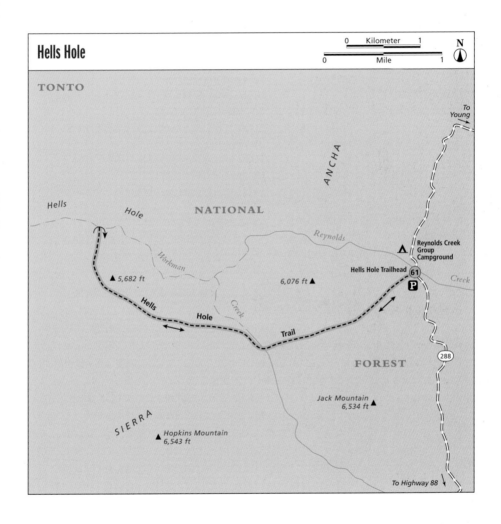

Hells Hole

0   Kilometer   1
0   Mile   1
N

TONTO

Hells

Hole

NATIONAL

ANCHA

Reynolds

To
Young

Reynolds Creek
Group
Campground

Workman

Hells Hole Trailhead

61

▲ 5,682 ft

6,076 ft ▲

Creek

Hells

Creek

Hole

P

Trail

288

FOREST

Jack Mountain
6,534 ft ▲

SIERRA

▲ Hopkins Mountain
6,543 ft

To Highway 88 ↓

62 Barks Canyon

This is a scenic hike up Peralta Canyon through a forest of stone towers to a viewpoint overlooking Weavers Needle, the most famous landmark in the Superstition Mountains. The hike uses a short section of cross-country hiking to return via Barks Canyon.

Distance: 5.2-mile loop
Hiking time: About 4 hours
Difficulty: Moderate
Trail surface: Dirt trails, cross-country
Best season: Fall through spring
Water: Seasonal water in Peralta and Barks Canyons
Other trail users: Horses on the Terrapin and Dutchmans Trails
Canine compatibility: Controlled dogs allowed

Land status: Superstition Wilderness, Tonto National Forest
Nearest town: Apache Junction
Fees and permits: None
Other: Group size limited to 15; 14-day stay limit
Schedule: Open all year
Maps: USGS Weavers Needle; USFS Superstition Wilderness
Trail contacts: Tonto National Forest, 2324 E. McDowell Rd., Phoenix, AZ 85006; (602) 225-5200; www.fs.usda.gov/tonto

Finding the trailhead: From Apache Junction drive about 8.5 miles east on US 60. Turn left onto Peralta Road (FR 77), which becomes maintained dirt after passing a subdivision. Continue 8 miles to the end of the road at the Peralta trailhead. GPS: N33 23.84'/W111 20.87'

The Hike

Start the loop on the well-graded but rocky Peralta Trail, which heads northwest up Peralta Canyon, climbing steadily. The trail generally stays near the bed of the canyon, occasionally crossing it. Numerous stone pinnacles, known locally as "stone ghosts," are scattered along the canyon and its rims. The pinnacles are mostly carved from rhyolite, a volcanic rock. As the mountains eroded, erosion followed cracks in the rock and carved out odd-looking fins and pinnacles. The trail steepens somewhat near the head of the canyon, and a few short switchbacks lead to Fremont Saddle at the head of Peralta Canyon.

The Cave Trail continues north from the saddle, but your route follows the unsigned Cave Trail east onto the broken plateau northeast of the saddle. Once on the plateau, turn left on the unsigned Weavers Needle Overlook Trail and head north across the plateau to its northern rim and a panoramic view of Weavers Needle. After enjoying the view, backtrack along the trail to a low saddle and descend east off

Weavers Needle from Barks Canyon ▶

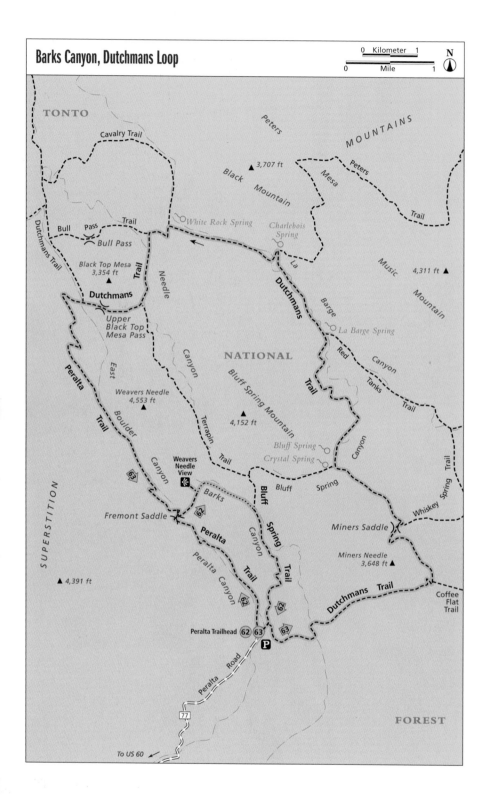

Barks Canyon, Dutchmans Loop

0 — Kilometer — 1
0 — Mile — 1

N

TONTO

Cavalry Trail

Peters

MOUNTAINS

Black Mountain

▲ 3,707 ft

Mesa

Peters

Trail

Dutchmans Trail

Bull Pass — Trail

White Rock Spring

Charlebois Spring

Bull Pass

La

Dutchmans

Music Mountain

4,311 ft ▲

Black Top Mesa 3,354 ft ▲

Needle Trail

Dutchmans

Barge

La Barge Spring

Upper Black Top Mesa Pass

Peralta

East

Canyon

NATIONAL

Trail

Red

Canyon

Tanks

Trail

Boulder

Weavers Needle 4,553 ft ▲

Bluff Spring Mountain

▲ 4,152 ft

Canyon

Terrapin

Trail

Bluff Spring

Crystal Spring

Canyon

Whiskey Spring Trail

Weavers Needle View

Barks

Bluff

Spring

SUPERSTITION

Canyon

63

Fremont Saddle

6

Bluff Spring Trail

Miners Saddle

Peralta

Spring

Canyon

Trail

Miners Needle 3,648 ft ▲

▲ 4,391 ft

Peralta Canyon

Peralta Trail

62

63

Dutchmans Trail

Coffee Flat Trail

Peralta Trailhead 62 63

P

Peralta Road

77

To US 60

FOREST

the rim, then follow the drainage northeast into Barks Canyon. The exact point at which you start the descent is not critical, because the entire eastern rim drains into Barks Canyon. Now turn right and follow Barks Canyon downstream. Volcanic pinnacles and stone grottos line both sides of the shallow canyon, and it's an interesting area to explore. After a major tributary joins from the left, watch for the Bluff Spring Trail, which descends the eastern slopes into Barks Canyon. Turn right, and follow this well-used trail back to the Peralta trailhead.

▶ Fremont Saddle is one of many places throughout the American West named for John C. Fremont, the noted American explorer who led several government-sponsored survey expeditions.

Miles and Directions

0.0 Start at the Peralta trailhead at the end of FR 77.

1.9 Reach Fremont Saddle and turn right on the unsigned Cave Trail.

2.1 Turn left on the unsigned Weavers Needle Overlook Trail

2.4 Come to a view of Weavers Needle, then backtrack to a low saddle and descend east into the Barks Canyon drainage

2.6 Reach Barks Canyon; turn right, downstream.

3.4 Turn right at junction onto the Bluff Spring Trail.

5.2 Arrive back at the trailhead.

63 Dutchmans Loop

This popular loop through the western Superstition Mountains, known by its many fans as "the Sups," takes in a lot of interesting country, following well-graded, easy trails throughout. The hike can be done as a long day hike but is an especially good overnight hike for those new to the sport of backpacking.

See map on page 198.
Distance: 14.8-mile loop
Hiking time: About 9 hours or 2 days
Difficulty: Moderate
Trail surface: Dirt trails
Best season: Fall through spring
Water: Seasonal at Crystal, Bluff, La Barge, Charlebois, and White Rock Springs
Other trail users: Horses
Canine compatibility: Controlled dogs allowed

Land status: Superstition Wilderness, Tonto National Forest
Nearest town: Apache Junction
Fees and permits: None
Other: Group size limited to 15; 14-day stay limit
Schedule: Open all year
Maps: USGS Weavers Needle; USFS Superstition Wilderness, Tonto National Forest
Trail contacts: Tonto National Forest, 2324 E. McDowell Rd., Phoenix, AZ 85006; (602) 225-5200; www.fs.usda.gov/tonto

Finding the trailhead: From Apache Junction drive about 8.5 miles east on US 60. Turn left onto Peralta Road (FR 77), which becomes maintained dirt after passing a subdivision. Continue 8 miles to the end of the road at the Peralta trailhead. GPS: N33 23.84' / W111 20.87'

The Hike

Hike east on the Dutchmans Trail over a low ridge. The trail passes the junction with the Coffee Flat Trail, then loops around the base of Miners Needle, climbing to Miners Summit via a couple of switchbacks. It then descends northwest to Crystal Spring at the base of Bluff Spring Mountain. Turning northeast, the good trail descends Bluff Spring Canyon, passing the spur trail to Bluff Spring, and then turns more to the north and works its way down to La Barge Canyon and the junction with the Red Tanks Trail. La Barge Spring is located just east of this junction, on the north side of the canyon. There are several campsites in the area.

Stay left on the Dutchmans Trail, and follow it down La Barge Canyon to the northwest. A spur trail leads to Music Spring. At the junction with the Peters Trail, you can reach Charlebois Spring by following the Peters Trail a short distance into the side canyon. There are several popular campsites near this spring. The main trail

Storm over Weavers Needle from East Boulder Canyon ▶

continues down La Barge Canyon to Marsh Valley and the junction with the Cavalry Trail. White Rock Spring usually has water, and there is limited camping nearby.

Again, stay left on the Dutchmans Trail and climb west to a low saddle. Here, at the junction with the Bull Pass Trail, the Dutchmans Trail turns south and drops into Needle Canyon. After following Needle Canyon for a while, turn right at the junction with the Terrapin Trail and follow the Dutchmans Trail up an unnamed drainage south of Black Top Mesa. The trail reaches Upper Black Top Mesa Pass, then descends northwest into East Boulder Canyon to meet the Peralta Trail. There are campsites in this scenic basin, which is dominated by towering Weavers Needle to the south. Seasonal water can be found in the bed of the wash.

Turn left onto the Peralta Trail, which climbs west in well-graded switchbacks to the ridge south of Palomino Mountain, then heads south on a slope above a small canyon. A few switchbacks take the trail over a saddle next to a rock outcrop, and then the trail descends back into East Boulder Canyon below triple-summited Weavers Needle. It then works its way up the scenic head of East Boulder Canyon. Water can sometimes be found in the creekbed. The Peralta Trail climbs to Fremont Saddle in a couple of switchbacks and then descends scenic Peralta Canyon to the Peralta trailhead.

Miles and Directions

0.0 Start at the Peralta trailhead at the end of FR 77, hiking east on the Dutchmans Trail.

2.2 Pass junction with the Coffee Flat Trail.

2.6 Reach Miners Summit and junction with the Whiskey Spring Trail. Stay on the Dutchmans Trail.

3.8 Pass the Bluff Spring Trail; turn right to stay on the Dutchmans Trail.

5.0 Stay left at Red Tanks Trail junction and La Barge Spring. (*FYI:* There are several campsites in the area.)

6.1 Stay left again at Peters Trail and Charlebois Spring. (*FYI:* There are several campsites near the spring.)

7.4 Reach Marsh Valley, White Rock Spring, and the Cavalry Trail; stay left. (*FYI:* There is limited camping near White Rock Spring.)

7.8 At junction with Bull Pass Trail, stay left on the Dutchmans Trail.

8.6 At junction with Terrapin Trail, stay right on the Dutchmans Trail.

9.4 Turn left onto the Peralta Trail in East Boulder Canyon. (*FYI:* There are campsites in the basin.)

13.0 Reach Fremont Saddle, and begin to descend Peralta Canyon.

14.8 Arrive back at the Peralta trailhead.

64 Fireline Loop

You'll find this to be an enjoyable hike through the surprising high country in the eastern Superstition Mountains. You'll have a chance to climb the highest peak in the range, visit the site of historic Reavis Ranch, and hike along beautiful Campaign Creek.

Distance: 14.5-mile loop
Hiking time: About 9 hours or 2 days
Difficulty: Strenuous
Trail surface: Dirt trails
Best season: Fall through spring
Water: Campaign Creek near the trailhead, Walnut Spring, seasonal in Pine Creek and Reavis Creek, Whiskey Spring, Black Jack Spring, Brushy Spring, seasonal in upper Campaign Creek
Other trail users: Horses
Canine compatibility: Controlled dogs allowed

Land status: Superstition Wilderness, Tonto National Forest
Nearest town: Globe
Fees and permits: None
Other: Group size limited to 15; 14-day stay limit
Schedule: Open all year
Maps: USGS Pinyon Mountain, Two Bar Mountain, Haunted Canyon, and Iron Mountain; USFS Superstition Wilderness, Tonto National Forest
Trail contacts: Tonto National Forest, 2324 E. McDowell Rd., Phoenix, AZ 85006; (602) 225-5200; www.fs.usda.gov/tonto

Finding the trailhead: From Apache Junction drive 20 miles northeast on Highway 88 to the end of the pavement. Continue another 20 miles on the gravel road to Roosevelt Dam, and then turn right to remain on Highway 88, which is now paved. Continue 8.6 miles, and then turn right onto FR 449, the Campaign Creek Road, which is maintained dirt. Go 1.9 miles; turn left at a fork onto FR 449A, and continue 5.2 miles to the end of the road at the Reavis Mountain School. FR 449A follows Campaign Creek and crosses it numerous times. This route requires a high-clearance vehicle and may be washed out and impassable after major storms. The Campaign trailhead is on private land—please park in the signed trailhead parking area. There is no camping at the trailhead. GPS: N33 31.81'/W111 4.85'

You can also reach FR 449 from Globe by driving about 20 miles west on Highway 88, which is paved.

The Hike

Hike through the Reavis Mountain School and continue southwest along Campaign Creek. This section of the creek has a permanent flow of water from several nearby springs. Just after a side canyon comes in from the right, turn right onto the Reavis Gap Trail. This trail is not shown on the USGS maps, and sections can be difficult to follow. The trail first climbs over a low ridge, then heads west up an unnamed canyon system, climbing steadily. After it crosses the normally dry wash, the grade steepens as it heads for Reavis Gap, a saddle on Two Bar Ridge. Just after passing through Reavis Gap, the Two Bar Ridge Trail branches right. (Walnut Spring is about 0.5 mile northwest on the Two Bar Ridge Trail.) Stay on the Reavis Gap Trail as it passes through another saddle,

FIRES

When Reavis Ranch was sold to the Forest Service in the 1960s, the historic ranch house was still intact and usable as an emergency shelter. Unfortunately, years of weather and vandalism took their toll, and careless campers finally burned the building to the ground. Although the ruins of the house were cleaned up and removed, you may find artifacts from the old ranching days—please leave everything as you find it.

Wildfires are common and difficult to fight in this remote country. In the early days of this wilderness, it was thought that all wildfires should be aggressively suppressed, and bulldozers were used to build access roads and construct fire lines, leaving scars that are still visible. The Forest Service now recognizes that lightning-caused fires are part of the natural forest cycle and are necessary to keep the wilderness wild. Such natural fires are allowed to burn uncontrolled, except for monitoring and containment efforts to keep the fire from threatening developed areas outside the wilderness. Another fire burned the area in the 1980s, but the use of low-impact firefighting techniques caused much less impact to the wilderness values.

then swings south and drops into Pine Creek. There is seasonal water in Pine Creek and several campsites scattered in the piñon pine–juniper forest along the creek.

After crossing Pine Creek, the trail again heads southwest and climbs gradually toward another saddle. It then drops gradually west down a tributary of Reavis Creek and ends at the Reavis Ranch Trail on the west side of Reavis Creek. Turn left onto the Reavis Ranch Trail. The trail passes an apple orchard and then emerges into a meadow next to Reavis Creek. This was the site of the old ranch house. There's plenty of camping both up- and downstream from the former ranch site, and you can usually find flowing water in the creek upstream for about 0.7 mile.

Continue the hike by heading south on the Reavis Ranch Trail. Turn left (east) onto the Fireline Trail before reaching the first major drainage that comes in on the left. Parts of this trail follow an old bulldozer track made by the Forest Service while fighting a forest fire in 1966.

You'll mostly be in piñon-juniper woodland with an understory of chaparral brush along the first part of the Fireline Trail. After passing Whiskey Spring the trail turns more to the northeast and climbs up a drainage to the divide between Reavis and Pine Creeks. Now it heads southeast and descends gradually into the head of Pine Creek. There are pockets of tall ponderosa pines growing in favored locations— hence the creek's name. The old dozer trail suddenly turns east and drops steeply into the bed of Pine Creek. It then follows the drainage for a short distance before climbing out to the east and crossing the divide between Pine and Campaign Creeks. Now it plunges steeply into Campaign Creek, passing Black Jack Spring just before ending

Fireline Loop

0 Kilometer 1
0 Mile 1

N

TONTO

Two Bar Ridge Trail

Walnut Spring

▲ 5,522 ft

Reavis Gap Trail

To Highway 88

449A

Campaign Trailhead 64 P

Reavis Mountain School

Reavis Gap

Pine

Creek

Campaign Creek Trail

Campaign

Creek

Creek

5,610 ft ▲

Reavis Gap Trail

Creek

NATIONAL

▲ 5,714 ft

▲ 4,922 ft

▲ 5,772 ft

Reavis Ranch (site)

Fireline

Reavis Ranch Trail

Whiskey Spring

Trail

Brushy Spring

Reavis Ranch Trail

Reavis Creek

SUPERSTITION

Black Jack Spring

Pinto Peak Trail

Pinto Peak Trail

FOREST

▲ 5,282 ft

Mound Mountain 6,266 ft

MOUNTAINS

at the Pinto Peak Trail in Campaign Creek. There are several good campsites, graced by more pines, at this trail junction.

Now turn left again, and follow the Pinto Peak Trail down Campaign Creek. After the rugged country you've just crossed, it's a joy to wander down the scenic canyon bottom. There's seasonal water in the creek bed. The Pinto Peak Trail veers right and climbs out of Campaign Creek at a trail junction; go left here onto the Campaign Creek Trail and continue north down Campaign Creek. Finally the trail climbs over a low saddle to avoid a narrow, rough section of the canyon bottom, and then meets the Reavis Gap Trail. Stay right to return to the Campaign trailhead.

Miles and Directions

0.0 Start at the Campaign trailhead on FR 449A.

0.7 Turn right onto Reavis Gap Trail.

3.0 Reach Reavis Gap. The Two Bar Ridge Trail branches right; stay on the Reavis Gap Trail.

3.3 Cross Pine Creek. (***FYI:*** There are several campsites in the forest along the creek.)

6.1 Turn left onto the Reavis Ranch Trail.

6.5 Reach the Reavis Ranch site. (***FYI:*** There is camping up- and downstream from the site.)

6.8 Turn left onto the Fireline Trail.

8.0 Cross the Reavis Creek–Pine Creek divide.

8.9 The trail leaves Pine Creek.

10.0 Turn left onto the Pinto Peak Trail, in Campaign Creek. (***FYI:*** There are several campsites at the trail junction.)

11.8 Turn left onto the Campaign Creek Trail, and continue down Campaign Creek.

13.9 Pass the junction with the Reavis Gap Trail; turn right to return to the trailhead.

14.5 Arrive back at the Campaign trailhead.

Cooking dinner on a Superstition backpack trip

Options

Option 1: At Reavis Gap turn right onto the Two Bar Ridge Trail. Hike 1.2 miles north, past Walnut Spring, to the point where the trail starts to drop into a tributary of Pine Creek. This point is a fine overlook of lower Pine Creek and Two Bar Ridge. This option adds 2.4 miles and 200 feet of elevation change to the hike.

Option 2: Where the Reavis Gap Trail crosses Pine Creek, turn left and hike cross-country up Pine Creek to the Fireline Trail. Sections of upper Pine Creek are rough and slow because of large boulders and dense brush. It's 1.8 miles to the Fireline Trail, and you'll climb about 620 feet. This option shortens the loop by 5.6 miles but is much more difficult than staying on the trails.

Option 3: When the Fireline Trail starts down into Pine Creek, leave the trail and hike cross-country south along the piñon-juniper-covered ridge. Although the upper part of this ridge is brushy, with some route finding you can find a reasonably brush-free route to the top of Mound Mountain. At 6,266 feet, this round summit is the highest point in the Superstition Mountains and has an appropriately commanding view of the range. This option adds 2.6 miles and 800 feet of elevation change to the trip.

Option 4: At the junction of the Fireline and Pinto Peak Trails, turn right and hike up the Pinto Peak Trail to the saddle at the head of Campaign Creek. You'll get good views of upper Pinto Creek and the rugged country around Iron Mountain and Pinto Peak in the southeast corner of the Superstition Mountains. This option adds 3.2 miles and 690 feet of elevation gain to the trip.

White Mountains

The White Mountains in east-central Arizona offer a cool respite from the desert lowlands. This area averages 8,000 feet above sea level and has a long, snowy winter season. Cloaked by spruce, fir, and pine forest interspersed with gorgeous alpine meadows, lakes, and streams, the region is the source for several of the Southwest's major rivers, including the Little Colorado, the Salt, and the Gila Rivers.

Big Lake, near the southern trailhead of the Apache Railroad Trail

65 Escudilla Mountain

This is an alpine hike to the summit plateau of Arizona's third-highest peak, Escudilla Mountain. Unfortunately, Escudilla Mountain was hard hit by the human-caused Wallow Fire and is now a study in forest regeneration. Within a few years large stands of quaking aspen should start to appear, replacing the fir and spruce forest that formerly covered most of the mountain.

Distance: 5.8 miles out and back
Hiking time: About 4 hours
Difficulty: Moderate
Trail surface: Dirt trails
Best season: Late spring through fall
Water: No water available
Other trail users: Horses
Canine compatibility: Controlled dogs allowed
Land status: Escudilla Wilderness, Apache-Sitgreaves National Forest

Nearest town: Alpine
Fees and permits: None
Other: Camping discouraged
Schedule: Open all year
Maps: USGS Escudilla Mountain; Apache-Sitgreaves National Forest
Trail contacts: Apache-Sitgreaves National Forest, PO Box 640, Springerville, AZ 85938; (928) 333-4301; www.fs.usda.gov/asnf

Finding the trailhead: From Alpine drive about 6 miles north on US 180, then turn right onto FR 56. Continue about 4.6 miles to Terry Flat Road; stay left and go another 0.3 mile to the Escudilla Mountain trailhead. GPS: N33 55.20' / W109 7.04'

The Hike

The Escudilla Mountain Trail starts up the south slopes of the mountain and steepens as it begins to switchback through stands of quaking aspen. The final switchbacks lead into an alpine meadow with excellent views of Terry Flat to the south. At the north side of this meadow, the trail crosses Profanity Ridge and then descends slightly into another beautiful meadow. Here the Government Trail joins from the left (west). Your trail continues north and climbs through fir and spruce forest to reach the rounded summit of the mountain. A fire lookout stands on the highest point—if it is staffed, be sure to ask permission before climbing the tower.

LEOPOLD WAS HERE

Escudilla Mountain was one of the favorite places of Aldo Leopold, a Forest Service employee. In the 1930s Leopold and other visionaries began to promote the idea of preserving roadless areas within the national forests. This resulted in the USDA Forest Service designating the first National Forest Wilderness Areas and then passage of the Wilderness Act of 1964, through which the US Congress created the National Wilderness Preservation System.

Escudilla Mountain

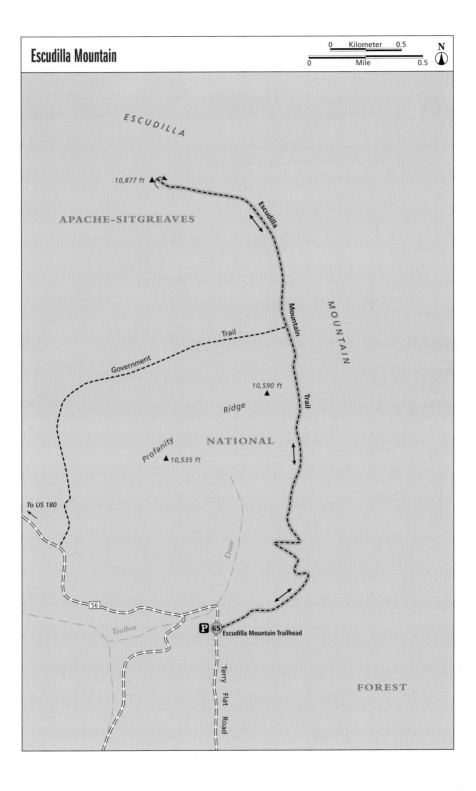

0 — Kilometer — 0.5
0 — Mile — 0.5

N

ESCUDILLA

10,877 ft ▲

APACHE-SITGREAVES

Escudilla

Mountain

MOUNTAIN

Trail

Government

10,590 ft ▲

Ridge

Trail

Profanity
▲ 10,535 ft

NATIONAL

To US 180

Draw

56

Toolbox

P 65

Escudilla Mountain Trailhead

Terry Flat Road

FOREST

Aspens and alpine meadows on the Escudilla Mountain Trail

Miles and Directions

0.0   Start at the Escudilla Mountain trailhead on Terry Flat Road.

1.5   Cross Profanity Ridge.

1.7   Pass junction with the Government Trail on the left.

2.9   Reach Escudilla Mountain. Retrace your steps.

5.8   Arrive back at the trailhead.

66 Apache Railroad Trail

This hike follows the old Apache Railroad grade through the scenic high country of the White Mountains, winding in and out of expansive meadows with sweeping views, as well as fir, aspen, and spruce forest. The trail is open to hikers, horses, and bicycles but closed to motor vehicles.

Distance: 19.1 miles one-way with a shuttle
Hiking time: About 12 hours or 2 days
Difficulty: Moderate
Trail surface: Dirt trails along former railroad grade
Best seasons: Summer and fall
Water: The West Fork of the Little Colorado River is the only reliable water that's easy to reach. Seasonally, there's water in several reservoirs and small lakes that you'll pass, but the shores are usually swampy and the water hard to reach.
Other trail users: Mountain bikes and horses

Canine compatibility: Controlled dogs allowed
Land status: Apache-Sitgreaves National Forest
Nearest towns: Show Low and Springerville
Fees and permits: None
Schedule: Open all year
Maps: USGS Big Lake North, Mount Baldy, Greer, and Greens Peak; Apache-Sitgreaves National Forest
Trail contacts: Apache-Sitgreaves National Forest, PO Box 640, Springerville, AZ 85938; (928) 333-4301; www.fs.usda.gov/asnf

Finding the trailhead: To reach the Highway 260 trailhead from Show Low, drive about 41 miles east on Highway 260, passing the junction with Highway 273. The trailhead is about 1.5 miles east of the Highway 273 turnoff, just after leaving the White Mountain Apache Reservation. If you plan to do the entire hike one-way, you'll need to leave a shuttle vehicle here. GPS: N34 3.25'/W109 34.10'

To reach the Sheep Crossing trailhead, drive 4 miles south on Highway 273, and then turn right into the trailhead parking area. This trailhead can be used to hike either the north or south portions of the trail, for a shorter hike. GPS: N33 57.94'/W109 29.99'

To reach the Big Lake trailhead and the start of the hike, continue on Highway 273 another 5.6 miles, then turn right onto FR 116. Continue 2.6 miles, and then turn left onto FR 249E. Go 2.1 miles, then turn left and go 0.4 mile to the trailhead. GPS: N33 53.05'/W109 25.77'

The Hike

Follow the old railroad grade north as it cuts through the rolling alpine meadow northwest of Big Lake. This high plateau is formed from basalt lava flows, and the White Mountains' volcanic origins are evidenced by the cinders underfoot. All the hills and mountains in this area are old volcanoes. As the trail turns more to the northwest, you'll pass Basin Lake and then cross Highway 273. Now the trail closely parallels Highway 273 for a time as it enters mixed fir-aspen-spruce forest along Burro Creek. Just after the trail emerges into a small meadow at the head of the creek, it crosses the divide between Burro Creek and the East Fork of the Little Colorado River—the high point of this nearly level hike. Now the old railroad grade swings around the

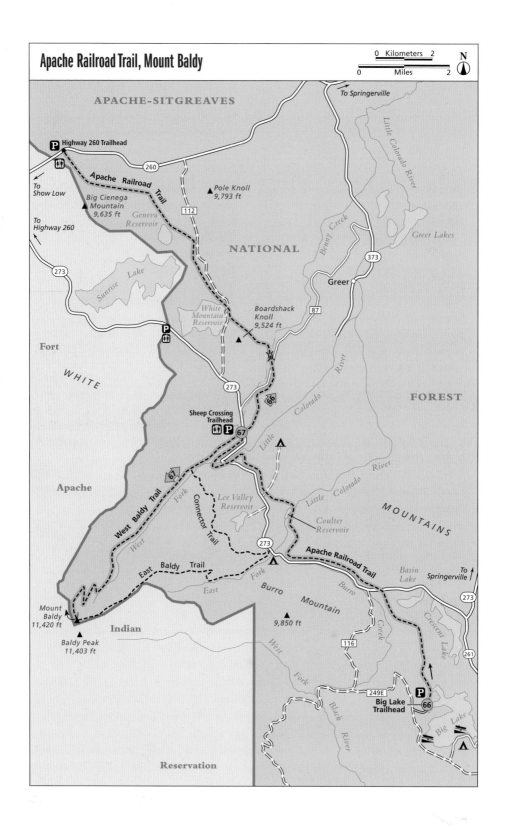

Apache Railroad Trail, Mount Baldy

0　Kilometers　2

0　Miles　2

N

To Springerville

APACHE-SITGREAVES

P Highway 260 Trailhead

260

To Show Low

Apache　Railroad　Trail

Big Cienega Mountain 9,635 ft

Geneva Reservoir

112

▲ *Pole Knoll* 9,793 ft

Little Colorado River

NATIONAL

Benny Creek

373

Greer Lakes

To Highway 260

273

Sunrise Lake

White Mountain Reservoir

Greer

Boardshack Knoll 9,524 ft

87

Fort

P

273

66

Colorado River

FOREST

WHITE

Sheep Crossing Trailhead

P 67

Apache

67

West Baldy Trail

West Fork

Connector Trail

Lee Valley Reservoir

Little

▲

Little Colorado River

MOUNTAINS

Coulter Reservoir

273

Basin Lake

To Springerville

East　Baldy　Trail

East Fork

▲

Burro　Mountain

Burro

273

Mount Baldy 11,420 ft

▲ *Baldy Peak* 11,403 ft

Indian

▲ 9,850 ft

West Fork

Creek

261

Crescent Lake

116

249E

P 66

Big Lake Trailhead

Black River

Big Lake

▲

Reservation

base of a hill, leaving Highway 273 behind as it parallels the East Fork. It crosses the East Fork on the dam below Coulter Reservoir, and then heads generally northwest again. A sharp (for a railroad) right then left turn mark the approach to the West Fork of the Little Colorado River at Sheep Crossing.

After crossing the river the trail closely parallels Highway 273 again. It passes the Sheep Crossing trailhead, then crosses Highway 273 a final time, and heads northeast through alternating meadows and forest. For a while the trail parallels FR 87, then crosses the road. It crosses Benny Creek on a bridge, then heads northwest along the northeast slopes of Boardshack Knoll and White Mountain Reservoir. After passing Boardshack Knoll the trail is in open meadow with only a few stands of trees nearby. It finally approaches the eastern side of Big Cienega Mountain and reaches the Highway 260 trailhead at the north end of this large hill, which is marked by a prominent red-and-white microwave tower.

▷ **Originally built as the main line of a logging railroad system, the Apache Railroad was later operated as a scenic railroad. It was finally closed for good and the tracks removed in the 1960s.**

Miles and Directions

0.0 Start at the Big Lake trailhead, 0.4 mile from FR 249E.

2.6 Pass Basin Lake.

3.0 Cross Highway 273.

5.2 Cross the divide between Burro Creek and the East Fork of the Little Colorado River, the high point of the hike.

6.5 Cross the East Fork on the dam below Coulter Reservoir.

9.2 Cross the West Fork of the Little Colorado River.

10.0 Pass the Sheep Crossing trailhead.

12.2 Cross Benny Creek on a bridge.

13.7 Pass White Mountain Reservoir.

19.1 Reach the Highway 260 trailhead and your shuttle.

67 Mount Baldy

This day hike takes you to the highest point of the White Mountains and Arizona's second-highest mountain. On the way you'll follow a trout stream as it winds through alpine meadows, then climb through a beautiful forest of Douglas fir, Colorado blue spruce, and quaking aspen to reach the alpine tundra along the summit ridge.

See map on page 212.
Distance: 12.0 miles out and back
Hiking time: About 7 hours
Difficulty: Strenuous
Trail surface: Dirt trails
Best season: Summer through fall
Water: West Fork of the Little Colorado River
Other trail users: Horses
Canine compatibility: Controlled dogs allowed
Land status: Mount Baldy Wilderness, Apache-Sitgreaves National Forest

Nearest towns: Show Low and Springerville
Fees and permits: None
Other: Baldy Peak on the Fort Apache Indian Reservation closed to all entry
Schedule: Open all year
Maps: USGS Mount Baldy; USFS Mount Baldy Wilderness
Trail contacts: Apache-Sitgreaves National Forest, PO Box 640, Springerville, AZ 85938; (928) 333-4301; www.fs.usda.gov/asnf

Finding the trailhead: From Show Low, drive about 39 miles east on AZ 260. Turn right on AZ 273 and drive 4 miles to the trailhead, on the right. GPS: N33 57.94' / W109 29.99'

The Hike

The popular West Baldy Trail begins along the bank of the West Fork of the Little Colorado River and climbs through lovely blue spruce forest and alpine meadows. During the short summer months, aster, fleabane, penstemon, cinquefoil, and iris bloom. There is evidence of past glacial activity—glacial erratics, large boulders deposited by flowing ice—along the valley floor.

West Fork contains brook, rainbow, and cutthroat trout, but the trail is only close to the stream near the trailhead. About 3 miles in, the trail crosses a tributary to West Fork. The trail then reaches the ridge leading to Mount Baldy and the junction with the East Baldy Trail, where you are treated to spectacular vistas of the White Mountain region. The boundary of the Fort Apache Indian Reservation runs along the west side of the summit ridge. (**Note:** The Apache Tribe has closed the reservation to all access, which includes Baldy Peak at the south end of the Mount Baldy ridge. Trespassers have had their packs confiscated and have been fined for trying to sneak to the top of Baldy Peak.)

According to the USGS Mount Baldy topo, the actual high point of the mountain is the Mount Baldy ridge, which has a final contour line at 11,420 feet. This makes the ridge 17 feet higher than Baldy Peak (11,403 feet). It's safe to leave the West Baldy

Sunset on Mount Baldy summit ridge

Trail where it runs along the tree line and walk to the high point of the ridge. If you look closely, you'll see small metal survey caps just below the ridge crest to the west. These mark the actual boundary of the reservation. Feel free to point these out to any Apache ranger who questions your presence on the ridge crest.

Although this is the turnaround point for the hike, the trail continues, descending into the East Fork of the Little Colorado River.

Miles and Directions

0.0 Start at the Sheep Crossing trailhead.

3.0 Cross a tributary to the West Fork of the Little Colorado River.

4.4 Reach ridge leading to Mount Baldy.

5.3 Reach the reservation boundary. (Do *not* trespass on reservation land.)

5.4 Reach junction with East Baldy Trail.

5.6 Reach a saddle just north of Baldy Peak.

6.0 Arrive at the true, unnamed summit of Mount Baldy, your turnaround point. (Again, do *not* trespass on the reservation.)

12.0 Arrive back at the trailhead.

68 KP Creek

KP Creek and its tributaries provide an opportunity for a fine backpack trip along the Mogollon Rim next to alpine creeks in the Blue Range Primitive Area.

Distance: 20.6-mile loop
Hiking time: About 12 hours or 2 days
Difficulty: Strenuous
Trail surface: Dirt trails
Best season: Summer through fall
Water: Grant Creek, KP Creek, seasonally at Willow and Mud Springs
Other trail users: Horses
Canine compatibility: Controlled dogs allowed

Land status: Blue Range Primitive Area, Apache-Sitgreaves National Forest
Nearest town: Alpine
Fees and permits: None
Schedule: Open all year
Maps: USGS Strayhorse, Hannagan Meadow, and Bear Mountain; USFS Blue Range Primitive Area
Trail contacts: Apache-Sitgreaves National Forest, PO Box 640, Springerville, AZ 85938; (928) 333-4301; www.fs.usda.gov/asnf

Finding the trailhead: From Alpine drive 24 miles south on US 191. Past Hannagan Meadow, turn left into the KP Rim trailhead. GPS: N33 36.86'/W109 19.69'

The Hike

Start the loop hike on Trail 315, which heads east along the north rim of KP Creek. (Trail 93, which comes in from the south, will be your return.) Although the trail closely follows the rim of the deep canyon containing KP Creek, views are limited in the dense spruce–fir–aspen forest. At 2 miles turn left onto Trail 73. A short descent to the northwest leads through a meadow at the head of an unnamed tributary of Grant Creek. After a short climb to a saddle, the trail turns more to the north and crosses two more tributaries; the second of these contains another nice meadow and Willow Spring. The trail drops down another tributary, crosses Grant Creek at 3.8 miles, and then climbs out via a tributary to the north. After the trail regains the Mogollon Rim at 5 miles, turn right onto Trail 76.

This trail works its way east along the forested ridge south of Hannagan Creek, passing Trail 326 (a short spur to US 191), and then meeting Trail 75 at P Bar Lake at 8.3 miles. Turn right onto Trail 75 and follow it down a steep descent in a side canyon to the south. The descent moderates at 9.3 miles. Turn right onto Trail 306 and follow it south and down to Grant Creek. Notice how ponderosa pines are now the dominant tree at this lower and drier elevation.

Here, at 10.2 miles, Trail 65 heads up Grant Creek. Our route turns left onto Trail 65. This trail follows Grant Creek downstream for 0.5 mile to Trail 74. Turn right and follow this trail southeast past Moonshine Park and then west into Steeple Creek at 12.3 miles. Turn left here onto Trail 73, which descends southeast along Steeple Creek to Mud Spring at 12.8 miles. Now turn right onto Trail 70, which contours

Falls along KP Creek

southwest into KP Creek. At just under 7,000 feet, this southeast-facing slope is quite a bit warmer and drier than the depths of Steeple Creek canyon that we just left.

At 15.8 miles the trail crosses the creek and passes Trail 72. Continue west up KP Creek past Trail 71, which also joins from the left. KP Creek is a beautiful alpine stream set in a forested, 2,000-foot-deep canyon, and the climb is steady but not too steep. At 18.5 miles turn right onto Trail 93. You may want to make a side trip of

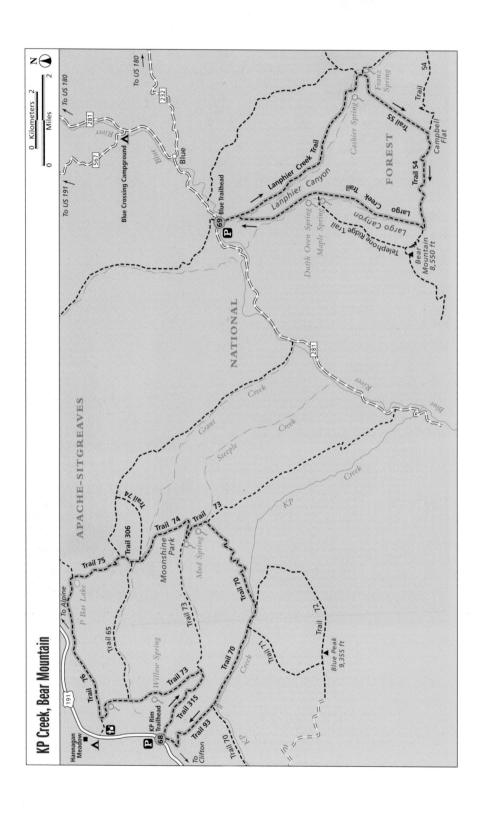

KP Creek, Bear Mountain

N

0 Kilometers 2
0 Miles 2

To US 191

To US 180

281

567

232

Blue River

Blue Crossing Campground

Blue

Blue

69 Blue Trailhead

P

Lanphier Creek Trail

Lanphier Canyon

Cashier Spring

Franz Spring

Trail 54

Trail 55

FOREST

Campbell Flat

Dutch Oven Spring

Maple Spring

Largo Creek Trail

Largo Canyon

Telephone Ridge Trail

Bear Mountain 8,550 ft

Trail 54

NATIONAL

281

Grant Creek

Steeple Creek

KP Creek

Blue River

APACHE-SITGREAVES

Trail 74

Trail 306

Trail 75

Trail 74

Trail 73

Moonshine Park

Mud Spring

Trail 73

Trail 70

Trail 70

Trail 72

Blue Peak 9,355 ft

To Alpine

P Bar Lake

Trail 65

Willow Spring

Trail 73

Trail 70

Trail 71

KP Creek

Hannagan Meadow

191

Trail 76

KP Rim Trailhead

68

Trail 315

Trail 93

Trail 70

To Clifton

about 100 yards on Trail 70 to a small waterfall on KP Creek.

The grade steepens as Trail 93 climbs up an unnamed tributary of KP Creek and turns more to the northwest. A couple of switchbacks lead to the top of the ascent at 20 miles. Now the trail follows the rim northwest 0.6 mile to the KP Rim trailhead.

Miles and Directions

0.0 Start at the KP Rim trailhead off US 191, and follow Trail 315.

2.0 Turn left onto Trail 73.

3.8 Cross Grant Creek.

5.0 Turn right onto Trail 76.

8.3 Meet Trail 75 at P Bar Lake; turn right onto Trail 75.

9.3 Turn right onto Trail 306.

10.2 Reach Grant Creek and junction with Trail 65; turn left onto Trail 65.

10.7 Turn right onto Trail 74.

10.9 Pass Moonshine Park.

12.3 Reach Steeple Creek and Trail 73; turn left onto Trail 73.

12.8 Turn right onto Trail 70.

15.8 Cross KP Creek and pass Trail 72.

16.5 Pass Trail 71.

18.5 Turn right onto Trail 93. (***Option:*** Walk 100 yards on Trail 70 to a small waterfall on KP Creek.)

20.0 Reach the top of the Mogollon Rim ascent.

20.6 Arrive back at the KP Rim trailhead.

DESERVING OF PROTECTION

The USDA Forest Service, under the guidance of such visionaries as Aldo Leopold, pioneered the concept of managing public lands for their wilderness values—places where man is a temporary visitor and neither permanent structures nor motorized uses are allowed. Starting during the 1930s the Forest Service designated numerous wilderness areas within the national forests. Realizing that these administratively designed wild areas needed the protection of federal law, conservationists succeeded in getting Congress to pass the landmark Wilderness Act in 1964. Most of the Forest Service Wilderness Areas immediately became part of the new National Wilderness Preservation System. A few areas, such as the Blue Range, were not included and were redesignated as Primitive Areas. In the years since, Congress has designated all the Primitive Areas as wilderness except one: the Blue Range Primitive Area. After experiencing the truly wild character of the Blue Range, you'll probably agree that the Blue Range deserves wilderness protection.

69 Bear Mountain

This is another fine backpack trip through two scenic canyons and along a remote section of the Mogollon Rim in the Blue Range Primitive Area.

See map on page 218.
Distance: 15.5-mile loop
Hiking time: About 10 hours or 2 days
Difficulty: Strenuous
Trail surface: Dirt trails
Best season: Late spring through fall
Water: Seasonally in lower Lanphier Canyon and at Cashier, Maple, and Dutch Oven Springs
Other trail users: Horses
Canine compatibility: Controlled dogs allowed

Land status: Blue Range Primitive Area, Apache-Sitgreaves National Forest
Nearest town: Alpine
Fees and permits: None
Schedule: Open all year
Maps: USGS Bear Mountain and Blue; Apache-Sitgreaves National Forest
Trail contacts: Apache-Sitgreaves National Forest, PO Box 640, Springerville, AZ 85938; (928) 333-4301; www.fs.usda.gov/asnf

Finding the trailhead: From Alpine drive about 2 miles east on US 180, then turn south onto FR 281. Continue about 21 miles to the Blue trailhead at the Blue Administrative Site. GPS: N33 35.73'/W109 7.90'

The Hike

Many of the trails in the Blue Range Primitive Area are faint and little used. They are shown accurately on the USGS topo maps; you should have these maps with you and be comfortable with map reading and route finding before attempting this hike.

The Lanphier Creek Trail first crosses the Blue River—like most rivers in Arizona, it's creek-size except when flooding—and skirts some private land before heading up Lanphier Canyon. There is usually water in the creek. During late summer water can be a problem on the southern part of this loop, so keep your bottles full. Where the creek turns east, the trail leaves the creek side and climbs steeply onto a bench, where it parallels the creek for about a mile. At the point where the trail again descends to meet the creek, there is limited camping. A short distance upstream the trail passes Cashier Spring and climbs out of the canyon to the southeast. After climbing over a low ridge, the trail meets Forest Trail 55, where you'll turn right.

This trail heads generally southwest, first climbing a short tributary of Lanphier Creek before swinging around a ridge and climbing over a broad saddle. Open pine forest offers plenty of camping, although there is no water. At Campbell Flat, where the trail reaches the Mogollon Rim, turn right onto Forest Trail 54. Charred trees in this area attest to the many wildfires that have burned in the Blue Range. At present, most lightning-caused fires are considered natural fires and are allowed to burn under close monitoring. If you hike the Blue Range in late summer, you may see smoke from some of these fires.

Now you're heading west along the Mogollon Rim. The trail climbs over several low hills and dips through several broad saddles before reaching the Largo Creek Trail at the base of Bear Mountain. By continuing straight, you can do a short and easy side trip to the top of Bear Mountain. A fire lookout here is manned during periods of high fire danger. There's plenty of camping available in the saddle and to the north, and possible water at an unnamed spring about 0.5 mile north.

Back at the trail junction, continue the loop by turning right (north) on the Largo Creek Trail, which heads down the gentle headwaters of this drainage. After a mile or so the drainage starts to deepen into a canyon, and fir trees are mixed with pines on the north-facing slopes. At Maple Spring the Telephone Ridge Trail joins from the left; there are several campsites in the area between Maple and Dutch Oven Springs. Below the springs the trail follows the creek for a while and then leaves it to the east, climbs over a ridge, and drops into Lanphier Creek, completing the loop. Turn left here on the Lanphier Creek Trail, and return to the Blue trailhead.

Wildfire on WS Mountain, Blue Range

Miles and Directions

0.0 Start at the Blue trailhead at the Blue Administrative Site.

0.7 Stay left on Lanphier Creek Trail at junction with the Largo Creek Trail.

3.1 The trail leaves Lanphier Creek.

4.5 The trail rejoins the creek.

5.4 Turn right onto Forest Trail 55.

7.6 Reach Campbell Flat; turn right onto Forest Trail 54.

10.3 Turn right onto the Largo Creek Trail.

12.3 Pass Maple Spring and junction with the Telephone Ridge Trail. Stay on Largo Creek Trail. (**FYI:** There are several campsites available between Maple and Dutch Oven Springs.)

14.9 Lanphier Creek Trail joins from the right.

15.5 Arrive back at the trailhead.

70 Bear Wallow Trail

This is an overnight backpack or long day hike along Bear Wallow Creek. The headwaters of Bear Wallow Creek are the location where campers failed to put out their campfire, resulting in the Wallow Fire of June 2011, which burned 588,240 acres (841 square miles) of the eastern Mogollon Rim and the White Mountains. This is the largest wildfire in Arizona history and the second largest in American history. Fortunately the fire moved to the northeast and spared most of Bear Wallow Canyon.

Distance: 15.2 miles out and back
Hiking time: About 2 days
Difficulty: Moderate
Trail surface: Dirt trails
Best season: Summer through fall
Water: Bear Wallow Creek
Other trail users: Horses
Canine compatibility: Controlled dogs allowed
Land status: Bear Wallow Wilderness, Apache-Sitgreaves National Forest

Nearest town: Alpine
Fees and permits: None
Schedule: Open all year
Maps: USGS Hoodoo Knob and Baldy Bill Point; Apache-Sitgreaves National Forest
Trail contacts: Apache-Sitgreaves National Forest, PO Box 640, Springerville, AZ 85938; (928) 333-4301; www.fs.usda.gov/asnf

Finding the trailhead: From Alpine drive about 27 miles south on US 191. Turn right (west) onto FR 25; go another 3.3 miles to the signed trailhead on your left. GPS: N33 36.20' / W109 23.84'

The Hike

The Bear Wallow Trail starts directly behind the trailhead sign following a shallow drainage. Don't take the old logging road (FR 8316) running to your left. The trail is a bit gullied and can be muddy, but it is fairly easy walking. In a little over a mile you will intersect the North Fork of Bear Wallow Creek. The creek meanders and splashes its way through virgin old-growth forest of Douglas fir, spruce, and ponderosa pine. Along the trail grow wild strawberries, wild geraniums, New Mexican locusts, limber pines, and poison ivy—beware. Red squirrels and chipmunks are common.

At mile 2.5 the trail meets the Reno Trail (Trail 62). At 3.4 miles the South Fork of Bear Wallow Creek comes in from the left, and the remainder of the Bear Wallow Trail descends along Bear Wallow Creek. At 7.1 miles the Bear Wallow Trail passes the Gobbler Point Trail (Trail 59). At about mile 7.6 a fence marks the national forest boundary with the San Carlos Apache Indian Reservation. Going any farther downstream requires a permit from the Apache.

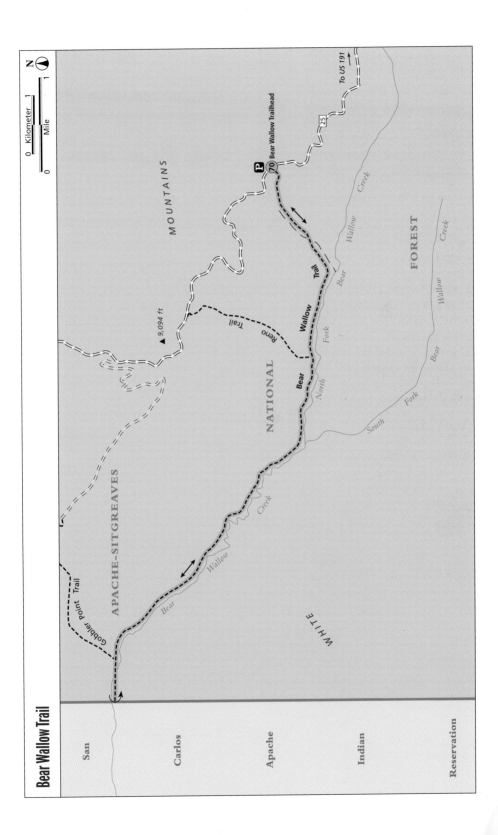

Bear Wallow Trail

San Carlos Apache Indian Reservation

APACHE-SITGREAVES NATIONAL FOREST

WHITE MOUNTAINS

Gobbler point Trail

Reno Trail

Bear Wallow Trail

▲ 9,094 ft

Bear Wallow Creek

North Fork

South Fork

Bear Wallow Creek

Bear Wallow Creek

P

70 Bear Wallow Trailhead

25

To US 191

N

0 Kilometer 1

0 Mile 1

BEAR WALLOW

Bear Wallow is one of the few creeks in Arizona where native Apache trout have been reintroduced. This trout was almost wiped out by overfishing, introduction of nonnative fish, and dam projects.

In 1884 rancher Pete Slaughter drove cattle into this valley and reported seeing numerous bear wallows along the creek where bruins had come to ward off pesky flies. Black bears still roam the area, as do elk, mule deer, and mountain lions. Also, the howl of a Mexican gray wolf might break the evening quiet. These small wolves became extinct in Arizona by 1970 but survived in northern Mexico. In 1998 Mexican gray wolves were released into the Apache-Sitgreaves National Forest as part of a wolf recovery program. The wolf recovery area has now been extended to the central Mogollon Rim, and efforts are being made to include the Grand Canyon country in the recovery area.

Miles and Directions

0.0 Start at the trailhead on FR 25.
1.3 Intersect the North Fork of Bear Wallow Creek.
2.5 Pass junction with the Reno Trail.
3.4 South Fork of Bear Wallow Creek comes in from the left.
7.1 Pass junction with the Gobbler Point Trail.
7.6 Reach boundary with the San Carlos Apache Indian Reservation. Retrace your steps.
15.2 Arrive back at the trailhead.

Phoenix Area

In this section you'll find hikes that are close to the greater Phoenix metropolitan area. These are great choices when you don't feel like a long drive. The region features a variety of hikes in city and country regional parks as well as national wilderness areas. These hikes are just a tiny sample of the many trails that are enjoyed by Phoenix hikers, and more trails are being developed all the time.

North Maricopa Mountains

71 Cave Creek Trail

Enjoy a desert day hike along a seasonal stream in the southern end of the New River Mountains (also known as the East Cedar Mountains).

Distance: 10.0-mile loop
Hiking time: About 6 hours
Difficulty: Moderate
Trail surface: Dirt trails
Best season: Fall through spring
Water: Seasonal in Cave Creek
Other trail users: Mountain bikes and horses
Canine compatibility: Controlled dogs allowed
Land status: Tonto National Forest

Nearest town: Carefree
Fees and permits: None
Schedule: Open all year
Maps: USGS New River Mesa and Humboldt Mountain; Tonto National Forest
Trail contacts: Tonto National Forest, 2324 E. McDowell Rd., Phoenix, AZ 85006; (602) 225-5200; www.fs.usda.gov/tonto

Finding the trailhead: From Carefree drive east on Cave Creek Road until it becomes FR 24. Drive 9 miles, past the Seven Springs and CCC campgrounds. Cross the creek twice before reaching the Cave Creek trailhead. GPS: N33 58.35' / W111 51.99'

The Hike

Along Cave Creek is a lovely riparian habitat with Fremont cottonwoods and Arizona sycamores. This is a great birding area, especially in late spring and early summer.

Start on the Cave Creek Trail (Forest Trail 4), which follows the creek, crossing it a few times. After about 4 miles turn left onto the Skunk Creek Trail, which will make you break into a sweat. After another 5 miles turn left onto Forest Trail 247 to return to the trailhead.

Miles and Directions

0.0 Start at the Cave Creek trailhead on FR 24.

4.0 Turn right onto Skunk Creek Trail to continue the main hike. (**Option:** Turn left onto Skunk Creek Trail to shorten the hike to about 6 miles.)

6.8 Reach the trail's high point.

9.0 Turn left onto Forest Trail 247.

10.0 Arrive back at the Cave Creek trailhead.

▶ **Just inside the forest boundary is a 0.5-mile side trip to Sears-Kay Ruin, the remains of a thousand-year-old Hohokam settlement. A self-guided tour includes signs explaining the site. The Hohokam built extensive irrigation canals to tap the rivers in the Salt River and Tucson Valleys. This effort supported large farms and a relatively large and sophisticated population.**

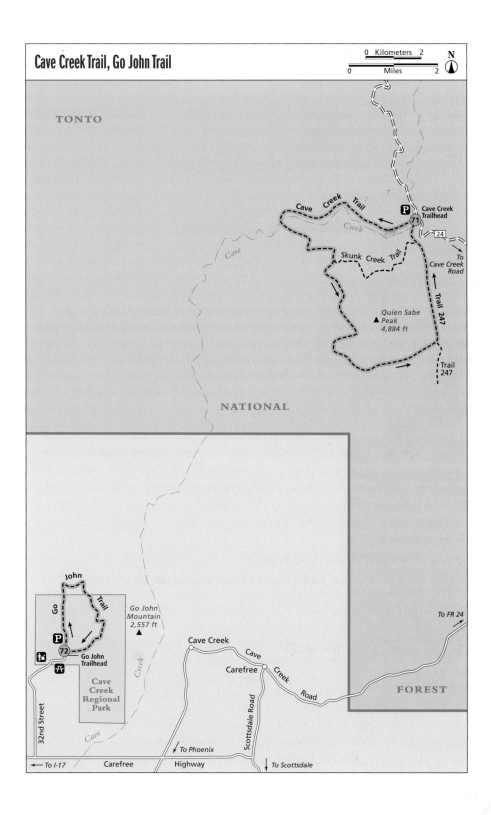

Cave Creek Trail, Go John Trail

TONTO

Cave Creek Trail

Creek

Cave

P Cave Creek
   Trailhead
71
24

To
Cave Creek
Road

Skunk Creek Trail

Quien Sabe
Peak
4,884 ft

Trail 247

Trail
247

NATIONAL

John

Go   Trail

Go John
Mountain
2,557 ft
▲

P
72
Go John
Trailhead

Cave
Creek
Regional
Park

Creek

To FR 24

Cave Creek

Cave

Carefree

Creek

Road

FOREST

32nd Street

Cave

Scottsdale Road

To Phoenix

To I-17   Carefree   Highway

To Scottsdale

72 Go John Trail

This gorgeous loop travels through the fascinating flora of the Sonoran Desert north of Phoenix. You'll also have good views of New River Mesa and the rugged southern end of the New River Mountains.

See map on page 227.
Distance: 4.8-mile loop
Hiking time: About 2 hours
Difficulty: Easy
Trail surface: Dirt trails
Best season: Fall through spring
Water: No water available
Other trail users: Mountain bikes and horses
Canine compatibility: Controlled dogs allowed

Land status: Cave Creek Regional Park
Nearest town: Cave Creek
Fees and permits: Park entrance fee
Schedule: Open all year
Maps: USGS Cave Creek
Trail contacts: Maricopa County Parks and Recreation, 234 N. Central Ave, Suite 6400, Phoenix, AZ 85004; (602) 506-2930; www.maricopa.gov/parks

Finding the trailhead: From I-17 drive east on Carefree Highway to 32nd Street. Turn north and go into the Cave Creek Regional Park. Pass the horse-rental and picnic areas, and then turn left at the second trailhead sign. The Go John Trail is signed. GPS: N33 49.94'/W112 0.10'

The Hike

This pleasant loop gives hikers a good introduction to the Sonoran Desert. The abundance and diversity of plant life surprise most first-time visitors. One factor that allows the Sonoran Desert to contain so many different kinds of plants—from cacti to small trees to shrubs to wildflowers—is that there are two rainy seasons. Certain plants tend to utilize the winter moisture, while other species rely upon the summer rains. Thus not every plant is competing all the time with its neighbor for the precious live-sustaining fluid.

The trail climbs north over a saddle in the low desert hills, then descends a drainage northward. Numerous unofficial trails come in from the right along the entire loop; stay right on the main trail, which is always obvious. The Go John Trail turns east and follows a drainage to a second saddle, drops a short distance into another drainage, and then turns south up this drainage.

After passing through a third saddle, the trail contours south and then east around the head of a small drainage before passing through a fourth saddle. Now the trail contours south across the desert slopes, passes through a fifth and final saddle, then descends west and crosses gentle slopes to return to the trailhead.

Teddybear cholla cactus, Go John Trail

Miles and Directions

0.0   Start at the Go John trailhead in the Cave Creek Regional Park; turn left onto the trail.

0.2   Pass over the first saddle.

1.4   Turn east up a drainage.

2.1   Pass over the second saddle, and turn south up a drainage.

2.7   Pass through the third saddle.

3.2   Pass through the fourth saddle.

3.7   Pass through the fifth saddle.

4.8   Arrive back at the trailhead.

73 Lookout Mountain

This is a short but scenic loop day hike around a small mountain in the middle of north Phoenix with an option to climb to the summit of Lookout Mountain. As you walk, it's easy to imagine a time not so long ago when the surrounding sea of houses was instead Sonoran Desert as far as the eye could see.

Distance: 2.6-mile loop
Hiking time: About 1 hour
Difficulty: Easy
Trail surface: Dirt trails
Best season: Fall through spring
Water: No water available
Other trail users: None
Canine compatibility: Controlled dogs allowed
Land status: Lookout Mountain Park

Nearest town: Phoenix
Fees and permits: None
Schedule: Open all year
Maps: USGS Union Hills and Sunnyslope
Trail contacts: Phoenix Parks and Recreation, Phoenix City Hall, 200 W. Washington St., 16th Floor, Phoenix, AZ 85003; (602) 262-6862; phoenix.gov

Finding the trailhead: From Bell Road in Phoenix, drive south about 1 mile on 16th Street to the Lookout Mountain Park entrance. The trailhead is at the parking area. GPS: N33 37.67'/W112 2.92'

The Hike

The Circumference Trail goes around Lookout Mountain. Start by going west (counterclockwise). In about 0.1 mile reach the junction with the Summit Trail, which climbs to the top of Lookout Mountain in about 0.6 mile. Take this side trail if you want a 360-degree view of the Valley of the Sun. Otherwise, stay on the main trail.

Although this park is in the heart of suburbia, it's not unusual to see a coyote or some of the typical desert birds such as roadrunners and Gila woodpeckers.

Miles and Directions

0.0 Start at the trailhead in the Lookout Mountain Park entrance parking area, and turn counterclockwise onto the Circumference Trail.

0.1 Reach junction with Summit Trail; stay on the Circumference Trail. (*Option:* Climb the Summit Trail 0.6 mile one-way to the top of Lookout Mountain and a panoramic view.)

2.6 Arrive back at the trailhead.

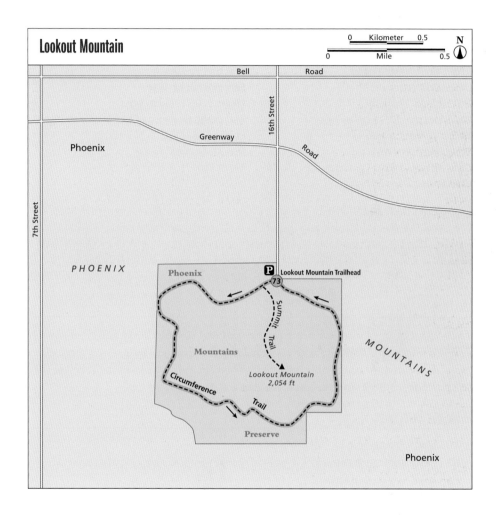

74 Cholla Trail

This is the original trail to the summit of Camelback Mountain, Phoenix's most distinctive landmark. Although fairly short, the trail climbs steeply for much of its length.

Distance: 2.5 miles out and back
Hiking time: About 3 hours
Difficulty: Moderate
Trail surface: Dirt trails
Best season: Fall through spring
Water: No water available
Other trail users: None
Canine compatibility: Controlled dogs allowed
Land status: City of Phoenix

Nearest town: Phoenix
Fees and permits: None
Schedule: Open all year
Maps: USGS Paradise Valley
Trail contacts: Phoenix Parks and Recreation, Phoenix City Hall, 200 W. Washington St., 16th Floor, Phoenix, AZ 85003; (602) 262-6862; phoenix.gov

Finding the trailhead: From East Camelback Road turn north onto North Invergordon Road. Drive about 0.8 mile and turn left onto East Cholla Lane. There is no official parking lot. Park where you can, but watch out for no-parking areas. You may have to park east of Invergordon Road and walk to the trailhead. GPS: N33 30.82' / W111 56.91'

The Hike

The well-marked Cholla Trail begins at the west end of East Cholla Lane and climbs steeply along the east ridge of the Camel's Hump, the highest part of the mountain. Near the top you must scramble over rocks. There are great views of the Valley of the Sun, including a peek into the "backyard" of the Phoenix Resort.

Miles and Directions

0.0 Start at the trailhead on East Cholla Lane.
1.2 Reach the ridgetop after a rock scramble. Enjoy the view before retracing your steps.
2.5 Arrive back at the trailhead.

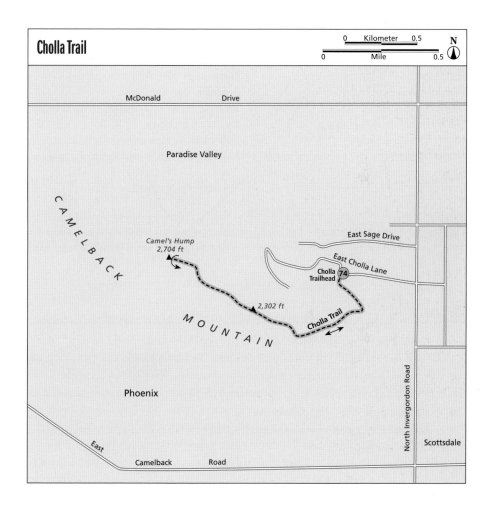

Cholla Trail

0   Kilometer   0.5

0   Mile   0.5

N

McDonald   Drive

Paradise Valley

C A M E L B A C K

Camel's Hump
2,704 ft

East Sage Drive

East Cholla Lane

Cholla
Trailhead

74

2,302 ft

Cholla Trail

M O U N T A I N

Phoenix

North Invergordon Road

Scottsdale

East

Camelback   Road

75 Pass Mountain Trail

This loop day hike through the western Goldfield Mountains northeast of Mesa offers a fine sense of remoteness, considering its location on the very edge of the greater Phoenix area. The backside of the loop offers a sweeping view of the wild Superstition and southern Mazatzal Mountains.

Distance: 7.7-mile loop
Hiking time: About 4 hours
Difficulty: Moderate
Trail surface: Dirt trails
Best season: Fall through spring
Water: No water available
Other trail users: Mountain bikes and horses
Canine compatibility: Controlled dogs allowed
Land status: Usery Mountain Regional Park, Tonto National Forest

Nearest town: Mesa
Fees and permits: Park entrance fee
Schedule: Open all year
Maps: USGS Apache Junction; Usery Mountain Recreation Area map
Trail contacts: Maricopa County Parks and Recreation, 234 N. Central Ave., Suite 6400, Phoenix, AZ 85004; (602) 506-2930; www.maricopa.gov/parks

Finding the trailhead: From Mesa go north on Ellsworth Road, which becomes Usery Pass Road. Turn right at the park entrance and go to the horse staging area, which is the trailhead. GPS: N33 27.99'/W111 36.43'

The Hike

Begin at the Pass Mountain trailhead. After a couple hundred yards, turn left at a T intersection to start the loop portion of the hike. The trail wanders north along the east side of the park facilities. After passing a final ramada and parking area, you'll pass the Wind Cave Trail; stay left. The trail works its way north along the west slopes of Pass Mountain. A fence marks the boundary of the Tonto National Forest. Now the trail climbs gradually around the north side of the mountain. As the trail crosses a ridge, the remainder of the Goldfield mountain range becomes visible to the northeast and, beyond, the distinctive summits of Four Peaks. Continuing to climb, the trail turns south into a canyon and climbs to a pass. This spot is the high point of the hike. With the bulk of Pass Mountain hiding the metropolitan area to the southwest, this saddle is a wild and rugged spot.

The descent is eroded and steep at first, but then a newer trail branches right and continues the descent at a more gradual rate. As you reach the mouth of the canyon and the southern foothills, the trail starts to swing west along the base of the mountain. Ignore an unsigned trail branching left and keep right. Stay right again at the junction with the Cat Peaks Trail. When you reach the T intersection near the horse staging area, turn left to return to the trailhead.

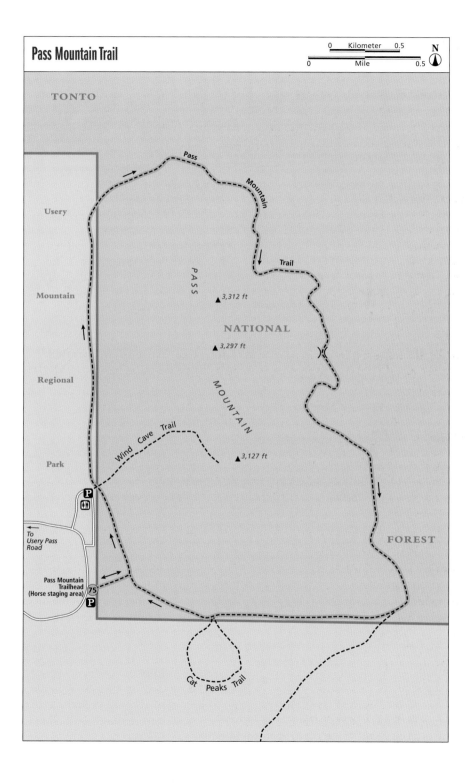

Pass Mountain Trail

TONTO

Usery

Mountain

Regional

Park

Pass
Mountain
Trail

PASS

NATIONAL

MOUNTAIN

▲ 3,312 ft

▲ 3,297 ft

▲ 3,127 ft

Wind Cave Trail

To
Usery Pass
Road

Pass Mountain
Trailhead
(Horse staging area)

75

Cat Peaks Trail

FOREST

N

0   Kilometer   0.5

0   Mile   0.5

Cholla and saguaro cactus along the Pass Mountain Trail

Miles and Directions

0.0   Start at the horse staging area near the park entrance. Head east on the Pass Mountain Trail and then turn left at the T intersection.

0.7   Stay left at the junction with the Wind Cave Trail.

2.3   Reach the Tonto National Forest boundary.

4.4   Reach a pass, the high point of the hike.

4.6   The old trail forks left; stay right, on the new trail.

6.1   Stay right at an unsigned trail junction.

7.1   Stay right at the junction with the Cat Peaks Trail.

7.6   Turn left at the T intersection to return to the trailhead.

7.7   Arrive back at the horse staging area.

76 Baseline Trail

This easy hike loops around a small hill in the foothills of the Sierra Estrella and gives you panoramic views of the surrounding Sonoran desert. As just one of many trails in Estrella Mountain Regional Park, this loop is a fine introduction to the many hiking possibilities in the park.

Distance: 2.9-mile loop
Hiking time: About 1 to 2 hours
Difficulty: Easy
Trail surface: Dirt trails
Best season: Fall through spring
Water: No water available
Other trail users: Mountain bikes and horses
Canine compatibility: Controlled dogs allowed
Land status: Estrella Mountain Regional Park
Nearest town: Phoenix

Fees and permits: Park entrance fee
Schedule: Open all year
Maps: USGS Perryville, Tolleson, Avondale SE, and Avondale SW; Estrella Mountain Regional Park map
Trail contacts: Maricopa County Parks and Recreation, 234 N. Central Ave, Suite 6400, Phoenix, AZ 85004; (602) 506-2930; www.maricopa.gov/parks

Finding the trailhead: From Phoenix drive west on I-10 about 25 miles to the Estrella Parkway exit. Go south 7 miles and turn left onto Vineyard Avenue. Go about 2.5 miles to the Estrella Mountain Regional Park entrance. Follow Casey Abbott Road south past the amphitheater to the parking area and signed trailhead. GPS: N33 22.95' / W112 22.18'

The Hike

This loop trail encircles one of the many peaks in the park. Although close to metropolitan Phoenix, the area has a remote feeling. From the trailhead, follow the barrier-free Gila Loop Trail south. This trail soon splits—you can take either the left or right fork. At the south end of the Gila Loop Trail, continue south on the Baseline Trail. At a junction, the Horseshoe Trail comes in from the left, and the loop portion of the Baseline Trail begins. Continue straight ahead on the Baseline Trail. (The trail on the right will be your return trail.)

CACTUS WREN

Look for football-size cactus wren nests in the abundant cholla cacti. The nest's interior is accessible only through a small opening at one end. At 8 to 9 inches in length, the cactus wren is North America's largest wren. Unlike most other birds, this wren can be heard singing year-round.

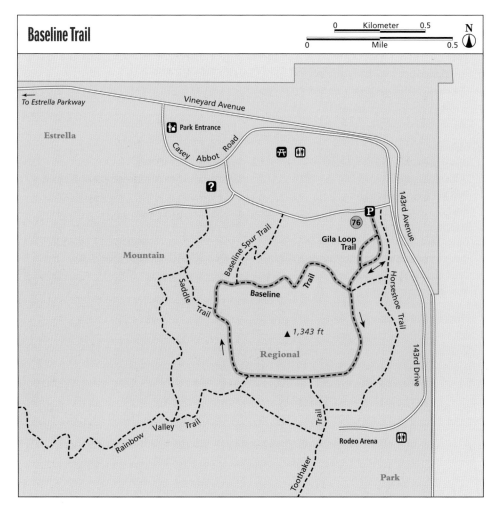

Kilometer

Mile

N

To Estrella Parkway

Vineyard Avenue

Estrella

Park Entrance

Casey Abbot Road

Mountain

Baseline Spur Trail

Saddle Trail

Gila Loop Trail

Baseline

Trail

143rd Avenue

Horseshoe Trail

▲ 1,343 ft

Regional

143rd Drive

Rainbow Valley Trail

Trail

Rodeo Arena

Toothaker

Park

Follow the Baseline Trail south along the east slopes of a low desert hill, and then west to the junction with the Toothaker Trail. Stay right and follow the Baseline Trail west toward a saddle. Here the Rainbow Valley Trail forks left; stay right on the Baseline Trail. After the trail swings around to the west slopes of the hill, it meets the Saddle Trail; again, stay right to remain on the Baseline Trail. Soon, the Baseline Spur Trail forks left; stay right and follow the Baseline Trail east across the north slopes of the hill to the junction with the Horseshoe Trail; stay left on the Baseline Trail to retrace your steps to the Gila Loop barrier-free trail and turn either right or left to return to the trailhead.

Miles and Directions

0.0   Start on the Gila Loop Trail.

0.1   The loop portion of the Gila Loop Trail begins; go either left or right.

0.3   Leave the Gila Loop Trail and continue south on the Baseline Trail.

0.4   Reach the junction with Horseshoe Trail; continue south on the Baseline Trail.

0.9   Intersect with Toothaker Trail; stay right on the Baseline Trail.

1.4   Rainbow Valley Trail enters from the left. Stay right on the Baseline Trail.

1.8   Reach the junction with Saddle Trail on the left; stay right on the Baseline Trail.

2.0   Baseline Spur Trail comes in from the left; stay right on the Baseline Trail.

2.5   Return to the junction with Horseshoe Trail; turn left (north) on the Baseline Trail.

2.6   At Gila Loop Trail, turn left or right to return to the trailhead.

2.8   Loop portion of Gila Loop Trail ends; follow the trail north to the trailhead.

2.9   Arrive at the trailhead.

77 Quartz Peak Trail

This rugged day hike takes you to the summit of a prominent peak in the seldom-visited Sierra Estrella Wilderness. As a reward for the steep climb, you'll have contrasting views of the greater Phoenix area to the northeast, and the almost unpopulated Sonoran Desert to the southwest.

Distance: 4.8 miles out and back
Elevation change: 2,502 feet
Difficulty: Strenuous
Best season: Fall through spring
Trail surface: Dirt trails; boulders and talus near summit
Water: No water available
Other trail users: None
Canine compatibility: Controlled dogs allowed
Land status: Sierra Estrella Wilderness, Bureau of Land Management

Nearest town: Phoenix
Fees and permits: None
Schedule: Open all year
Maps: USGS Montezuma Peak
Trail contacts: Bureau of Land Management, Lower Sonoran Field Office, 21605 N. Seventh Ave., Phoenix, AZ 85027-2929; (623) 580-5500; www.blm.gov/az/st/en/fo/lower_sonoran_field.html

Finding the trailhead: Although distinguished as one of the closest wilderness areas to metropolitan Phoenix, four-wheel-drive vehicles are required to approach the wilderness boundary. Primitive dirt roads near the boundary are extremely sandy or silty, and wash crossings are rugged and deep. From Phoenix take I-10 to exit 126 and travel 8.3 miles south to Elliot Road. Turn right and go 2.6 miles to Rainbow Valley Road. Turn left and drive 9.3 miles south until the pavement ends. Turn left onto Riggs Road, and continue 4 miles to an intersection. Go straight through the intersection another 5.3 miles to a power line road. Turn right and drive 1.9 miles. Turn left onto a road and travel 1.9 miles east to the Quartz Peak trailhead. Some lands around and within the wilderness are not federally administered. Please respect the property rights of the owners—do not cross or use these lands without their permission. GPS: N33 11.94'/W112 14.41'

The Hike

Quartz Peak Trail, in the 14,400-acre Sierra Estrella Wilderness, leads visitors from the floor of Rainbow Valley (elevation 1,550 feet) to the summit ridge of the Sierra Estrella at Quartz Peak (elevation 4,052 feet) in just 3 miles. The trail is extremely steep and difficult to follow in places. This is a hike for experienced and well-conditioned hikers only!

From the Quartz Peak trailhead, follow a closed four-wheel-drive track approximately 0.3 mile. Look to the left as you walk up the old road to find a narrow trail ascending the ridge to the north. The trail is poorly marked in places and does not extend to the summit. The final 0.3 mile to Quartz Peak is a scramble over boulder and talus slopes that requires careful footing. Quartz Peak is a point on the spine of the Sierra Estrella capped by an outcrop of white quartz.

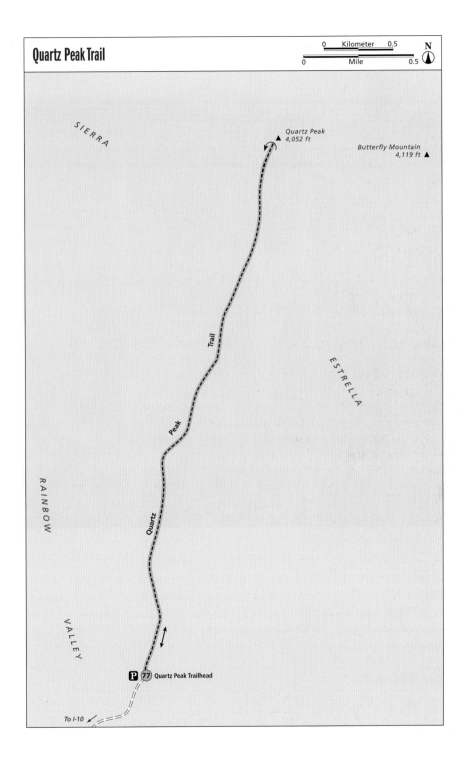

Quartz Peak Trail

0 Kilometer 0.5

0 Mile 0.5

N

SIERRA

Quartz Peak
▲ 4,052 ft

Butterfly Mountain
4,119 ft ▲

ESTRELLA

Trail

Peak

RAINBOW

Quartz

VALLEY

P 77 Quartz Peak Trailhead

To I-10

Saguaro cactus, Estrella Mountains

Along the way visitors are treated to a variety of Sonoran Desert plants and wildlife, scenic vistas, and evidence of the area's volcanic history. The views from the summit are spectacular. To the west is a dramatic panorama of rugged mountain ranges and desert plains; to the east metropolitan Phoenix unfolds over the valley of the lower Salt River.

Miles and Directions

- **0.0** Start at the Quartz Peak trailhead.
- **2.4** Reach Quartz Peak; retrace your steps. (**Caution:** The final 0.3-mile rock scramble requires careful footing.)
- **4.8** Arrive back at the trailhead.

78 Margies Cove Trail

This hike takes you across Sonoran Desert plains and into a scenic canyon in the North Maricopa Mountains, part of the Sonoran Desert National Monument.

Distance: 7.6 miles out and back
Difficulty: Moderate
Trail surface: Dirt trails
Best season: Fall through spring
Water: No water available
Other trail users: Horses
Canine compatibility: Controlled dogs allowed
Land status: North Maricopa Mountains Wilderness, Sonoran Desert National Monument, Bureau of Land Management

Nearest town: Phoenix
Fees and permits: None
Schedule: Open all year
Maps: USGS Cotton Center SE
Trail contacts: Bureau of Land Management, Lower Sonoran Field Office, 21605 N. Seventh Ave., Phoenix, AZ 85027-2929; (623) 580-5500; www.blm.gov/az/st/en/fo/lower_sonoran_field.html

Finding the trailhead: From Phoenix drive about 30 miles west on I-10, then exit south on Highway 85. Drive about 21 miles south and exit at Woods Road. Turn left, cross the overpass, and turn left again onto the frontage road. Drive north about 1 mile to reach the Margies Cove Road; turn right (east). After 4 miles, turn right (south) and continue 5.2 miles to the Margies Cove Trailhead. These dirt roads are passable to cars if driven with care. GPS: N33 7.54' / W112 34.92'

The Hike

Starting from the Margies Cove West trailhead, the trail follows a closed road and meanders up the broad, gently sloping valley. You'll pass an old windmill site in the first 0.5 mile. Gradually the mountains close in on either side. After about 3.1 miles

THE NORTH MARICOPA MOUNTAINS

The North Maricopa Mountains are a jumble of long ridges and isolated peaks separated by extensive, saguaro-studded bajadas and wide desert washes. Cholla, ocotillo, prickly pear, paloverde, ironwood, and Mexican jumping bean complement the thick stands of saguaro to form classic Sonoran Desert vistas. Commonly seen wildlife include desert mule deer, javelinas, desert bighorn sheep, coyotes, desert tortoises, and numerous varieties of lizards and birds.

A segment of the 1850s Butterfield Stageline runs along the southern boundary of the wilderness. This stageline was the first reliable, relatively fast method of transportation between the eastern United States and California. The stage carried people, mail, and freight more than 2,700 miles in less than twenty-five days. The stage boasted that it was late only three times in its three-year history.

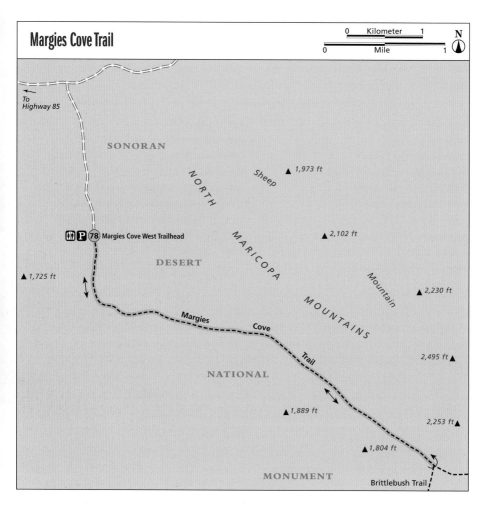

Margies Cove Trail

0 —— Kilometer —— 1

0 —— Mile —— 1

N

To Highway 85

SONORAN

▲ 1,973 ft

Sheep

NORTH

MARICOPA

DESERT

🏞️ 🅿️ ⑦⑧ Margies Cove West Trailhead

▲ 2,102 ft

▲ 1,725 ft

Margies

Cove

MOUNTAINS

Mountain

▲ 2,230 ft

Trail

2,495 ft ▲

NATIONAL

▲ 1,889 ft

2,253 ft ▲

▲ 1,804 ft

MONUMENT

Brittlebush Trail

the trail starts following a gravelly wash as the old road veers away. Watch for rock cairns and BLM trail markers along this section. The rugged peaks and canyon walls add to the wilderness atmosphere. Your hike ends where the Brittlebush Trail comes in from the right, about 3.8 miles from the trailhead.

Miles and Directions

0.0 Start at the Margies Cove West trailhead.

2.8 The trail leaves the old road and starts following a gravelly wash.

3.8 The Brittlebush Trail comes in from the right. This is the end of the hike and your turn-around point.

7.6 Arrive back at the trailhead.

79 Table Top Trail

A great winter hike, this trail takes you to the top of Table Top Mountain through lush Sonoran Desert.

Distance: 6.6 miles out and back
Hiking time: About 5 hours
Difficulty: Moderate
Trail surface: Dirt trails
Best season: Fall through spring
Water: No water available
Other trail users: None
Canine compatibility: Controlled dogs allowed
Land status: Table Top Wilderness, Sonoran Desert National Monument, Bureau of Land Management

Nearest town: Casa Grande
Fees and permits: None
Schedule: Open all year
Maps: USGS Little Table Top
Trail contacts: Bureau of Land Management, Lower Sonoran Field Office, 21605 N. Seventh Ave., Phoenix, AZ 85027-2929; (623) 580-5500; www.blm.gov/az/st/en/fo/lower_sonoran_field.html

Finding the trailhead: At the junction of I-8 with I-10, go west about 38 miles on I-8. Exit at Vekol Road (exit 144). Turn south onto the maintained gravel road. The maintenance road ends 1.9 miles from I-8; bear right here, at the turnoff to Vekol Ranch. The rest of the road is seldom maintained; use caution for washouts, loose sand, and rocks. A high-clearance vehicle is recommended. Go straight at a fork 7.8 miles from I-8. Stay right at a fork 12.1 miles from the interstate. You'll reach the Lava Flow South trailhead 14.9 miles from I-8. The road ends at the Table Top trailhead at 15.7 miles. The trailhead has a small campground and day-use parking but no water. GPS: N32 43.00'/W112 9.53'

The Hike

A pleasant stroll through magnificent saguaro forest starts the hike. This section wanders up a gentle valley between rugged, low hills. After crossing a dry wash, the trail follows a gentle ridge with good views of the surrounding mountains. While the surrounding hills are covered with basalt boulders, the rock underfoot is schist. The trail crosses another wash. The rock underfoot becomes granite, and the climb becomes steeper. As the trail approaches the base of the mountain, it becomes steeper yet. It swings right and crosses two ravines, which show plain evidence of massive flooding from some past storm. Switchbacks lead up the steep southwest slopes of the mountain. Near the summit the trail is briefly bordered by 3- to 4-foot-high stone walls. Although the construction was skillfully done, the origin and purpose of these structures is unknown. A final meander up a ridge leads to the end of the trail. Notice that there are no saguaros on the summit plateau. The summit supports an unusual 40-acre island of desert grassland, where the rare Gila spotted whiptail lizard or Ajo mountain whipsnake may be encountered.

Saguaros can't stand prolonged frost—the climate at the top of the mountain is evidently a little too cool for them. The view is open in all directions except the

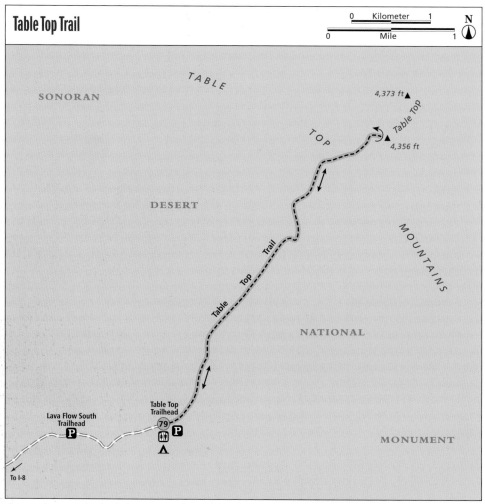

northeast, where the summit plateau blocks it. The Bradshaw Mountains are visible to the north and the Santa Catalina and Santa Rita Mountains to the southeast. The distinctive square tower of Baboquivari Peak is obvious to the south, and the bulk of Harquahala Mountain is visible to the distant northwest.

Miles and Directions

0.0 Start at the Table Top trailhead.

2.3 Reach the base of the mountain.

3.3 Reach Table Top Mountain after climbing a ridge. Retrace your steps.

6.6 Arrive back at the trailhead.

▶ Visitors may see Cooper's hawks, red-tailed hawks, prairie falcons, Gambel's quails, and turkey vultures. Mule deer, javelinas, desert bighorn sheep, coyotes, and antelope jackrabbits are also present within this 43,400-acre wilderness.

Tucson Area

Surrounded by dramatic mountain ranges rising up to 7,000 feet above the city, Tucson offers a range of hiking—from easy desert day hikes in the classic Sonoran Desert of the Tucson Mountains to strenuous multiday hikes in the forested high-country wilderness of the Santa Catalina Mountains and Rincon Mountains. And all of this is within an easy drive from Tucson.

Fishhook barrel cactus in the Tucson Mountains

80 Hunter Trail

This is a popular day hike to the top of Picacho Peak, a rugged landmark that is visible for many miles.

Distance: 4.0 miles out and back
Hiking time: About 4 hours
Difficulty: Moderate
Trail surface: Dirt trails
Best season: Fall through spring
Water: No water available
Other trail users: None
Canine compatibility: Controlled dogs allowed

Land status: Picacho Peak State Park
Nearest town: Eloy
Fees and permits: Park entrance fee
Schedule: Open all year
Maps: USGS Newman Peak
Trail contacts: Arizona State Parks, 1300 West Washington, Phoenix, AZ 85007; (602) 542-4174; azstateparks.com

Finding the trailhead: From Tucson drive 50 miles north on I-10 to the well-marked exit for Picacho Peak State Park. The trailhead is located in the southwest corner of the park's Barrett Loop, near the Saguaro Ramada. GPS: N32 38.56' / W111 24.15'

The Hike

In 1933 the Civilian Conservation Corps built a trail to the summit that now sees 10,000 or more hikers a year. In the early 1970s an Explorer Scout troop constructed a new trail to replace the lower half of the original CCC trail. Frequent trail signs and steel-cable handrails show the way over the eastern headwall to the main saddle. From the saddle, railroad-tie wooden steps, steel cables, wire mesh–enclosed catwalks, and gangplanks lead to the summit. On a clear day there are 100-mile views in all directions. Unfortunately, with each passing year there is less of the natural desert landscape and more urban development surrounding the park.

CIVIL WAR BATTLE SITE

Rising 1,500 vertical feet above the surrounding desert floor, 3,317-foot Picacho Peak is an isolated, 22-million-year-old volcanic mountain situated midway between the Gila River and Tucson. This is the site of Arizona's only Civil War battle. The Battle of Picacho Pass took place on April 15, 1862, lasted about an hour and a half, and cost the lives of four "Johnny Rebs" and three "Yanks." Petroglyphs abound in the area, testifying that the prehistoric Hohokam were here long before the white man.

Hunter Trail

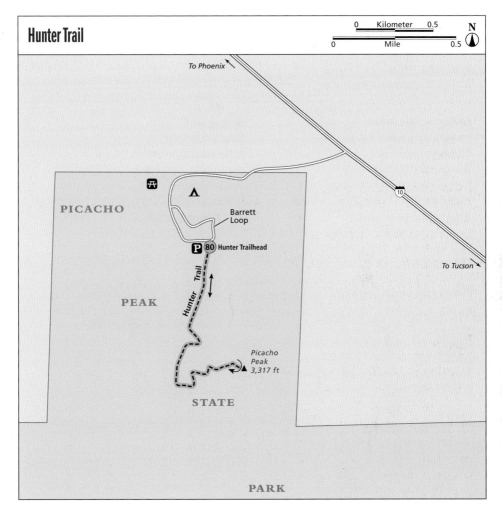

Miles and Directions

0.0   Start at the trailhead in the southwest corner of Barrett Loop.

2.0   Reach summit of Picacho Peak. Enjoy the view before retracing your steps.

4.0   Arrive back at the trailhead.

81 Wilderness of Rocks

This hike takes you through cool pine-fir forest to the edge of the Wilderness of Rocks in the high country of the Santa Catalina Mountains.

Distance: 3.2-mile loop
Hiking time: About 2 hours
Difficulty: Easy
Trail surface: Dirt trails
Best season: Spring through fall
Water: None
Other trail users: Horses
Canine compatibility: Controlled dogs allowed
Land status: Pusch Ridge Wilderness, Coronado National Forest

Nearest town: Tucson
Fees and permits: None
Schedule: Open all year
Maps: USGS Mount Lemmon; USFS Pusch Ridge Wilderness
Trail contacts: Coronado National Forest, 300 West Congress, Tucson, AZ 85701; (520) 388-8300; www.fs.usda.gov/coronado

Finding the trailhead: From I-10 in Tucson exit at Grant Road, then drive 8.5 miles east. Turn left onto Tanque Verde Road; go 3.2 miles and turn left onto Catalina Highway, which becomes General Hitchcock Highway (FR 833) as it starts up the Santa Catalina Mountains. (There is a recreation fee, payable at the entrance station.) Continue about 32 miles, and then turn left into Summerhaven. Continue 1.4 miles south on the main road through Summerhaven to its end at the Marshall Gulch trailhead. GPS: N32 25.68'/W110 45.34'

The Hike

Start on the Marshall Gulch Trail, which climbs west along the north side of Marshall Gulch. This cool, shady ravine is densely forested with ponderosa pine, Douglas fir, and quaking aspen. At the head of the gulch, the trail emerges onto broad, pine-covered Marshall Saddle. Turn left here, at 1.2 miles, onto the Aspen Trail, which climbs gradually as it heads south along the east slopes of Marshall Peak. At 1.7 miles the trail passes through a broad saddle and turns more easterly. You can leave the trail here and follow an informal trail southwest to a rocky viewpoint overlooking the Wilderness of Rocks, named for its granite outcrops. Back on the main trail, follow it east as it climbs gently to the highest elevation of the hike, then descends rapidly east toward Sabino Canyon. It swings north and descends to the Marshall Gulch trailhead, completing the loop.

Miles and Directions

0.0 Start at the Marshall Gulch trailhead, 1.4 miles south of Summerhaven.
1.2 Turn left onto the Aspen Trail.
1.7 Pass through a broad saddle. (***Option:*** Follow an informal trail southwest to a viewpoint overlooking the Wilderness of Rocks.)
3.2 Arrive back at the Marshall Gulch trailhead.

Wilderness of Rocks, Butterfly Trail, Finger Rock Trail, West Fork Sabino Canyon

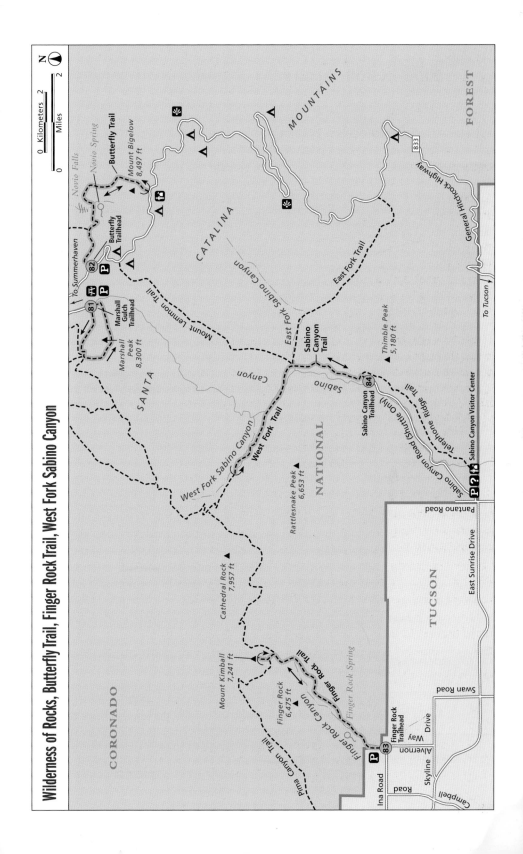

82 Butterfly Trail

A great choice when the deserts below are scorching hot, this hike takes you across the cool northeast slopes of Mount Bigelow in the Santa Catalina Mountains.

See map on page 251.
Distance: 10.4 miles out and back
Hiking time: About 7 hours
Difficulty: Moderate
Trail surface: Dirt trails
Best season: Spring through fall
Water: Seasonal at Novio Spring
Other trail users: Mountain bikes and horses
Canine compatibility: Controlled dogs allowed

Land status: Coronado National Forest
Nearest town: Tucson
Fees and permits: None
Schedule: Open all year
Maps: USGS Mount Bigelow
Trail contacts: Coronado National Forest, 300 West Congress, Tucson, AZ 85701; (520) 388-8300; www.fs.usda.gov/coronado

Finding the trailhead: From I-10 in Tucson exit at Grant Road, then drive 8.5 miles east. Turn left onto Tanque Verde Road; go 3.2 miles, then turn left onto Catalina Highway, which becomes General Hitchcock Highway (FR 833) as it starts up the Santa Catalina Mountains. (There is a recreation fee, payable at the entrance station.) Continue about 27 miles to the Palisade Ranger Station, and then drive another 2.9 miles to the Butterfly trailhead, the start of the hike. GPS: N32 25.64'/W110 44.44'

The Hike

The Butterfly Trail starts out as an old jeep road, which descends rapidly to the north but soon becomes a foot trail. Now the trail contours east, heads several drainages, then descends to the junction with Trail 17, southeast of Butterfly Peak, at 1.3 miles. Again the trail contours east, then descends sharply to the lowest elevation of the hike. There are seasonal waterfalls in the drainage below the trail. Novio Spring is located in a drainage near the trail, at 2.3 miles. The trail swings north around the drainage, an unnamed tributary of Alder Creek. It then turns east again and starts to climb. Switchbacks lead south onto the north end of a ridge at 3.3 miles, and the climb moderates for a while. The trail climbs east across a north-facing slope, then

MICROCLIMATES

The north-facing slopes along the Butterfly Trail are mostly covered with a lush, green pine-fir forest. As the trail crosses slopes with slightly different aspects, you can clearly see the effect of microclimates. West- and south-facing slopes are drier and warmer, and the tall trees give way to chaparral.

swings south for the final climb to the Bigelow–Kellogg Saddle at 4.7 miles. A gradual descent leads to the Palisades Ranger Station, the turnaround point.

Miles and Directions

0.0 Start at the Butterfly trailhead, descending rapidly on an old jeep road that becomes a foot trail.

1.3 Reach junction with Trail 17; stay on the Butterfly Trail.

2.3 Pass Novio Spring.

3.3 Reach north end of ridge.

4.7 Reach Bigelow-Kellogg Saddle after a climb.

5.2 Arrive at Palisades Ranger Station, your turnaround point.

10.4 Arrive back at the trailhead.

83 Finger Rock Trail

This is a hike up a rugged, scenic canyon in the desert foothills of the Santa Catalina Mountains. It leads to the 7,241-foot summit of Mount Kimball, a prominent peak in the Catalina Front Range.

See map on page 251.
Distance: 8.8 miles out and back
Hiking time: About 7 hours
Difficulty: Strenuous
Trail surface: Dirt trails
Best season: Fall through spring
Water: Seasonal at Finger Rock Spring
Other trail users: None
Canine compatibility: Dogs prohibited
Land status: Pusch Ridge Wilderness, Coronado National Forest
Nearest town: Tucson

Fees and permits: None
Other: To protect bighorn sheep, day hike group size limit is 15 persons; overnight group size limit is 6 persons. Jan 1 through Apr 30, no camping beyond 400 feet from system trails. No hiking on unofficial trails.
Schedule: Open all year
Maps: USGS Tucson North and Oro Valley; USFS Pusch Ridge Wilderness
Trail contacts: Coronado National Forest, 300 West Congress, Tucson, AZ 85701; (520) 388-8300; www.fs.usda.gov/coronado

Finding the trailhead: From I-10 exit onto Orange Grove Road and go 6.7 miles east. Turn right onto Skyline Drive, and drive 1.8 miles. Turn left onto Alvernon Way; continue 1 mile north to the end of the road and the Finger Rock trailhead. GPS: N32 20.24'/W110 54.65'

The Hike

Start on the Finger Rock Trail, which heads north into the mouth of Finger Rock Canyon. Now the trail climbs gradually northeast up the canyon to Finger Rock Spring at 0.9 mile. The main trail turns right here and switchbacks up the slope to the east—it stays on this slope nearly all the way to the head of the canyon. It's a steep climb but worth it. As you ascend, the vegetation changes from saguaro-forested desert to piñon pine–juniper forest. After about 3 miles the trail swings east into a basin—watch for a spur trail that goes east to Linda Vista Saddle. This beautiful saddle with its sweeping view is a good destination for a shorter hike.

Continuing on the main trail, climb to a saddle at the head of Finger Rock Canyon, where it meets the Pima Canyon Trail at 3.9 miles. Turn left and follow this trail as it climbs onto the summit ridge of Mount Kimball. Turn right at 4.2 miles and continue 0.2 mile to the summit of Mount Kimball. It's been a long climb, but from this vantage point you can see much of the front range of the Santa Catalina Mountains.

Finger Rock high on the skyline above Finger Rock Canyon

Miles and Directions

0.0 Start at Finger Rock trailhead.

0.9 Pass Finger Rock Spring. The main trail turns right here.

3.4 Pass spur trail to Linda Vista Saddle. (***Option:*** Visit the saddle, enjoy the view, and then retrace your steps for a shorter hike.)

3.9 At junction turn left onto the Pima Canyon Trail.

4.2 Turn right onto the Mount Kimball Trail.

4.4 Reach the summit of Mount Kimball. Retrace your steps.

8.8 Arrive back at the trailhead.

84 West Fork Sabino Canyon

This hike takes you up two gorgeous canyons to fine seasonal pools in the Front Range of the Santa Catalina Mountains.

See map on page 251.
Distance: 8.8 miles out and back
Hiking time: About 6 hours
Difficulty: Moderate
Trail surface: Dirt trails
Best season: Fall through spring
Water: Seasonal in Sabino Canyon and West Fork Sabino Canyon
Other trail users: None
Canine compatibility: Controlled dogs allowed

Land status: Pusch Ridge Wilderness, Coronado National Forest
Nearest town: Tucson
Fees and permits: Entrance and tram fees
Schedule: Open all year
Maps: USGS Sabino Canyon and Mount Lemmon; USFS Pusch Ridge Wilderness
Trail contacts: Coronado National Forest, 300 West Congress, Tucson, AZ 85701; (520) 388-8300; www.fs.usda.gov/coronado

Finding the trailhead: From I-10 in Tucson exit at Grant Road and go 8.5 miles east. Turn left onto Tanque Verde Road and continue 0.5 mile; turn left onto Sabino Canyon Road and drive 4.4 miles to the Sabino Canyon Visitor Center. Take the Sabino Canyon Tram (fee) to the Sabino Canyon Trailhead. GPS: N32 20.63' / W110 46.85'

Hikers cross Sabino Creek in flood. The water here is only a few inches deep because most of the flood is going under the roadway. It would be very dangerous to cross the main creek.

The Hike

The Sabino Canyon Trail switchbacks up the slope east of Sabino Creek, passes the Telephone Ridge Trail, and then climbs more gradually. After passing through a saddle at 0.9 mile, the trail contours along the east side of Sabino Canyon, well above the canyon bed. The trail crosses an unnamed drainage and then meets the West Fork, East Fork, and Mount Lemmon Trails at 2.2 miles; turn left onto the West Fork Trail. After crossing the East Fork of Sabino Canyon, the trail heads west along the north side of Sabino Canyon. At 3.6 miles the trail meets the West Fork of Sabino Canyon. Follow the trail across the West Fork and up the slope to the west. Watch for several spur trails to the right. These go to several large pools along the bed of the creek, our goal for the hike.

Miles and Directions

0.0 Start at the Sabino Canyon trailhead and begin to climb on switchbacks.

0.2 Pass junction with the Telephone Ridge Trail; stay left.

0.9 Pass through a saddle.

2.2 At junction with multiple trails, turn left onto the West Fork Trail.

3.6 Reach the West Fork of Sabino Canyon. Follow the trail across the fork and up the slope.

4.4 Watch for spur trails to large pools along the creek bed. Retrace your steps.

8.8 Arrive back at the trailhead.

85 Mica Mountain

This backpack trip takes you to the pine-forested summit of the Rincon Mountains. As the only forested mountain range in southeast Arizona without a road to the top, the remote crest of the Rincon Mountains is the province of the backpacker.

Distance: 23.8 miles out and back
Hiking time: About 4 days
Difficulty: Strenuous
Trail surface: Dirt trails
Best seasons: Spring and fall
Water: Seasonal at Douglas Spring, Italian Spring, and Manning Camp
Other trail users: Horses
Canine compatibility: Dogs prohibited
Land status: Saguaro Wilderness, Saguaro National Park

Nearest town: Tucson
Fees and permits: Permit (fee) required for backcountry camping
Other: Camping allowed only in designated wilderness campsites
Schedule: Open all year
Maps: USGS Tanque Verde and Mica Mountain; Trails Illustrated Saguaro National Park
Trail contacts: Saguaro National Park, 3693 S. Old Spanish Trail, Tucson, AZ 85730; (520) 733-5100; www.nps.gov/sagu

Finding the trailhead: From I-10 in Tucson exit at Speedway Boulevard and drive 17.4 miles to the Douglas Spring trailhead at the end of the road. GPS: N32 14.12'/W110 41.21'

The Hike

Start on the Douglas Spring Trail, which heads eastward through classic Sonoran Desert. Several trails join from the right for the first mile or so; be sure to stay left on the Douglas Spring Trail. The trail climbs steadily, then levels somewhat as you pass the Three Tank Trail at 2.1 miles. Just after this junction, watch for a spur trail to Bridal Wreath Falls, a 0.4-mile round-trip. The main trail crosses the remainder of the mesquite flat and then starts to climb again. At 5.6 miles you'll reach Douglas Spring, a seasonal water source and a designated campsite.

Now the trail turns south and begins to climb in earnest, heading up a ridge next to Canyon del Pino. After about a mile, the trail enters the forested canyon itself and climbs to its head at Cow Head Saddle. The curious rock formation responsible for the name is visible as you approach the saddle at 7.7 miles. Turn left onto the Cow Head Saddle Trail, which heads east up a broad ridge.

Southeast of Helens Dome, at mile 10.8, you'll pass the North Slope Trail on the left; the trail contours southeast. Just 0.1 mile farther, turn left onto the Fire Loop Trail, which climbs northeast toward Spud Rock. (The Cow Head Saddle Trail continues 0.4 mile to Manning Camp, another designated campsite with a spring.) A trail branches right near Spud Rock; continue straight ahead to Mica Mountain at 11.9 miles, the goal for our hike. The summit is marked with the foundation of an old fire lookout tower.

Rincon Peak from near Mica Mountain

Mica Mountain, Tanque Verde Ridge

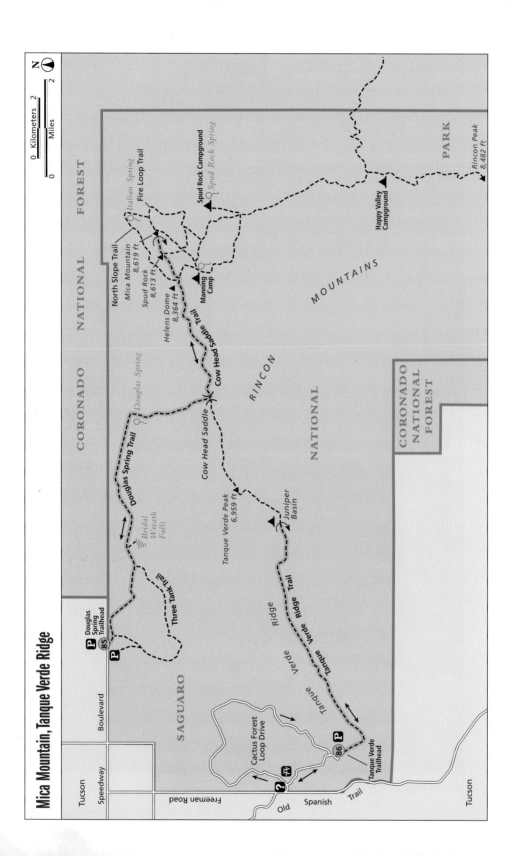

Miles and Directions

0.0 Start at the Douglas Spring trailhead. Ignore the several trails on the right for the first mile or so.

2.1 Pass Three Tank Trail.

2.3 Pass spur trail to Bridal Wreath Falls. (**Option:** Take this 0.4-mile round-trip trail to the falls.)

5.6 Reach Douglas Spring. (**FYI:** This is a seasonal water source and a designated campsite.)

7.7 Reach Cow Head Saddle, and turn left onto the Cow Head Saddle Trail.

10.8 Pass the North Slope Trail on the left.

10.9 Turn left onto the Fire Loop Trail. (**FYI:** Manning Camp campsite and spring are 0.4 mile farther on the Cow Head Saddle Trail.)

11.5 Stay straight at trail junction near Spud Rock.

11.9 Reach Mica Mountain, your goal for this hike. Retrace your steps.

23.8 Arrive back at the trailhead.

Options

There are a number of options in the Mica Mountain area. One is to hike about 0.5 mile east on the Fire Loop Trail to a meadow with open views to the east. You could continue on the Fire Loop Trail to loop south past Manning Camp and then northwest back to the Cow Head Saddle Trail. This loop is about 1.7 miles longer than the normal return via Spud Rock. Another loop, this time to the north, uses the North Slope Trail, which traverses the heavily forested northern slopes of Mica Mountain and also meets the Cow Head Saddle Trail near Helens Dome. This loop is 1.9 miles farther than the direct return.

86 Tanque Verde Ridge

This is a long day hike up a scenic desert ridge in the Rincon Mountains. It takes you from saguaro cactus "forest" to piñon pine–juniper woodland.

See map on page 260.
Distance: 12.4 miles out and back
Hiking time: About 8 hours
Difficulty: Strenuous
Trail surface: Dirt trails
Best season: Fall through spring
Water: No water available
Other trail users: Horses
Canine compatibility: Dogs prohibited
Land status: Saguaro Wilderness, Saguaro National Park

Nearest town: Tucson
Fees and permits: Permit (fee) required for backcountry camping
Other: Camping allowed only in designated wilderness campsites
Schedule: Open all year
Maps: USGS Tanque Verde Peak; Trails Illustrated Saguaro National Park
Trail contacts: Saguaro National Park, 3693 S. Old Spanish Trail, Tucson, AZ 85730; (520) 733-5100; www.nps.gov/sagu

Finding the trailhead: From I-10 in Tucson exit at Speedway Boulevard and drive 12.4 miles east to Houghton Road. Turn right; go 2.7 miles and turn left onto Old Spanish Trail. Go another 2.7 miles, and turn left into Saguaro National Park. Turn right at the visitor center and go about 2 miles to the Tanque Verde trailhead. GPS: N32 9.93' / W110 43.46'

The Hike

The Tanque Verde Ridge Trail first heads southeast across the desert foothills, climbing onto the west end of Tanque Verde Ridge. Here the trail swings northeast and starts a steady climb up this long ridge. The trail dips and winds around small hills and across small drainages but always tends to follow the main ridge. At first you will be in the saguaro cactus "forest." The national park was established to protect this unique and beautiful desert landscape, as well as its plants and animals.

As the trail climbs along the ridge, the cactus forest gradually gives way to high-desert grassland and piñon pine–juniper forest. Saguaros are not tolerant of frost, so they disappear from the cooler, north-facing slopes first. There are many points with good views of the Tucson area and its mountains along the lower portion of the ridge. As the miniature piñon-juniper forest becomes thicker, views become limited. Below an unnamed peak (6,300 feet), the trail turns southeast and contours to cross a drainage. The trail then turns east and follows another shallow drainage to Juniper Basin. This wilderness campground is a good turnaround point for a day hike and a good goal for an overnight backpack trip.

Manning Camp Ranger Station, Rincon Mountains

Miles and Directions

0.0   Start at the Tanque Verde trailhead and head southeast across the desert foothills.

0.8   Reach the west end of Tanque Verde Ridge.

3.4   Pass through a small saddle.

3.6   Pass through a second small saddle.

4.7   Cross a small drainage.

4.9   The trail turns southeast below an unnamed peak.

6.2   Reach Juniper Basin, your turnaround or overnight point.

12.4   Arrive back at the trailhead.

87 Hugh Norris Trail

This is the standard trail to the highest point in the Tucson Mountains, and although it is very popular, the hike is worth it just for the climb along a very scenic desert ridge.

Distance: 8.4 miles out and back
Hiking time: About 5 hours
Difficulty: Moderate
Trail surface: Dirt trails
Best season: Fall through spring
Water: No water available
Other trail users: None
Canine compatibility: Dogs prohibited
Land status: Saguaro Wilderness, Saguaro National Park

Nearest town: Tucson
Fees and permits: Entrance fee
Schedule: Open all year
Maps: USGS Avra; Trails Illustrated Saguaro National Park
Trail contacts: Saguaro National Park, 3693 S. Old Spanish Trail, Tucson, AZ 85730; (520) 733-5100; www.nps.gov/sagu

Finding the trailhead: From I-10 in Tucson, drive west on Speedway Boulevard, which becomes Gates Pass Road. Continue 9.5 miles, and then turn right onto Kinney Road. Go 6.3 miles; turn right onto Hohokam Road, and drive 0.8 mile to the Hugh Norris trailhead. GPS: N32 16.35'/W110 12.20'

The Hike

The trail heads southeast into a drainage and then climbs up a ravine. A few switchbacks lead to the crest of the long ridge trending west from Wasson and Amole Peaks. After dipping through a saddle, the trail climbs gradually eastward across the north side of a peak and through another saddle. Now the trail stays near the ridge crest, generally avoiding small peaks on their north sides. At 2.4 miles you'll cross the Sendero Esperanza Trail in a saddle. The Hugh Norris Trail continues east, climbing a bit more steeply to regain the crest, then turns slightly northeast. After passing south of

OUTSTANDING SAGUAROS

The Tucson Mountains contain one of the best stands of saguaro cactus in the Sonoran Desert, and Saguaro National Park was created to protect these giant cacti. Saguaros are widely regarded as a symbol of the American desert, but actually they occur only in the Sonoran Desert of northwest Mexico and southwest Arizona and not in the other three American deserts. Young saguaros generally get their start under the protection of a nurse tree such as a paloverde. Saguaro cactus can't stand prolonged freezes, so you'll only find them where snow is rare. Nevertheless, every few years an especially cold storm will dust the cactus forests with a few inches of snow, which quickly melts when the sun comes out.

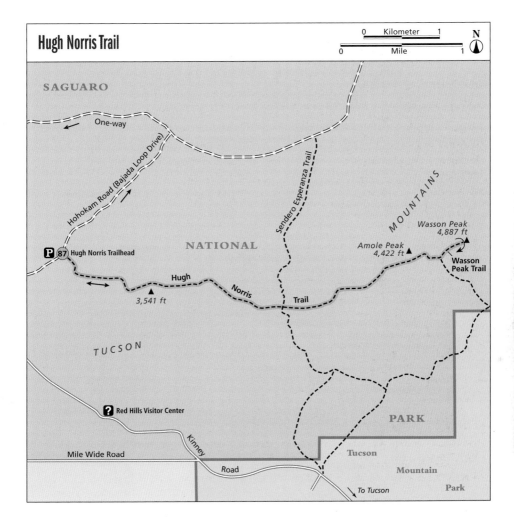

SAGUARO

One-way

Hohokam Road (Bajada Loop Drive)

Sendero Esperanza Trail

MOUNTAINS

Wasson Peak
4,887 ft

P 87 Hugh Norris Trailhead

NATIONAL

Amole Peak
4,422 ft

Wasson
Peak Trail

Hugh

Norris

3,541 ft

Trail

TUCSON

? Red Hills Visitor Center

PARK

Kinney

Mile Wide Road

Road

Tucson

To Tucson

Mountain

Park

Amole Peak, the trail climbs to meet the Wasson Peak Trail at 4.0 miles. Turn left and hike 0.2 mile to the summit of Wasson Peak.

Wasson Peak is the highest summit in the Tucson Mountains, and the view is appropriately sweeping. Saguaro National Park is laid out before you, and the Tucson urban area sprawls to the east below the massive Rincon and Santa Catalina ranges.

Miles and Directions

0.0 Start at the Hugh Norris trailhead and head southeast into a drainage.

0.8 Reach a ridge crest.

2.4 Cross the Sendero Esperanza Trail; continue east on the Hugh Norris Trail.

4.0 Turn left onto the Wasson Peak Trail.

4.2 Reach Wasson Peak. Retrace your steps.

8.4 Arrive back at the trailhead.

Southern Mountains

The high mountains of southeastern Arizona are also known as Sky Islands because they are isolated forested mountain ranges scattered across a sea of desert. The Santa Catalina, Rincon, Pinaleño, Chiricahua, and other mountain ranges rise thousands of feet above the surrounding desert. Their cool, moist forested tops really are biological islands set within the desert sea.

Cave Creek area, Chiricahua Mountains

88 Aravaipa Canyon

This delightful hike along one of Arizona's best desert riparian areas follows a desert stream through a canyon cut across the northern end of the Galiuro Mountains.

Distance: 10.0 miles one-way with a shuttle
Hiking time: About 7 hours
Difficulty: Moderate
Trail surface: Cross-country walking along and in Aravaipa Creek
Best season: Year-round
Water: Aravaipa Creek
Other trail users: None
Canine compatibility: Dogs prohibited
Land status: Aravaipa Canyon Wilderness, Bureau of Land Management

Nearest town: Winkelman
Fees and permits: Advance permit and fee required
Schedule: Open all year
Maps: USGS Brandenburg Mountain and Booger Canyon
Trail contacts: Bureau of Land Management, Safford Field Office, 711 14th Ave., Safford, AZ 85546-3337; (928) 348-4400; www.blm.gov/az/st/en/fo/safford_field_office.html

Finding the trailhead: From Winkelman take Highway 77 south for 11 miles to the Aravaipa Road. Follow the Aravaipa Road 12 miles east to the western trailhead. GPS: N32 54.19'/W110 33.99'

Access to the eastern trailhead is 10 miles northwest of Klondyke on the Aravaipa Canyon Road, which requires a high-clearance vehicle. Some lands around and within the wilderness are not federally administered. Please respect the property rights of the owners, and do not cross or use these lands without permission. GPS: N32 53.92'/W110 26.40'

The Hike

There is no established trail through Aravaipa Canyon. You simply follow the stream. Stream wading and numerous crossings (up to knee deep), as well as hiking through dense riparian brush, can slow your pace and extend your travel time. It takes a strong hiker about 10 hours to hike the length of the canyon. Topographic maps are handy for keeping track of your progress. The main attraction along the route, other than delightful Aravaipa Creek itself, is the numerous side canyons along the way, each of which invites exploration. Such side trips can add hours to the hike, so if you plan much side exploration, you may want to do this hike as an overnight backpack trip.

Aravaipa Canyon

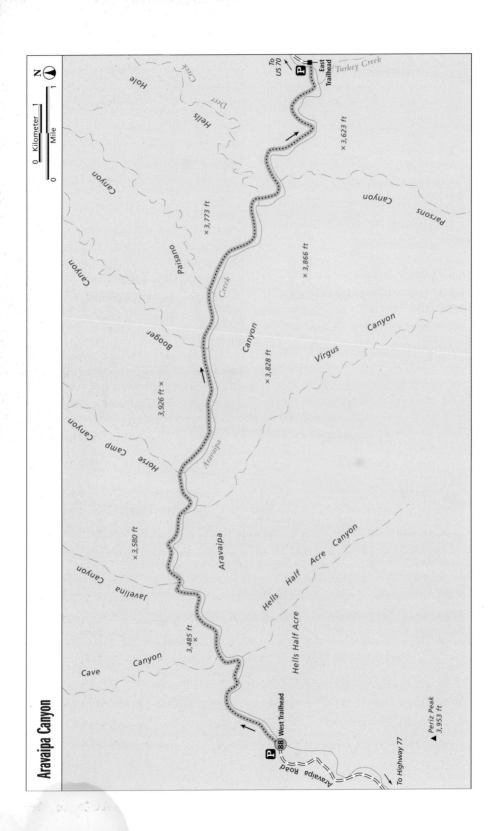

N

0   Kilometer   1

0   Mile   1

Cave   Canyon

3,485 ft ×

Javelina   Canyon

× 3,580 ft

Horse   Camp   Canyon

3,926 ft ×

Canyon

Canyon

Paisano

× 3,773 ft

Booger

Creek

Hole

Hells   Deer   Creek

× 3,623 ft

East
Trailhead

To
US 70

Turkey Creek

Parsons   Canyon

× 3,866 ft

Virgus   Canyon

× 3,828 ft

Aravaipa   Creek

Canyon

Aravaipa

Hells   Half   Acre   Canyon

Hells Half Acre

88   West Trailhead

Aravaipa   Road

To Highway 77

▲ Periz Peak
3,953 ft

Miles and Directions

0.0 Start at the western trailhead and begin following the stream. Be prepared for stream wading and numerous crossings.

1.3 Hells Half Acre Canyon enters from the right.

1.6 Cave Canyon enters from the left.

2.7 Javelina Canyon enters from the left.

3.7 Virgus Canyon enters from the right.

4.1 Horse Camp Canyon enters from the left.

5.7 Booger Canyon enters from the left.

6.3 Paisano Canyon enters from the left.

7.5 Deer Creek enters from the left.

8.0 Parsons Canyon enters from the right.

9.9 Turkey Creek enters from the right.

10.0 Arrive at the eastern trailhead and your shuttle.

Aravaipa Creek

ARAVAIPA CANYON

Aravaipa Canyon, which cuts through the northern part of the Galiuro Mountains, has long been recognized for its spectacular scenery and important wildlife habitat. A 19,410-acre designated wilderness area consists of Aravaipa Canyon plus surrounding tablelands and nine side canyons. Thousand-foot cliffs rise above a green ribbon of rich riparian habitat found along the 11-mile segment of Aravaipa Creek that flows through the wilderness. More than 200 species of birds live among the shady cottonwoods and willows growing along the perennial waters of Aravaipa Creek. During late spring and summer, birders can expect yellow-billed cuckoos, vermilion flycatchers, northern beardless-tyrannulets, yellow warblers, yellow-breasted chats, and summer tanagers. Two federally listed threatened fish occur in the creek—spikedace and loach minnow. There are an additional five species of native fish, which makes Aravaipa Creek one of the best native fisheries remaining in Arizona. The stream has been recommended to be designated a National Wild and Scenic River.

89 Powers Garden

This long day hike or overnight backpack takes you to a historic ranch in a scenic canyon in the Galiuro Mountains, one of Arizona's most remote and least-visited wilderness areas.

Distance: 14.4 miles out and back
Hiking time: About 9 hours or 2 days
Difficulty: Strenuous
Trail surface: Dirt trails
Best season: Spring through fall
Water: Seasonal at Mud and Powers Garden Springs
Other trail users: Horses
Canine compatibility: Controlled dogs allowed
Land status: Galiuro Wilderness, Coronado National Forest

Nearest town: Safford
Fees and permits: None
Schedule: Open all year
Maps: USGS Kennedy Peak; Coronado National Forest (Safford and Santa Catalina Ranger Districts)
Trail contacts: Coronado National Forest, 300 West Congress, Tucson, AZ 85701; (520) 388-8300; www.fs.usda.gov/coronado

Finding the trailhead: From Safford drive about 15 miles northwest on US 70, then turn left onto the graded-dirt Klondyke Road. Go about 24 miles, then turn left on Aravaipa Road. Continue 4.6 miles; turn right onto FR 253, and go 7.4 miles to Deer Creek trailhead. GPS: N32 40.28' / W110 16.93'

The Hike

The trail climbs west up a grassy hillside dotted with juniper trees and climbs over a broad saddle. A gradual descent leads across Oak Creek at 0.9 mile. Now the trail climbs west past Mud Spring and then contours around several unnamed tributaries of Oak Creek, climbing gradually. Note how the junipers have been joined by a few piñon pines on this cooler, north-facing slope. At 2.7 miles the trail swings south around the end of a ridge and passes the junction with the Sycamore Creek Trail. It then works its way across the headwaters of Sycamore Creek, reaching Topout Divide,

THE POWER BROTHERS SHOOTOUT

The Power family established a homestead here before World War I and were soon involved in cattle ranching as well as mining. News of the war was slow to reach this isolated region, and either the Powers didn't know about the draft or pretended they didn't. Eventually the authorities came to arrest them for draft evasion. The resulting shootout left Jeff Power and three lawmen dead. Tom and John Power fled to Mexico and were caught after the largest (to date) manhunt in Arizona history.

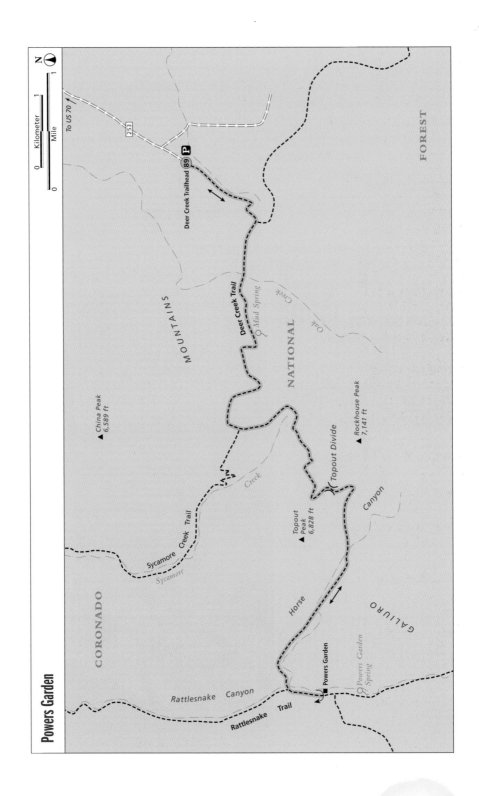

Powers Garden

CORONADO

MOUNTAINS

▲ China Peak
6,589 ft

Sycamore Creek Trail

Sycamore Creek

Creek

▲ Topout Peak
6,828 ft

Topout Divide

Canyon

Horse

Rattlesnake Canyon

Powers Garden

Rattlesnake Trail

Powers Garden Spring

GALIURO

▲ Rockhouse Peak
7,141 ft

NATIONAL

Mud Spring

Deer Creek Trail

Oak Creek

FOREST

Deer Creek Trailhead 89 P

253

To US 70

0   Kilometer   1

0   Mile   1

a pass that marks the high point of the trail at 4.5 miles. The trail drops south into Horse Canyon, then turns sharply northwest and follows the bed of the canyon. A couple of sharp bends mark the end of the canyon. The trail emerges into Rattlesnake Canyon. Turn left onto the Rattlesnake Trail at 6.9 miles, and continue 0.3 mile to the old ranch site at Powers Garden. The beautiful meadow, set in a picturesque canyon, is graced with towering ponderosa pines. There is seasonal water in Powers Garden Spring, just south of the old ranch site.

Miles and Directions

0.0 Start at the Deer Creek trailhead and begin to climb a grassy hillside.

0.9 Cross Oak Creek.

2.7 Pass junction with the Sycamore Creek Trail (Trail 278).

4.5 Reach Topout Divide, the trail's high point.

6.9 Turn left onto the Rattlesnake Trail.

7.2 Reach the old ranch site at Powers Garden, your turnaround point. (**FYI:** Seasonal water is available in Powers Garden Spring, just south of the ranch site.)

14.4 Arrive back at the trailhead.

Options

There are many options for exploring the trail system in the Galiuro Mountains, but be prepared for faint, brushy trails. Many of the trails receive little use or maintenance.

Near Deer Creek trailhead, Galiuro Mountains

90 Ash Creek Falls

This hike leads you through the cool alpine forest high on the Pinaleño Mountains to a high waterfall that can be spectacular just after spring snowmelt.

Distance: 4.8 miles out and back
Hiking time: About 3 hours
Difficulty: Easy
Trail surface: Dirt trails
Best season: Summer through fall
Water: Ash Creek
Other trail users: Horses
Canine compatibility: Controlled dogs allowed
Land status: Coronado National Forest

Nearest town: Safford
Fees and permits: None
Schedule: Open all year
Maps: USGS Webb Peak; Coronado National Forest (Pinaleño Mountains)
Trail contacts: Coronado National Forest, 300 West Congress, Tucson, AZ 85701; (520) 388-8300; www.fs.usda.gov/coronado

Finding the trailhead: From Safford drive 7 miles south on US 191, then turn right onto the Swift Trail (Highway 366). Go about 28 miles, just past the Forest Service Columbine Work Center, then turn right into the Columbine trailhead. GPS: N32 42.28' / W109 54.62'

The Hike

The trails in the Pinaleño Mountains offer high, cool hikes, a welcome escape from the furnace-like desert below. Snow lingers into May and may return in October. Access to this hike is provided by the Swift Trail. This amazing road, now paved for most of its length, climbs the north slopes of the range, crosses Ladybug Pass, then traverses high on the south slopes. Numerous trails start from the Swift Trail and its spur roads and descend the mountain to trailheads in the foothills. These hikes are long, strenuous—and rewarding. The hike to Ash Creek Falls, in contrast, remains in the alpine forest just below the mountain crest and takes you to a high waterfall.

The Ash Creek Trail starts from the east side of the parking area and descends gradually into the headwaters of the creek. A delightful mix of quaking aspen and Douglas fir shade the trail. At 0.5 mile a signed trail forks left to Webb Peak. Your trail continues down Ash Creek and soon swings around a fine alpine meadow at 1.3 miles, marked Mount Graham Mill Site on the USGS map. During the settling of Arizona, "sky-island mountains" such as the Pinaleños provided timber for the ranches and towns in the valleys below. Often, small mills located near the logging site would mill the logs into lumber.

A short distance below the mill site meadow, a horse bypass trail branches left. The reason for the bypass becomes apparent when you reach Slick Rock, a horse-unfriendly section of trail blasted from the granite bedrock. Below this section the trail veers left, out of the creek bed. Just where the view to the north opens up, you'll hear and see 200-foot Ash Creek Falls below the trail to the east. The view includes

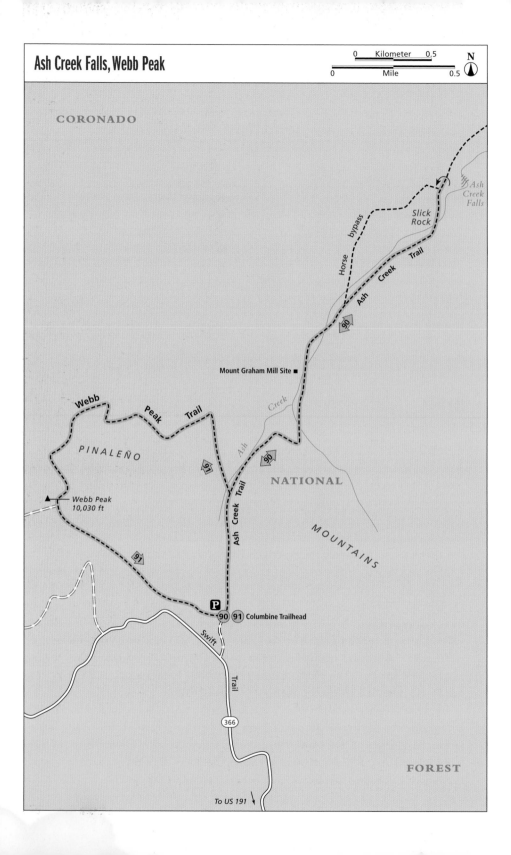

Ash Creek Falls, Webb Peak

CORONADO

Ash
Creek
Falls

Slick
Rock

Horse bypass

Ash Creek Trail

90

Mount Graham Mill Site ■

Creek

Webb Peak Trail

PINALEÑO

Ash

91

90

Ash Creek Trail

NATIONAL

▲ Webb Peak
10,030 ft

MOUNTAINS

91

P
90 91 Columbine Trailhead

Swift

Trail

366

FOREST

To US 191

Pinaleño Mountains trailhead

the Mogollon Mountains in New Mexico, the Mogollon Rim in Arizona, and the towns of Thatcher and Safford far below in the Gila River Valley.

Miles and Directions

0.0 Start at the Columbine trailhead on the east side of the parking area and begin to descend on the Ash Creek Trail.

0.5 The Webb Peak Trail forks left; stay on the Ash Creek Trail.

1.3 Reach the Mount Graham Mill site.

1.7 Pass the horse bypass trail.

2.2 Reach Slick Rock. The trail veers left.

2.4 Reach Ash Creek Falls. Retrace your steps.

4.8 Arrive back at the trailhead.

91 Webb Peak

This easy hike takes you to a 10,030-foot summit along the crest of the alpine-forested Pinaleño Mountains.

See map on page 274.
Distance: 2.7-mile loop
Hiking time: About 2 hours
Difficulty: Easy
Trail surface: Dirt trails
Best season: Summer through fall
Water: No water available
Other trail users: Mountain bikes and horses
Canine compatibility: Controlled dogs allowed

Land status: Coronado National Forest
Nearest town: Safford
Fees and permits: None
Schedule: Open all year
Maps: USGS Webb Peak; Coronado National Forest (Pinaleño Mountains)
Trail contacts: Coronado National Forest, 300 West Congress, Tucson, AZ 85701; (520) 388-8300; www.fs.usda.gov/coronado

Finding the trailhead: From Safford drive 7 miles south on US 191, then turn right onto the Swift Trail (Highway 366). Go about 28 miles, just past the Forest Service Columbine Work Center, then turn right into the Columbine trailhead. GPS: N32 42.28' / W109 54.62'

The Hike

Start on the Ash Creek Trail, turning left onto the Webb Peak Trail at 0.5 mile. The trail is actually an old road, probably built for logging or firefighting. Meandering through beautiful alpine forest, the trail eventually reaches an old burn and turns south toward the summit. Follow the trail carefully here, as it is easy to lose in the meadows. There are excellent views into Blair Canyon as the trail climbs steeply to the summit. Turn left onto a maintained dirt road and walk the last 100 yards to the old fire lookout on the summit, at 2.1 miles. Next to the Forest Service cabin, a sign marks the start of the return trail. This trail drops directly down the southeast ridge to the Columbine trailhead.

▷ The fir forests of the Pinaleño Mountains are home to the endangered Mount Graham red squirrel (Tamiasciurus hudsonicus grahamensis). Controversy continues over the ongoing development of an astronomical observatory on Mount Graham, the highest peak in the range, and the effect of the observatory and associated facilities on the survival of the squirrel.

Mountain lion, also know as cougar

Miles and Directions

0.0 Start at the Columbine trailhead on the east side of the parking area and begin to descend on the Ash Creek Trail.

0.5 Turn left onto the Webb Peak Trail.

2.1 Reach Webb Peak and the old fire lookout. (*FYI:* A sign next to the Forest Service cabin marks the return trail.)

2.7 Arrive back at the trailhead.

92 Safford-Morenci Trail

This is a backpack trip along a historic trail in the Gila Box Riparian National Conservation Area.

Distance: 18.0-mile shuttle
Hiking time: About 2 to 3 days
Difficulty: Strenuous
Trail surface: Dirt trails
Best seasons: Spring and fall
Water: Bonita Creek
Other trail users: Horses
Canine compatibility: Controlled dogs allowed
Land status: Gila Box Riparian National Conservation Area
Nearest town: Safford
Fees and permits: A recreation permit is required for crossing Arizona state trust land 1 mile southward of the East Trailhead. Permits are available by mail or in person at the Arizona State Land Department in Phoenix, Tucson, and Flagstaff and from the Arizona Public Lands Information Center in Phoenix.
You should obtain a San Carlos Apache Tribal recreation permit if you wish to cross the short section of the trail that passes through the reservation near the East Trailhead. Permits are available from the Tribal Recreation and Wildlife Department in San Carlos or from convenience stores in Safford and Pima.
Schedule: Open all year
Maps: USGS Bonita Spring, Weber Peak, Copperplate Gulch, and Lone Star Mountain
Trail contacts: Bureau of Land Management, Safford Field Office, 711 14th Ave., Safford, AZ 85546-3337; (928) 348-4400; www.blm.gov/az/st/en/fo/safford_field_office.html. Arizona State Land Department, 1616 W. Adams St., Phoenix, AZ 85007; (602) 542-4631; www.azland.gov. San Carlos Apache Nation, Recreation and Wildlife Department, PO Box 97, San Carlos, AZ 85550; (928) 475-2343; http://scatrw.com/

Finding the trailhead: The West Trailhead near Bear Springs is about 12 miles northeast of Safford via the Solomon Pass and Salt Trap Roads. To reach the trailhead, take 8th Avenue north out of Safford. A half mile after crossing the Gila River bridge, take the right fork onto Airport Road. Drive 4.3 miles to Aviation Way. Turn left onto Aviation Way, then another immediate left onto the paved unsigned road. This is the Solomon Pass Road, follow it 8 miles to the Solomon Pass–Salt Trap Road Junction. Take the left fork onto Salt Trap Road and follow 1.8 miles. Turn left and continue about 4 miles west to the West Trailhead. If you reach Salt Trap tank and corrals, you've missed the turn. A 4WD high-clearance vehicle is needed for sections of the last 4 miles. GPS: N32 58.37'/W109 37.33'

To reach the East Trailhead (6 air miles west of Morenci), take the Lower Eagle Creek/Black River Road off of Highway 191, just north of Morenci. The turnoff is about 0.25 mile past a historic hillside cemetery on your right. Take the left into what appears to be a dirt parking area. The Eagle Creek road begins there. You will need to ford Eagle Creek just below the water pipeline at the ranch house. Continue on for about another 4 miles. The trailhead is signed. Although the Lower Eagle Creek/Black River Road is maintained gravel, the river crossing may require a high-clearance vehicle during high-water events. (GPS location not available)

Safford-Morenci Trail

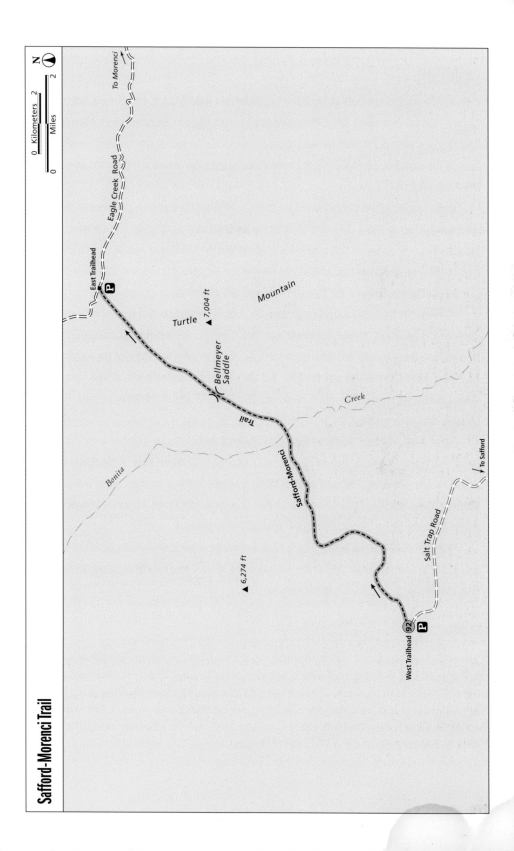

To Morenci

Eagle Creek Road

East Trailhead

P

N

0 Kilometers 2

0 Miles 2

Turtle

▲ 7,004 ft

Mountain

Bellmeyer
Saddle

Trail

Creek

Bonita

Safford-Morenci

▲ 6,274 ft

West Trailhead

92

P

Salt Trap Road

To Safford

AMBUSH!

Pioneer farmers and ranchers in the Gila River Valley and Bonita Creek area gouged out the Safford-Morenci Trail about 1874. They needed a shorter route to Morenci, where booming copper mines offered a market for their produce and meat. The mines also required wood to burn in the smelters, so Mexican wood haulers and their pack trains of mules and burros also used the trail.

Horse rancher Albert Bellmeyer and his foreman rode up this trail from the Morenci side on a fine fall day in 1892. They wanted to check on their herd grazing on Turtle Mountain because there were rumors that renegades from the nearby San Carlos Apache Reservation were in the area. Geronimo had surrendered six year earlier, ending for all practical purposes the threat of hostile Indians, but the ranchers were still concerned.

What exactly happened next is conjecture, but evidence suggests that the two men were ambushed at Bellmeyer Saddle. Bellmeyer was shot twice and apparently died instantly. The foreman, however, spurred his horse down the trail. Another shot rang out, and the foreman fell to the ground. The wound was not fatal, but the attackers crushed his head with a rock. When their bodies were discovered, a posse was dispatched to search for the murderers, but no suspects were ever caught.

Other people of note who have lived near the trail include Toppy Johnson, whose real name was Presley Cantrell. Before coming to Arizona he had served time in the Santa Fe prison for cattle rustling. The local Fulcher family was also involved in illegal horse trading. Mother Fulcher committed suicide where the trail crosses Bonita Creek. A couple of cowboys loaded her body onto a large mule and transported her to Morenci.

With the advent of the automobile, a road was constructed farther south and the trail was slowly abandoned. Remnants of the old homesteads mark these early days, and prehistoric cliff dwellings tell of even earlier residents.

The Hike

This well-established trail winds through rugged and beautiful canyons whose walls are composed of volcanic rocks such as basalt, rhyolite, and andesite. After crossing Bonita Creek the trail climbs along Midnight Canyon and over Bellmeyer Saddle. The vegetation varies from mesquite and creosote bush at the West Trailhead to riparian species such as Fremont cottonwood, willow, and Arizona sycamore along Bonita Creek to piñon-juniper-oak woodland in Smith Canyon. Wildlife is abundant. Look for signs of mule deer, mountain lions, javelinas, coyotes, and gray foxes.

Miles and Directions

0.0 Start at the West Trailhead.

8.0 Cross Bonita Creek.

12.0 Cross Bellmeyer Saddle.

18.0 Reach the East Trailhead and your shuttle.

93 Cochise Stronghold East

This is an enjoyable hike through a granite canyon in the rugged Dragoon Mountains to one of the hideouts of the famous Apache chief.

Distance: 5.6 miles out and back
Hiking time: About 4 hours
Difficulty: Easy
Trail surface: Dirt trails
Best seasons: Spring and fall
Water: Seasonal at Cochise Spring
Other trail users: Mountain bikes and horses
Canine compatibility: Controlled dogs allowed
Land status: Coronado National Forest

Nearest town: Willcox
Fees and permits: None
Schedule: Open all year
Maps: USGS Cochise Stronghold; USFS Coronado National Forest (Chiricahua, Peloncillo, and Dragoon Mountain Ranges)
Trail contacts: Coronado National Forest, 300 West Congress, Tucson, AZ 85701; (520) 388-8300; www.fs.usda.gov/coronado

Finding the trailhead: From Willcox drive 9 miles west on I-10. Turn onto US 191, and drive about 18 miles south to Sunsites; turn right onto Cochise Stronghold Road (FR 84). Continue on this maintained dirt road to its end at Cochise Stronghold Campground and park here. GPS: N31 55.34'/W109 58.03'

The Hike

The trail first climbs south into upper Stronghold Canyon East. You'll pass a spur trail; stay right here, and continue past Cochise Spring, at 1 mile. The canyon turns northwest, and the trail follows it through rugged, beautiful country dotted with granite boulders, domes, and cliffs. The trail then swings left onto the south slopes of the canyon and contours to a pass overlooking Stronghold Canyon West, your goal for this hike.

APACHE RAIDERS

What is now a peaceful hike might have been a different experience when the Chiricahua Apache were using the Dragoon Mountains as a base for raiding settlements in the surrounding valleys. Led by wily Chief Cochise, the warriors led their pursuers into the mountains, where the Apache's skill at rapid travel through very difficult terrain made them impossible to follow.

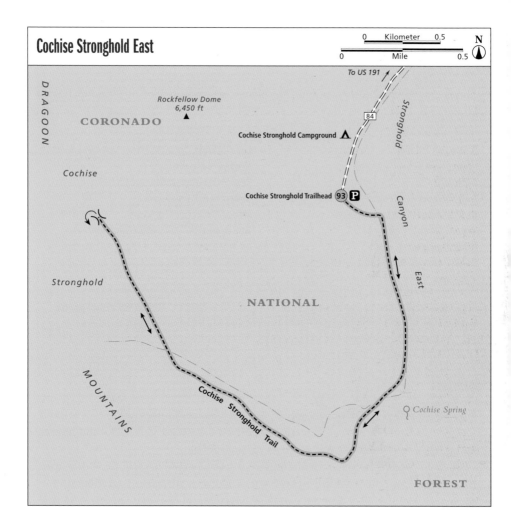

Cochise Stronghold East

0 Kilometer 0.5

0 Mile 0.5

N

To US 191

DRAGOON

Rockfellow Dome
6,450 ft ▲

CORONADO

Stronghold

84

Cochise Stronghold Campground ▲

Cochise

Canyon

Cochise Stronghold Trailhead 93 P

East

Stronghold

NATIONAL

Cochise Spring

M O U N T A I N S

Cochise Stronghold Trail

FOREST

Miles and Directions

0.0 Start at the Cochise Stronghold trailhead and begin climbing south.

0.8 Pass a spur trail; stay right.

1.0 Reach Cochise Spring.

2.8 Reach the pass overlooking Stronghold Canyon West. Retrace your steps.

5.6 Arrive back at the trailhead.

94 Sugarloaf Mountain

This is an easy day hike to one of the highest viewpoints in Chiricahua National Monument, which is also the site of a fire lookout.

Distance: 2.0 miles out and back
Hiking time: About 2 hours
Difficulty: Easy
Trail surface: Dirt trails
Best season: Spring through fall
Water: No water available
Other trail users: None
Canine compatibility: Dogs prohibited

Land status: Chiricahua National Monument
Nearest town: Willcox
Fees and permits: Entrance fee
Schedule: Open all year
Maps: USGS Cochise Head
Trail contacts: Chiricahua National Monument, 12856 E. Rhyolite Creek Rd., Willcox, AZ 85643; (520) 824-3560; www.nps.gov/chir

Finding the trailhead: From Willcox on I-10 drive 34 miles southeast on Highway 186. Turn left onto Highway 181, and continue 5.1 miles to the Chiricahua National Monument Visitor Center. Take Bonita Canyon Drive for about 5.5 miles to the Sugarloaf Mountain turnoff. Another mile brings you to a picnic area and the trailhead. GPS: N32 0.99' / W109 19.25'

The Hike

This well-maintained trail takes you to the old Civilian Conservation Corps–built fire lookout atop Sugarloaf Mountain, where you'll have great views of the monument's renowned fractured and sculpted volcanic rhyolite formations. The plant life is equally intriguing. Seven varieties of oak, as well as pines, cypress, fir, and juniper, grow in the monument. Mixed in with the woodlands are yuccas, agave, and sotol. Javelinas and white-tailed deer are common. Many birds breed in or migrate through the area, including hummingbirds, rose-throated becards, and elegant trogons.

Miles and Directions

0.0 Start at the trailhead at the picnic area.
1.0 Reach Sugarloaf Lookout. Retrace your steps.
2.0 Arrive back at the trailhead.

Sugarloaf Mountain, Echo Canyon, Heart of Rocks

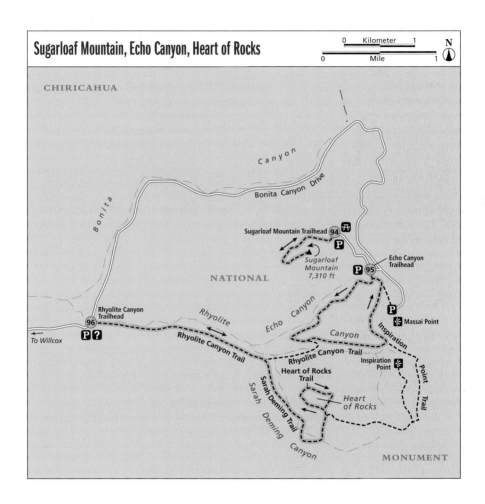

0 — Kilometer — 1

0 — Mile — 1

N

CHIRICAHUA

Canyon

Bonita Canyon Drive

Bonita

Sugarloaf Mountain Trailhead 94

Echo Canyon Trailhead

Sugarloaf Mountain 7,310 ft

NATIONAL

95

Rhyolite Canyon Trailhead

Rhyolite

Echo Canyon

Massai Point

96

To Willcox

Rhyolite Canyon Trail

Canyon

Inspiration

Rhyolite Canyon Trail

Inspiration Point

Point Trail

Heart of Rocks Trail

Sarah Deming Trail

Heart of Rocks

Sarah Deming Canyon

MONUMENT

95 Echo Canyon

This is the classic hike through the hoodoos—weirdly eroded rock formations—in Chiricahua National Monument.

See map on page 285.
Distance: 2.8-mile loop
Hiking time: About 2 hours
Difficulty: Easy
Trail surface: Dirt trails
Best season: Year-round
Water: No water available
Other trail users: None
Canine compatibility: Dogs prohibited

Land status: Chiricahua National Monument
Nearest town: Willcox
Fees and permits: Entrance fee
Schedule: Open all year
Maps: USGS Cochise Head; Chiricahua National Monument brochure
Trail contacts: Chiricahua National Monument, 12856 E. Rhyolite Creek Rd., Willcox, AZ 85643; (520) 824-3560; www.nps.gov/chir

---

Finding the trailhead: From Willcox on I-10 drive 34 miles southeast on Highway 186. Turn left onto Highway 181, and continue 5.1 miles to the Chiricahua National Monument Visitor Center. Take Bonita Canyon Drive for about 5.6 miles to the Echo Canyon trailhead, just before the end of the road. GPS: N32 0.73'/W109 18.94'

The Hike

The trail descends gradually from the trailhead and at 0.2 mile meets the Rhyolite Canyon Trail, which will be the return. Stay right, and follow the Echo Canyon Trail into Echo Park. Here the trail winds between tall rock towers, which remind one of the artificial canyons of a large city. Next you'll enter the cool depths of Echo Canyon, which is shaded with Apache and ponderosa pines. The trail swings around a point into Rhyolite Canyon and meets the Rhyolite Canyon Trail at 1.2 miles. Turn left, and follow the trail east along the north side of the canyon. Notice how this slope is brushy, warmer, and drier than the more-sheltered bottom of Echo Canyon. You'll have great views of the rock pinnacles and formations on both sides of the canyon. At 2.1 miles stay left at the Inspiration Point Trail. The trail swings north and works its way up a side canyon. A side trail leads right to Massai Point; stay left. At 2.6 miles you'll rejoin the Echo Canyon Trail; turn right and walk 0.2 mile back to the Echo Canyon trailhead.

Miles and Directions

0.0 Start at the Echo Canyon trailhead.
0.2 Stay right at junction with the Rhyolite Canyon Trail.
1.2 Turn left onto the Rhyolite Canyon Trail.
2.1 Stay left at the Inspiration Point Trail.
2.6 Turn right onto the Echo Canyon Trail.
2.8 Arrive back at the trailhead.

96 Heart of Rocks

This aptly named hike takes you away from the crowds and into a remote area featuring some of the best of the stone hoodoos in Chiricahua National Monument.

See map on page 285.
Distance: 6.7-mile lollipop
Hiking time: About 5 hours
Difficulty: Moderate
Trail surface: Dirt trails
Best season: Year-round
Water: No water available
Other trail users: None
Canine compatibility: Dogs prohibited

Land status: Chiricahua National Monument
Nearest town: Willcox
Fees and permits: Entrance fee
Schedule: Open all year
Maps: USGS Cochise Head; Chiricahua National Monument brochure
Trail contacts: Chiricahua National Monument, 12856 E. Rhyolite Creek Rd., Willcox, AZ 85643; (520) 824-3560; www.nps.gov/chir

Finding the trailhead: From Willcox on I-10, drive 34 miles southeast on Highway 186. Turn left onto Highway 181. Continue 5.1 miles to the Chiricahua National Monument Visitor Center and the trailhead. GPS: N32 0.34' / W109 21.39'

The Hike

The trail starts at the national monument visitor center parking lot and heads east along the south side of Rhyolite Canyon, climbing gradually. At 1.5 miles turn right onto the Sarah Deming Trail, which ascends a little faster as it turns southeast up Sarah Deming Canyon. Near the head of the canyon, the trail turns abruptly north and climbs out of the canyon into a land of strange-shaped rock formations. You'll meet the Heart of Rocks Trail at 2.9 miles; turn left to hike this scenic loop. The trail returns to the same junction at 3.8 miles. Stay left, and return to the visitor center via the Sarah Deming and Rhyolite Canyon Trails.

The Heart of Rocks Loop features rock caricatures of people and animals and the most massive balanced rock in the monument. There are sweeping views of Sulphur Springs Valley, Cochise Head, and the Chiricahua Mountains.

Balanced Rock, Heart of Rocks

GEOLOGY LESSON

The story behind this fantastic collection of rocks is not completely understood, but geologists believe that about 27 million years ago violent volcanic eruptions spewed red-hot pumice and ash over a 1,200-square-mile area. The hot particles became "welded" together to form an 800-foot-thick layer of tuff with a composition of rhyolite. As cooling took place, the tuff contracted and vertical cracks (joints) formed. The extent and thickness of this deposit indicates eruptions substantially greater than the Mount St. Helens eruption in 1980.

From 25 to 5 million years ago, the earth's crust stretched and broke into large fault-bounded blocks. One uplifted block created the Chiricahua Mountains, and the masters of erosion—water, wind, and ice—began to sculpt the rock into odd formations. The horizontal bedding planes and joints provided weak places for erosion to act upon. Fanciful names such as Organ Pipe, Sea Captain, China Boy, Punch and Judy, and Duck on a Rock describe some of the strange rock shapes. Although many pinnacles and rocks appear to be precariously balanced, they were sufficiently stable to withstand the magnitude-7.2 earthquake that shook southeastern Arizona in 1887.

Miles and Directions

0.0 Start at the Rhyolite Canyon trailhead and head east.

1.5 Turn right onto the Sarah Deming Trail.

2.9 Reach junction with the Heart of Rocks Trail; turn left onto the loop.

3.8 Complete the loop and turn left onto the Sarah Deming Trail.

5.2 Turn left onto the Rhyolite Canyon Trail.

6.7 Arrive back at the trailhead.

97 Buena Vista Peak

This short hike to a rock summit and the site of a former fire lookout features panoramic views of the northern Chiricahua Mountains.

Distance: 2.4 miles out and back
Hiking time: About 2 hours
Difficulty: Easy
Trail surface: Dirt trails
Best season: Spring through fall
Water: No water available
Other trail users: None
Canine compatibility: Controlled dogs allowed
Land status: Coronado National Forest

Nearest town: Willcox
Fees and permits: None
Schedule: Open all year
Maps: USGS Rustler Park; USFS Coronado National Forest (Chiricahua, Peloncillo, and Dragoon Mountain Ranges)
Trail contacts: Coronado National Forest, 300 West Congress, Tucson, AZ 85701; (520) 388-8300; www.fs.usda.gov/coronado

Finding the trailhead: From Willcox on I-10 drive 34 miles southeast on Highway 186. Turn left onto Highway 181, and continue 3 miles. Turn left onto Pinery Canyon Road (FR 42), a maintained dirt road. Go 12 miles to Onion Saddle. Turn right onto Rustler Park Road (FR 42D), and drive 3 miles to Rustler Park trailhead. GPS: N31 54.36'/W109 16.69'

The Hike

Turn right at a junction just 100 yards from the start of the trail. The trail now heads north, climbing gradually through the forest on the east slopes of a ridge and reaching the crest after 0.5 mile. Stay right at an unsigned junction. The trail stays close to the ridgetop for a short distance and then contours the east slope to a second saddle at 1.1 miles. A final short climb brings you to Barfoot Lookout, a Forest Service fire lookout station built on the rocky summit of Buena Vista Peak. *Buena Vista* is Spanish for "good view," and that's certainly true of this 8,753-foot peak at the north end of the Chiricahua Mountains. To the south you can see the high peaks in the Chiricahua Wilderness; to the southeast lies the exceptionally scenic Portal area with its dramatic cliffs towering above Cave Creek.

Barfoot Peak from Buena Vista Peak

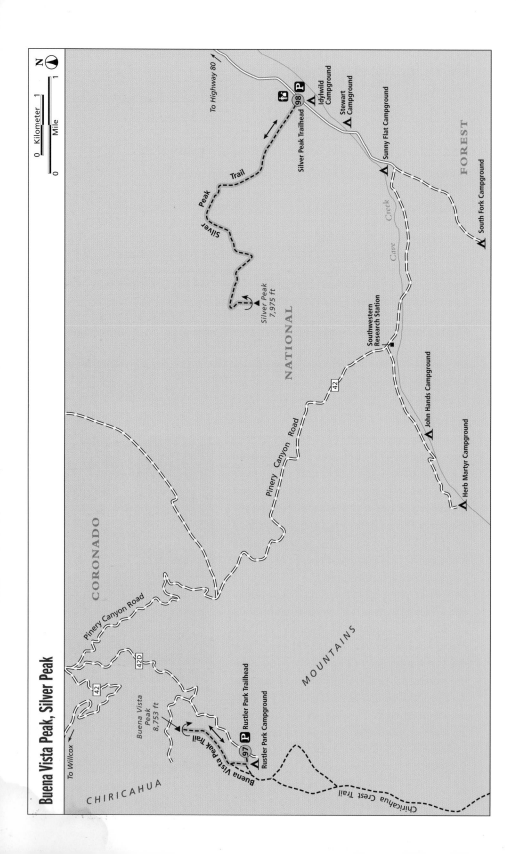

Buena Vista Peak, Silver Peak

CHIRICAHUA

CORONADO

NATIONAL

FOREST

To Willcox

Pinery Canyon Road

42

42D

Buena Vista Peak
8,753 ft

97 P Rustler Park Trailhead

Rustler Park Campground

Buena Vista Peak Trail

MOUNTAINS

Chiricahua Crest Trail

Pinery Canyon Road

42

Southwestern
Research Station

John Hands Campground

Herb Martyr Campground

Silver Peak
7,975 ft

Silver Peak Trail

Cave Creek

98 P

Silver Peak Trailhead

To Highway 80

Idylwild
Campground

Stewart
Campground

Sunny Flat Campground

South Fork Campground

N

0 Kilometer 1

0 Mile 1

Miles and Directions

0.0 Start at the Rustler Park trailhead and turn right at a junction in just 100 yards.

0.5 Reach the first saddle and an unsigned trail junction; stay right.

1.1 Reach the second saddle.

1.2 Climb to Barfoot Lookout on Buena Vista Peak, your turnaround point.

2.4 Arrive back at the trailhead.

98 Silver Peak

This hike leads to a summit east of the main Chiricahua Crest, overlooking the cliff-bound Portal area and the eastern portion of the Chiricahua Mountains.

See map on page 290.
Distance: 7.8 miles out and back
Hiking time: About 6 hours
Difficulty: Strenuous
Trail surface: Dirt trails
Best season: Spring through fall
Water: No water available
Other trail users: None
Canine compatibility: Controlled dogs allowed
Land status: Coronado National Forest

Nearest town: Douglas
Fees and permits: None
Schedule: Open all year
Maps: USGS Portal Peak; USFS Coronado National Forest (Chiricahua, Peloncillo, and Dragoon Mountain Ranges)
Trail contacts: Coronado National Forest, 300 West Congress, Tucson, AZ 85701; (520) 388-8300; www.fs.usda.gov/coronado

Finding the trailhead: From Douglas drive about 54 miles northeast on Highway 80, then turn left onto Portal Road. Go 9.1 miles to the Silver Peak trailhead, just past the ranger station. GPS: N31 53.88' / W109 9.75'

The Hike

You'll be climbing Silver Peak, the massive mountain west of the trailhead. The actual summit is hidden from the trailhead. A few yards up the trail, an unsigned trail goes to the ranger station; turn left here and start up the slope toward the west. This slope appears to be gentle, but it's deceiving. The trail actually climbs 700 feet to reach the base of the mountain. This is a good goal for those desiring an easy hike, and it offers good views of the Portal area.

Now the trail swings around the north slope of the mountain and enters stands of shady pine forest. Final steep switchbacks lead to the rock summit and the ruins of the fire lookout building. To the west the high, forested crest of the Chiricahua Mountains dominates the skyline, and the mountains of New Mexico are visible to the northeast. Closer at hand, to the east and south, lie Cave Creek and the small settlement of Portal.

Miles and Directions

0.0 Start at the Silver Peak trailhead; turn left just past the trailhead.
1.7 Trail enters a pine forest.
3.3 Begin the final switchbacks to the summit.
3.9 Reach Silver Peak and the fire lookout ruins. Retrace your steps.
7.8 Arrive back at the trailhead.

Paint Rock from the Chiricahua Crest Trail ▶

99 Chiricahua Peak

This long day hike or overnight backpack starts from a major canyon in the western foothills and leads you to the highest point in the Chiricahua Mountains.

Distance: 15.5-mile loop
Hiking time: About 10 hours or 2 days
Difficulty: Strenuous
Best season: Spring through fall
Trail surface: Dirt trails
Water: Seasonal at Booger, Anita, and Mormon Springs
Other trail users: Horses
Canine compatibility: Controlled dogs allowed
Land status: Chiricahua Wilderness, Coronado National Forest

Nearest town: Douglas
Fees and permits: None
Schedule: Open all year
Maps: USGS Rustler Park and Chiricahua Peak; USFS Coronado National Forest (Chiricahua, Peloncillo, and Dragoon Mountain Ranges)
Trail contacts: Coronado National Forest, 300 West Congress, Tucson, AZ 85701; (520) 388-8300; www.fs.usda.gov/coronado

Finding the trailhead: From Tucson drive about 72 miles east on I-10; exit at US 191, and go south 27 miles. Turn left onto Highway 181, and drive east 12 miles. Highway 181 turns left; continue straight onto maintained-dirt Turkey Creek Road (FR 41). Go 9 miles, and then turn left onto a short spur road to the Salisbury trailhead. GPS: N31 51.88' / W109 20.52'

The Hike

The Salisbury Trail heads northeast and ambles up through a lovely forest of oak, Apache and Chiricahua pine, and Arizona cypress. The route steepens, but you are treated to magnificent views across the Chiricahua Wilderness and Sulphur Springs Valley. At 2.3 miles the trail passes through Salisbury Saddle and turns southeast. Generally following a ridge, the trail climbs over Little Baldy Mountain. As you continue to climb, the vegetation changes to Douglas fir, Engelmann spruce, and eventually some quaking aspen.

At 4.7 miles turn right onto the Crest Trail. Shortly you'll come to Round Park. A spur trail leads to Booger Spring. Back on the Crest Trail, continue south past Cima Park to Anita Park, at 6.6 miles. Another spur trail leads to Anita Spring, which like Booger Spring may be dry in drought years. A few yards south of Anita Park, you come to a multiple trail junction at Junction Saddle. Continue straight ahead here on the Chiricahua Peak Trail to reach the round, forested summit of the Chiricahua Mountains at 6.9 miles. Unfortunately, the dense forest blocks

▶ **Many birds are found in the Chiricahua Mountains, not only typical Arizona and Mexican species but also some eastern birds such as warblers, which pass through on their migrations to and from Mexico. Black bears and mountain lions are also found in these mountains.**

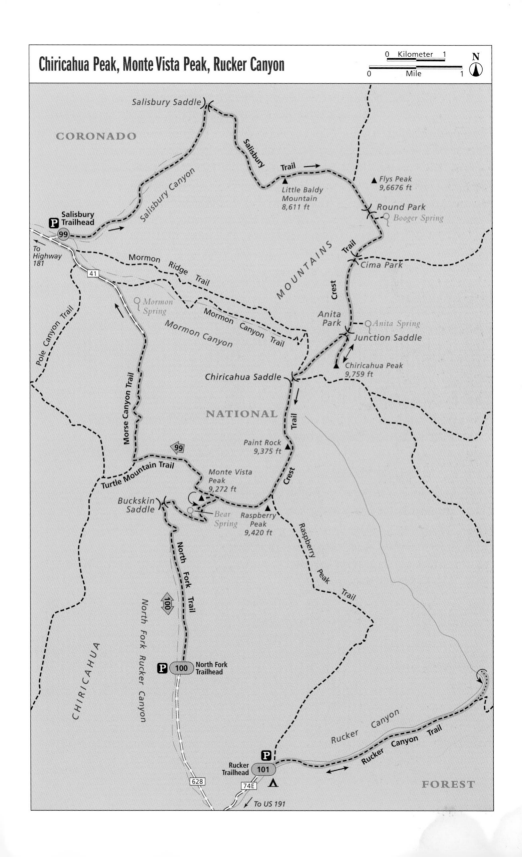

Chiricahua Peak, Monte Vista Peak, Rucker Canyon

0 Kilometer 1

0 Mile 1

N

CORONADO

Salisbury Saddle

Salisbury Trail

Little Baldy
Mountain
8,611 ft

Flys Peak
9,6676 ft

Round Park

Booger Spring

Salisbury Canyon

Salisbury Trailhead
99

To Highway 181

41

Mormon Ridge Trail

Mormon Spring

Mormon Canyon Trail

Mormon Canyon

MOUNTAINS

Crest Trail

Cima Park

Anita Park

Anita Spring

Junction Saddle

Chiricahua Peak
9,759 ft

Pole Canyon Trail

Morse Canyon Trail

Chiricahua Saddle

NATIONAL

Paint Rock
9,375 ft

Crest Trail

99

Turtle Mountain Trail

Monte Vista
Peak
9,272 ft

Buckskin
Saddle

Bear
Spring

Raspberry
Peak
9,420 ft

Raspberry Peak Trail

North Fork Trail

North Fork Rucker Canyon

100

North Fork
Trailhead
100

CHIRICAHUA

628

Rucker
Trailhead
101

74E

To US 191

Rucker Canyon

Rucker Canyon Trail

FOREST

the view. Return to Junction Saddle, and then turn left onto the Crest Trail to resume the loop.

The trail contours along the west slopes of Chiricahua Peak, then passes through Chiricahua Saddle at 8.1 miles. Now the trail stays pretty much on the crest of the range, passing Paint Rock and then turning west at the junction with Raspberry Peak Trail. At 10 miles the Monte Vista Peak Trail branches left; turn right onto the Morse Canyon Trail. This trail drops down the northwest slopes of the peak, then follows a ridge to a saddle east of Johnson Peak at 11.3 miles, where it meets the trail to Turtle Mountain. Stay right here, and follow the trail as it switchbacks steeply down into Morse Canyon. The grade moderates as the trail drops into the bottom of the canyon; you'll reach the Morse Canyon trailhead at 13.5 miles. Walk down the road 1.7 miles, then turn right onto the Salisbury spur road and go 0.3 mile to the Salisbury trailhead.

Miles and Directions

0.0 Start at the Salisbury trailhead and head northeast.

2.3 Pass through Salisbury Saddle.

4.7 Turn right onto the Crest Trail.

5.0 Reach Round Park.

5.8 Reach Cima Park.

6.6 Reach Anita Park and Junction Saddle. Continue straight on the Chiricahua Peak Trail.

6.9 Reach the summit of Chiricahua Peak.

7.2 Return to Anita Park and Junction Saddle. Turn left onto the Crest Trail.

8.1 Pass through Chiricahua Saddle.

9.5 Raspberry Peak Trail joins from the left; stay right on Crest Trail.

10.0 Turn right onto the Turtle Mountain Trail.

11.3 Turn right onto the Morse Canyon trail.

13.5 Reach the Morse Canyon trailhead; walk down the road.

15.2 Turn right onto the Salisbury spur road.

15.5 Arrive back at the trailhead.

100 Monte Vista Peak

This day hike takes you to the southermost of the high summits in the Chiricahua Mountains—and the one with the best view.

See map on page 295.
Distance: 7.8 miles out and back
Hiking time: About 6 hours
Difficulty: Strenuous
Trail surface: Dirt trails
Best season: Spring through fall
Water: Seasonal at Bear Spring
Other trail users: Horses
Canine compatibility: Controlled dogs allowed
Land status: Chiricahua Wilderness, Coronado National Forest

Nearest town: Douglas
Fees and permits: None
Schedule: Open all year
Maps: USGS Chiricahua Peak; USFS Coronado National Forest (Chiricahua, Peloncillo, and Dragoon Mountain Ranges)
Trail contacts: Coronado National Forest, 300 West Congress, Tucson, AZ 85701; (520) 388-8300; www.fs.usda.gov/coronado

Finding the trailhead: From Douglas drive 34 miles north on US 191, and turn right onto Rucker Canyon Road. Go 16 miles; turn left to remain on Rucker Canyon Road, 9 more miles. Turn left onto FR 74E, and drive 4.6 miles. Turn left onto FR 628 (you'll need a high-clearance vehicle), and drive 1.8 miles to the North Fork trailhead. GPS: N31 47.98' / W109 19.19'

The Hike

The North Fork Trail climbs north along the North Fork of Rucker Canyon through pine-oak woodland. After a couple of switchbacks lead out of the canyon, the trail climbs along the east slopes of the canyon, and the grade becomes steeper. You're hiking through a fine example of a mature ponderosa pine forest. Large trees (known as "yellow pines") predominate, and the forest is open and spacious. You'll also see Apache pine, which is found only in southeast Arizona, southwest New Mexico, and northern Mexico. Its longer, lighter-colored needles distinguish Apache pine from ponderosa pine.

The trail passes through Buckskin Saddle at the head of the canyon, at 2.6 miles, and then swings out onto the south slopes for the final ascent of Monte Vista Peak. The effects of several forest fires are obvious on this steep slope. Many of the trees were killed. Those that survived lost their lower branches; these are called "flag" trees. Now, young pines are growing in dense "dog hair" stands. Only a few trees will win the competition for sunlight and grow to maturity.

A spur trail goes to Bear Spring; shortly afterward, at 3.8 miles, the trail ends at the Crest Trail junction. Turn left and walk 0.1 mile to the top. Unlike most other Chiricahua summits, Monte Vista Peak is bald and offers terrific views. A fire tower stands on the summit and is used by Forest Service personnel during the fire season. Ask permission from the observer before climbing the stairs.

Monte Vista Lookout

Miles and Directions

0.0 Start at the North Fork trailhead and head north.

2.6 Pass through Buckskin Saddle.

3.8 Turn left at the junction with the Crest Trail.

3.9 Reach Monte Vista Peak. Retrace your steps.

7.8 Arrive back at the trailhead.

101 Rucker Canyon

This hike follows an easy trail to a short cross-country walk into a rugged portion of Rucker Canyon in the southern Chiricahua Mountains. The cascades of a perennial stream add to the charm of this walk.

See map on page 295.
Distance: 5.6 miles out and back
Hiking time: About 3 hours
Difficulty: Easy
Trail surface: Dirt trails, cross-country
Best season: Spring through fall
Water: Rucker Creek
Other trail users: Horses
Canine compatibility: Controlled dogs allowed
Land status: Chiricahua Wilderness, Coronado National Forest

Nearest town: Douglas
Fees and permits: None
Schedule: Open all year
Maps: USGS Chiricahua Peak; USFS Coronado National Forest (Chiricahua, Peloncillo, and Dragoon Mountain Ranges)
Trail contacts: Coronado National Forest, 300 West Congress, Tucson, AZ 85701; (520) 388-8300; www.fs.usda.gov/coronado

Finding the trailhead: From Douglas drive 34 miles north on US 191, and turn right onto Rucker Canyon Road. Go 16 miles; turn left to remain on Rucker Canyon Road, and continue 9 miles. Turn left onto FR 74E, and drive 5.5 miles to the end of the road at Rucker Campground and the trailhead. GPS: N31 47.03' / W109 18.28'

The Hike

The Rucker Canyon Trail starts from the east end of the campground and follows Rucker Creek upstream to the east through the shady pine forest. At 2.5 miles the trail abruptly climbs out of the canyon via a series of switchbacks. Leave the trail here and continue up the canyon, following the stream. After 0.3 mile the canyon turns north and becomes much rougher. This secluded spot is our destination.

COPPER STRIKE

Rucker Canyon is named for Lieutenant John A. Rucker, who led an Army detachment based at Fort Bowie at the northern end of the Chiricahua Mountains in the late 1800s. His mission took him to the Mule Mountains in search of an Apache band who had fled their reservation. Although he found no trace of the fugitives, he did discover traces of copper near their camp in what is now downtown Bisbee. The resulting copper strike turned out to be one of the richest copper mines in the world. Unfortunately, Lieutenant Rucker was cheated by his partners and didn't share in the bonanza.

Rucker Creek

Here beside the musical stream, it's easy to imagine that modern civilization does not exist—and that an Apache warrior may glide into view at any moment. The wilderness seems complete, and there are tantalizing views of the crags and forested peaks of upper Rucker Canyon.

Miles and Directions

0.0 Start at the Rucker trailhead at the east end of Rucker Campground.

2.5 Start the cross-country portion of the hike. Leave the trail, following the stream upcanyon.

2.8 Reach Rucker Canyon, your turnaround point.

5.6 Arrive back at the trailhead.

102 Mount Wrightson

This long day hike or overnight backpack follows a well-graded trail to the summit of Mount Wrightson, the highest peak in the Santa Rita Mountains. The trail starts alongside Madera Creek, a small perennial stream that is a destination for Mexican bird species rarely sighted in Arizona. The views along this hike encompass much of southern Arizona and extend well into northern Mexico.

Distance: 13.7-mile loop with a cherry stem
Hiking time: About 9 hours or 2 days
Difficulty: Strenuous
Trail surface: Dirt trails
Best season: Spring through fall
Water: Seasonally in Madera Canyon; at Sprung, Baldy, and Bellows Springs
Other trail users: Horses
Canine compatibility: Controlled dogs allowed
Land status: Mount Wrightson Wilderness, Coronado National Forest

Nearest town: Tucson
Fees and permits: Trailhead parking fee
Schedule: Open all year
Maps: USGS Mount Wrightson; USFS Coronado National Forest (Nogales and Sierra Vista Ranger Districts)
Trail contacts: Coronado National Forest, 300 West Congress, Tucson, AZ 85701; (520) 388-8300; www.fs.usda.gov/coronado

Finding the trailhead: From Tucson go about 24 miles south on I-19. Exit at Continental, and drive east through Continental. Continue on paved Madera Canyon Road to its end at the Roundup trailhead. GPS: N31 42.81'/W110 52.41'

The Hike

This hike uses the newer, well-graded Super Trail to take you most of the way to the summit of Mount Wrightson, the highest point in the Santa Rita Mountains. The steeper but shorter Old Baldy Trail is used for the final ascent of the peak and for part of the return hike.

The Super Trail almost immediately crosses Madera Creek, then switchbacks up the east side of the canyon through chaparral brush and oak. This trail is well named because the ascent, though steady, is always moderate. After climbing along the east side of the creek for a bit, the trail gradually returns to the creek side. Beautiful Arizona sycamores grace the creek, which is nearly always flowing. More switchbacks take the trail out on the east side of the canyon once again. The trail works its way south toward the head of the canyon through silverleaf, Emory, and Arizona white oaks; Arizona madrone; and alligator junipers. You'll get occasional views of Mount Wrightson high to the east, but usually the summit is hidden behind closer ridges. After the trail passes Sprung Spring, it climbs into Josephine Saddle at 3.5 miles. Here a sign memorializes three Boy Scouts who died while camping here during a severe late-fall snowstorm.

Mount Wrightson, Santa Rita Crest Trail

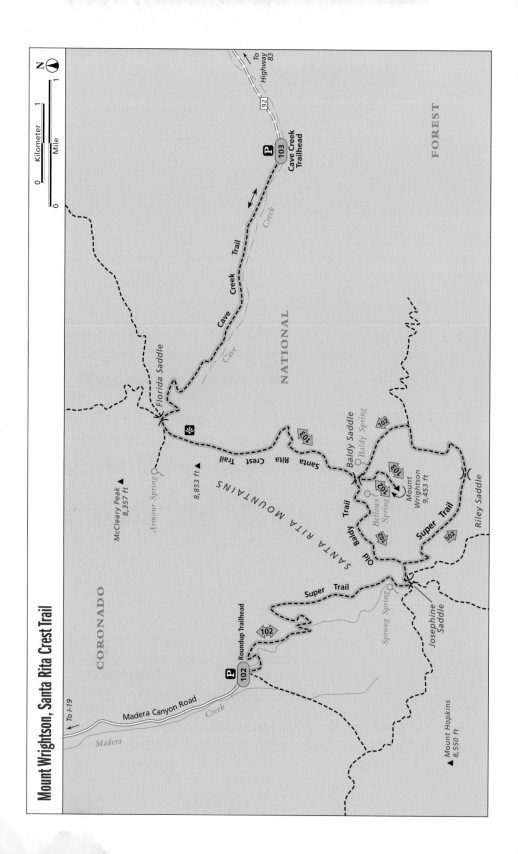

Madera Creek, Super Trail, Santa Rita Mountains

Several trails depart Josephine Saddle, but your route remains on the Super Trail, which switchbacks northeast out of the saddle. At 3.7 miles you'll pass the Old Baldy Trail in a minor saddle, which will be your return. The Super Trail now heads southeast across the slopes of Mount Wrightson, passing through Riley Saddle at 5.2 miles. Continuing to circle the mountain, the trail climbs northeast and then northwest, passing Baldy Spring. The Super Trail ends at Baldy Saddle at 6.8 miles; turn left onto the Old Baldy Trail. At first the Old Baldy Trail heads across the northeast slopes of Mount Wrightson, but it soon begins to switchback steeply, climbing around to the southeast face. The open, rocky terrain gives you great views. Early in the season, snow and ice can be a hazard on this section. A final climb takes you to the rocky summit dome, 7.6 miles from the start at the Roundup trailhead.

BIRDING DESTINATION

Madera Canyon is a favorite destination for birders, who come here to see more than 200 species. Many of these birds are found primarily in Mexico and in a few southern Arizona ranges such as the Santa Ritas. Among these are solitary vireo, acorn woodpeckers, Mexican jays, black-headed grosbeaks, red-shafted flickers, western tanagers, sulphur-bellied flycatchers, yellow-eyed juncos, and the rare elegant trogon.

As you would expect, the view is stupendous from Mount Wrightson. You can see the Tucson area and the Tucson, Santa Catalina, and Rincon Mountains to the north. Eastward the view includes the Huachuca Mountains and the sweeping oak and grassland country around Sonoita. Southward you can see far into Mexico; closer at hand, the Patagonia Mountains lie just north of the border.

Return to Baldy Saddle and the junction with the Super Trail, and then stay left to remain on the Old Baldy Trail. This trail switchbacks steeply down the rugged terrain below the saddle, then swings south past Bellows Spring and descends through stands of Mexican white pine and Douglas fir to meet the Super Trail just above Josephine Saddle. Turn right, and follow the Super Trail through Josephine Saddle and back to the Roundup trailhead.

Miles and Directions

0.0 Start at the Roundup trailhead and almost immediately cross Madera Creek on the Super Trail.

3.5 Reach Josephine Saddle.

3.7 Pass the Old Baldy Trail. (*FYI:* This will be the return trail.)

5.2 Pass through Riley Saddle.

6.8 Reach Baldy Saddle, and turn left onto the Old Baldy Trail.

7.6 Reach the summit of Mount Wrightson.

8.4 Return to Baldy Saddle; turn left to remain on the Old Baldy Trail.

10.0 Turn right onto the Super Trail.

10.2 Pass through Josephine Saddle.

13.7 Arrive back at the trailhead.

103 Santa Rita Crest Trail

This alternate, less-traveled route to the summit of Mount Wrightson climbs up a scenic east-side canyon and then follows the Santa Rita Crest Trail to the top of the mountain.

See map on page 302.
Distance: 13.2 miles out and back
Hiking time: About 9 hours or 2 days
Difficulty: Strenuous
Trail surface: Dirt trails
Best season: Spring through fall
Water: Seasonally in Cave Creek; at Armour and Baldy Springs (both side hikes)
Other trail users: Horses
Canine compatibility: Dogs under control allowed

Land status: Mount Wrightson Wilderness, Coronado National Forest
Nearest town: Tucson
Fees and permits: None
Schedule: Open all year
Maps: USGS Mount Wrightson; USFS Coronado National Forest (Nogales and Sierra Vista Ranger Districts)
Trail contacts: Coronado National Forest, 300 West Congress, Tucson, AZ 85701; (520) 388-8300; www.fs.usda.gov/coronado

Finding the trailhead: From Highway 83, 4 miles north of Sonoita (about 23 miles south of I-10), go west on the Gardner Canyon Road (FR 92) about 9 miles to its end. The last 2 miles will require a high-clearance vehicle. GPS: N31 42.55'/W110 48.28'

The Hike

The trail starts as an old road that follows Cave Creek to the west, climbing steadily. At 1.4 miles you'll pass the old Rock Candy Mine. Shortly after the mine the trail climbs away from Cave Creek up the north side of the canyon. Steep switchbacks lead to Florida Saddle at 3.4 miles. Turn left onto the Santa Rita Crest Trail, which climbs steeply southward through fine Douglas fir forest past the Armour Spring Trail junction. The climb moderates as the Crest Trail continues south along the east slopes of the range. Watch for a clearing below the trail at about 4 miles; rock outcrops provide a fine view to the east. This point makes a good goal for a shorter day hike.

At 4.2 miles the trail passes through a saddle on the crest of the range, then heads out across the east slopes again. A short, steep climb leads back to the crest, where the trail works its way south to end at Baldy Saddle. At this junction the Super Trail goes left; the Old Baldy Trail goes right. To continue to the summit of Mount Wrightson via the Old Baldy Trail, go straight ahead. The trail swings around the northeast side of the mountain, then switchbacks steeply to the summit, 6.6 miles from the start. From the summit the Santa Rita Mountains are spread out below you, as well as distant ranges in all directions.

Miles and Directions

0.0   Start at the Cave Creek trailhead, and follow an old road.

1.4   Pass the Rock Candy Mine.

3.4   Reach Florida Saddle, and turn left onto the Santa Rita Crest Trail.

3.6   Pass the Armour Spring Trail.

4.0   Reach a clearing with a view to the east. (***Option:*** Turn around here for an 8-mile out-and-back hike.)

4.2   Pass through a saddle.

5.8   The trail ends at Baldy Saddle. Go straight ahead onto the Old Baldy Trail.

6.6   Reach the Mount Wrightson summit. Retrace your steps.

13.2   Arrive back at the trailhead.

104 Carr Peak

This trail leads to a less-visited 9,235-foot summit in the Huachuca Mountains.

Distance: 6.2 miles out and back
Hiking time: About 4 hours
Difficulty: Moderate
Trail surface: Dirt trails
Best season: Spring through fall
Water: No water available
Other trail users: Horses
Canine compatibility: Dogs under control allowed
Land status: Miller Peak Wilderness, Coronado National Forest

Nearest town: Sierra Vista
Fees and permits: None
Schedule: Open all year
Maps: USGS Miller Peak; USFS Coronado National Forest (Nogales and Sierra Vista Ranger Districts)
Trail contacts: Coronado National Forest, 300 West Congress, Tucson, AZ 85701; (520) 388-8300; www.fs.usda.gov/coronado

Finding the trailhead: From Sierra Vista drive about 8 miles south on Highway 92. Turn right onto Carr Canyon Road. Continue to the end of this maintained dirt road at Ramsey Vista Campground; park at the Ramsey Vista trailhead at the west side of the loop road. GPS: N31 25.68'/W110 18.32'

The Hike

The Carr Peak Trail heads southeast up a gentle ridge through the 1977 Carr Peak burn. After you pass through a stand of surviving tall timber, the trail steepens as it switchbacks up the north ridge of Carr Peak. The fine, unlimited views are a bit of compensation for the burned forest. On the north side of the peak, the trail passes through thick stands of quaking aspen and then swings around to the south slopes. Here the forest survived the fire. At 2.8 miles turn right to stay on the Carr Peak Trail, and climb 0.3 mile to the rounded summit.

Miles and Directions

0.0 Start at the Ramsey Vista trailhead at the west side of the loop road.
2.8 Turn right to stay on the Carr Peak Trail.
3.1 Reach the Carr Peak summit. Retrace your steps.
6.2 Arrive back at the trailhead.

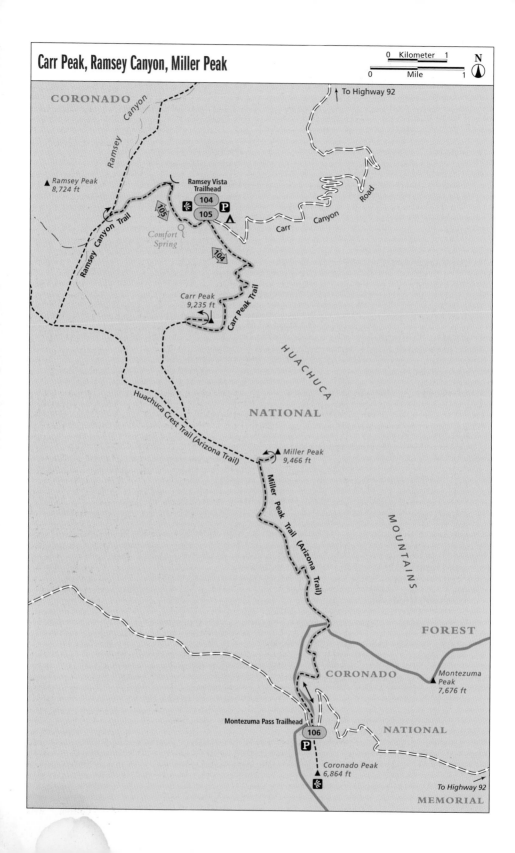

Carr Peak, Ramsey Canyon, Miller Peak

0   Kilometer   1
0   Mile   1

N

CORONADO

Ramsey Canyon

To Highway 92

▲ Ramsey Peak
8,724 ft

Ramsey Vista
Trailhead

104

P

105

Ramsey Canyon Trail

Comfort
Spring

104

Carr Canyon Road

Carr Peak
9,235 ft

Carr Peak Trail

HUACHUCA

NATIONAL

Huachuca Crest Trail (Arizona Trail)

▲ Miller Peak
9,466 ft

Miller Peak Trail (Arizona Trail)

MOUNTAINS

FOREST

CORONADO

▲ Montezuma
Peak
7,676 ft

Montezuma Pass Trailhead

106

P

NATIONAL

▲ Coronado Peak
6,864 ft

To Highway 92

MEMORIAL

105 Ramsey Canyon

This short but very scenic hike takes you into upper Ramsey Canyon in the Huachuca Mountains. Lower Ramsey Canyon is a world-famous birding site, but this hike takes you into the upper reaches of this rugged canyon where you have just as much opportunity to see rare birds.

See map on page 308.
Distance: 4.0 miles out and back
Hiking time: About 3 hours
Difficulty: Easy
Trail surface: Dirt trails
Best season: Spring through fall
Water: Seasonally at Comfort Spring
Other trail users: Horses
Canine compatibility: Controlled dogs allowed
Land status: Miller Peak Wilderness, Coronado National Forest

Nearest town: Sierra Vista
Fees and permits: None
Schedule: Open all year
Maps: USGS Miller Peak; USFS Coronado National Forest (Nogales and Sierra Vista Ranger Districts)
Trail contacts: Coronado National Forest, 300 West Congress, Tucson, AZ 85701; (520) 388-8300; www.fs.usda.gov/coronado

Finding the trailhead: From Sierra Vista drive about 8 miles south on Highway 92. Turn right onto Carr Canyon Road, and continue to the end of this maintained dirt road at Ramsey Vista Campground. Park in the signed trailhead parking area at the west side of the loop road. GPS: N31 25.68'/W110 18.32'

Coyote, serenader of desert nights

The Hike

The Ramsey Canyon Trail descends southwest below the campground, then contours west to Comfort Spring. A very gradual climb through isolated stands of pines leads to a saddle overlooking Ramsey Canyon at 0.9 mile. After the starkness of the Carr Peak burn, it's a relief to start the descent southwest into Ramsey Canyon across the cool, forested mountainside. At 2 miles the trail ends at the bottom of Ramsey Canyon. You can explore either up or down Ramsey Canyon. This is a popular area for birding—many rare species are found here.

Miles and Directions

0.0 Start at the Ramsey Vista trailhead, and descend on the Ramsey Canyon Trail.

0.4 Pass Comfort Spring.

0.9 Reach saddle overlooking Ramsey Canyon.

2.0 The trail ends at the bottom of Ramsey Canyon. Explore up or down the canyon before retracing your steps.

4.0 Arrive back at the trailhead.

106 Miller Peak

This hike follows the southern end of the 800-mile Arizona Trail along the crest of the Huachuca Mountains to the range's highest summit and the site of a former fire lookout station.

See map on page 308.
Distance: 9.2 miles out and back
Hiking time: About 6 hours
Difficulty: Strenuous
Trail surface: Dirt trails
Best season: Spring through fall
Water: No water available
Other trail users: Horses
Canine compatibility: Controlled dogs allowed
Land status: Miller Peak Wilderness, Coronado National Forest

Nearest town: Sierra Vista
Fees and permits: None
Schedule: Open all year
Maps: USGS Miller Peak and Montezuma Peak; USFS Coronado National Forest (Nogales and Sierra Vista Ranger Districts)
Trail contacts: Coronado National Forest, 300 West Congress, Tucson, AZ 85701; (520) 388-8300; www.fs.usda.gov/coronado

Finding the trailhead: From Sierra Vista drive about 15 miles south on Highway 92. Turn right onto Coronado National Memorial Road, which is paved at first but becomes maintained dirt. Continue 8.2 miles and park at Montezuma Pass. GPS: N31 21.05' / W110 17.12'

The Hike

The Miller Peak Trail starts up the grassy slopes south of the parking lot, climbs across the slope to a saddle, then begins switchbacking up a south-facing slope. This section offers fine views of Montezuma Canyon to the southeast. At 2.1 miles the trail reaches the ridge crest and follows it north toward Miller Peak. Notice the contrast between the grassy slopes you have just left and the densely vegetated slopes of Ash Canyon below you. Although the elevations are the same, the north-facing slopes of Ash Canyon are cooler and moister than the south-facing slopes. An alpine mix of vegetation, including ponderosa pine and Douglas fir, begins to dominate as you leave the dry, brushy ridge for the final ascent. The trail winds through scenic granite terrain before meeting the Huachuca Crest Trail at 4.2 miles. The Miller Peak Trail now swings right and switchbacks to the summit of Miller Peak. The old fire lookout building commands a view far into Mexico as well as nearer ranges such as the Chiricahua Mountains to the east and the Pinaleño Mountains to the northeast.

Miles and Directions

0.0 Start at the Miller Peak trailhead at Montezuma Pass.

2.1 Reach the ridge crest; follow it north.

4.2 Pass junction with the Huachuca Crest Trail; stay right on the Miller Peak Trail.

4.6 Reach Miller Peak and the old fire lookout. Retrace your steps.

9.2 Arrive back at the trailhead.

107 San Pedro River Trail

This long trail follows the San Pedro River, one of the last free-flowing rivers in Arizona and an important wildlife habitat area.

Distance: 27.0 miles one-way with a shuttle
Hiking time: About 2 to 3 days
Difficulty: Moderate
Trail surface: Dirt trails, old roads
Best season: Year-round
Water: San Pedro River; day hikers should bring their own water
Other trail users: Horses
Canine compatibility: Controlled dogs allowed
Land status: San Pedro Riparian National Conservation Area

Nearest town: Sierra Vista
Fees and permits: Camping and entrance fees
Schedule: Open all year
Maps: USGS Hereford SW, Stark, Nicksville, Hereford, Lewis Springs, Fairbank, and Land
Trail contacts: San Pedro Riparian National Conservation Area Office, 4070 S. Avenida Saracino, Hereford, AZ 85615, (520) 439-6400, www.blm.gov/az/st/en/prog/blm_special_areas/ncarea/sprnca.html

Finding the trailheads: To reach the starting trailhead from Sierra Vista, drive north on Highway 90. Turn right onto Highway 82, and drive 8.5 miles. Turn left onto Kellar Road, and drive approximately 2.2 miles to the Terrenate trailhead. GPS: N31 45.19'/W110 13.23'

To reach the ending trailhead from Sierra Vista, drive south on Highway 92. Turn left onto Hereford Road, and drive 7.5 miles. Turn right onto South Palomino Road, and drive 2 miles. Turn left onto Waters Road; continue east about 1 mile to the Waters Road trailhead. GPS: N31 24.55'/W110 6.46'

There are numerous other trailheads along the San Pedro River Trail. See the map in this hike for locations.

The Hike

The San Pedro Trail parallels the river through most of the San Pedro Riparian National Conservation Area (NCA) and is open to hiking, mountain biking, and horseback riding. Along the way you pass old mills, townsites, ranch ruins, and other historic and prehistoric sites. Several highways cross the trail, and several connector trails allow users to do shorter sections. Check with the San Pedro Riparian National Conservation Area Office, which has current trail information.

From the Terrenate trailhead, follow the trail east across the river, and then follow the trail south along the east side of the river. After crossing Highway 82 and passing Fairbank trailhead, you'll pass the hamlet of Fairbank. The San Pedro River Trail stays on the east side of the river and continues south to cross the dirt Charleston Road and pass Charleston Bridge trailhead. South of Charleston Road the trail crosses to the west side of the river and remains there for the rest of the hike. Unless it is flooding, the San Pedro River is shallow and easy to ford.

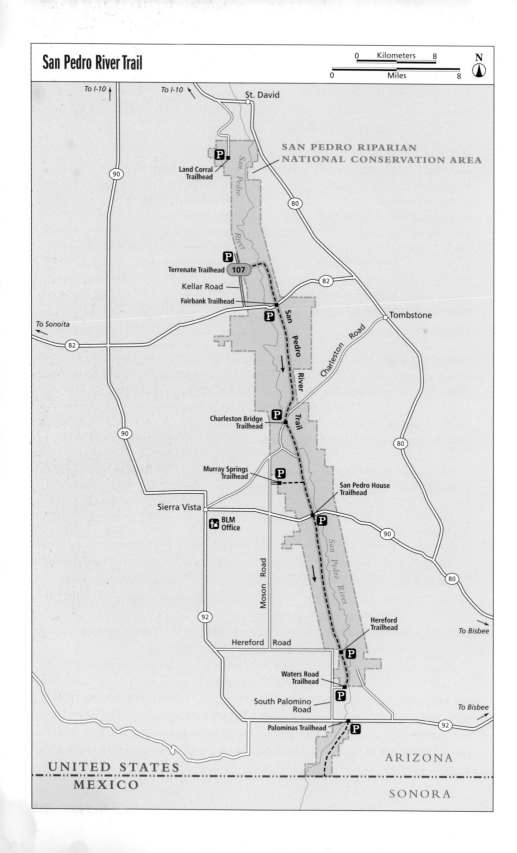

San Pedro River Trail

Kilometers 0 — 8
Miles 0 — 8

N

To I-10   To I-10   St. David

**SAN PEDRO RIPARIAN
NATIONAL CONSERVATION AREA**

90

San Pedro River

80

P Land Corral Trailhead

P Terrenate Trailhead   107

Kellar Road

Fairbank Trailhead

P

82

Tombstone

To Sonoita

82

San Pedro River Trail

90

Charleston Road

P Charleston Bridge Trailhead

P Murray Springs Trailhead

San Pedro House Trailhead

P

Sierra Vista

BLM Office

San Pedro River

90

80

Moson Road

P Hereford Trailhead

To Bisbee

92

Hereford Road

P Waters Road Trailhead

P South Palomino Road

To Bisbee

Palominas Trailhead P

92

ARIZONA

UNITED STATES

MEXICO   **SONORA**

Though perennial streams are rare in Arizona, they support critical wildlife habitat.

You'll soon pass the junction with the spur trail to the Murray Springs trailhead. The main trail continues south, crosses Highway 90, and then passes San Pedro House trailhead. A long stretch of trail leads to Hereford Road and the Hereford trailhead. After crossing Hereford Road, follow the trail a final 2 miles to the end of the hike at the Waters Road trailhead.

THE SAN PEDRO RIVER

This area offers opportunities for world-class bird watching, wildlife viewing, photography, hiking, mountain biking, camping, seasonal hunting, horseback riding, nature study, and environmental education. The San Pedro River has been called one of America's last great places. It's one of the few rivers of any size in the desert Southwest that isn't bone-dry most of the year. Preservation of this riparian habitat was recognized as being so important that in 1988 Congress created the 58,000-acre San Pedro Riparian National Conservation Area (NCA), the first such preserve in the nation.

The NCA stretches from the international border nearly 40 miles north to St. David. The San Pedro River enters Arizona from Sonora, Mexico; flows north between the Huachuca and Mule Mountains; and joins the Gila River 140 miles downstream near the town of Winkelman. Sometimes the river's flow is only a trickle, but perennial springs keep the ecosystem alive.

Fremont cottonwood and Goodding willow dominate the river corridor. Lesser amounts of Arizona ash, Arizona black walnut, netleaf hackberry, and soapberry occur as well. Chihuahuan desert-scrub, typified by thorny species such as tarbush, creosote, and acacia, characterize the uplands bordering both sides of the river. Mesquite and sacaton grass dominate the bottomland adjacent to the riparian corridor.

Wildlife abounds in the NCA because of abundant food, water, and cover. The area supports more than 350 species of birds, 80 species of mammals, 2 native and several introduced species of fish, and more than 40 species of amphibians and reptiles.

Miles and Directions

0.0 Start at the Terrenate trailhead on Kellar Road.

1.2 Cross the San Pedro River; turn right (south) along the east side of the river.

3.9 Cross Highway 82, and pass the Fairbank trailhead.

4.5 Pass the hamlet of Fairbank.

10.8 Cross Charleston Road and pass the Charleston Bridge trailhead.

14.7 Reach junction with the spur trail to the Murray Springs trailhead. Continue south on the main San Pedro River Trail.

16.8 Cross Highway 90.

17.0 Pass the San Pedro House trailhead.

25.0 Cross Hereford Road, and pass the Hereford trailhead.

27.0 Reach the end of the hike at the Waters Road trailhead.

Prehistoric and historic sites are also plentiful. The Clovis Culture, named for a unique type of stone projectile point, were the first human occupants in the upper San Pedro River Valley, dating back approximately 11,000 years. Stone tools and weapons used by these people to butcher large mammals, such as mammoths and bison, were found with the bones of their prey at the Lehner Mammoth Kill and Murray Springs Clovis sites. Directions to these sites can be obtained from the San Pedro NCA Office. Remains of other cultures include the Archaic people (6000 BC to AD 1) and the Mogollon and Hohokam (AD 1 to 1500).

The historic cultures can be divided into three major periods. First came the Spanish. Francisco Vasquez de Coronado led his 1540 expedition through the San Pedro Valley. Around 1775, Spanish troops led by an Irish mercenary began to build the Presidio (fortified settlement) Santa Cruz de Terrenate. It was never completed and was abandoned by 1780 due to continuous Apache raids. Directions to the ruins of the Presidio can be obtained from the San Pedro NCA Office.

Next came the Mexicans. After Mexico declared independence from Spain in 1821, Mexicans moved into the San Pedro Valley to homestead and ranch. They, too, fell victim to the Apaches.

With the Gadsden Purchase of 1853, the area became US territory. The latter nineteenth century witnessed more cattle ranching and farming and the discovery of silver in nearby Tombstone and other locations. Most Apache raiding ended in 1886 with the surrender of Geronimo and his followers.

In terms of natural and cultural history, exploring the San Pedro River NCA is one of the most interesting walks in southern Arizona.

108 Summit Trail

This beautiful day hike takes you through the desert foothills of the Baboquivari Mountains to the base of one of the most distinctive peaks in Arizona, and one of the few that requires technical climbing to reach its summit.

Distance: 8.0 miles out and back
Hiking time: About 6 hours
Difficulty: Moderate
Trail surface: Dirt trails
Best season: Fall through spring
Water: No water available
Other trail users: None
Canine compatibility: Controlled dogs allowed
Land status: Tohono O'odham Nation
Nearest town: Tucson

Fees and permits: Permit required from Tohono O'odham Nation. Payment for the permit can be made to the manager at Baboquivari Park daily except Wed and Thurs. On those days obtain permits from the Baboquivari District Office in Topawa.
Schedule: Open all year
Maps: USGS Chiuli Shaik and Baboquivari Peak
Trail contacts: Tohono O'odham Nation, www.tonation-nsn.gov

Finding the trailhead: The old "standard route" up the west slope on the Tohono O'odham Reservation may be reached by taking Indian Highway 19 south of Sells 12.2 miles to Topawa. At Topawa a sign directs you to the east on a graded road, Indian Highway 10. It's another 12 miles to Baboquivari Park, where there is a picnic area and primitive campground. GPS: N31 46.85'/W111 37.80'

Baboquivari Peak

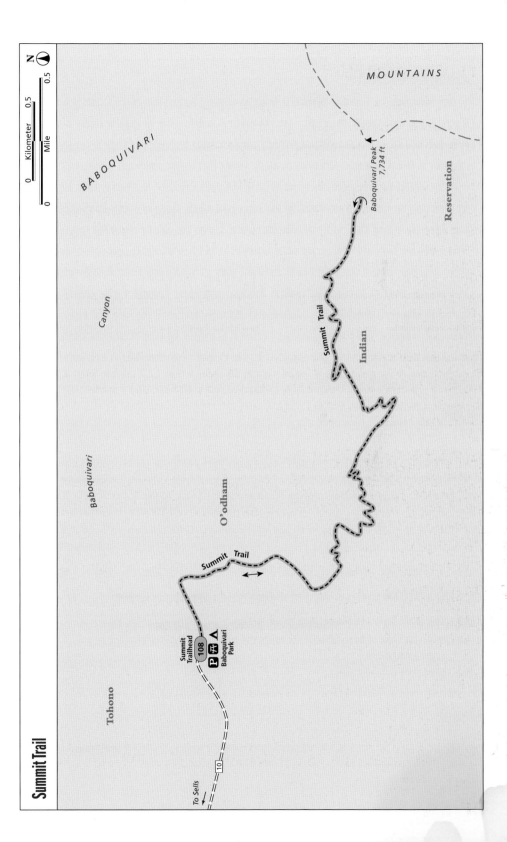

Summit Trail

N

0 Kilometer 0.5

0 Mile 0.5

BABOQUIVARI

Canyon

Baboquivari

MOUNTAINS

Baboquivari Peak
7,734 ft

Summit Trail

Indian

Reservation

Tohono

O'odham

Summit Trail

Summit
Trailhead

108

P

Baboquivari
Park

10

To Sells

CLIMBING HISTORY

The late Supreme Court Justice William O. Douglas climbed Baboquivari in 1951 and wrote, "It was a mountain wholly detached from the earth—a magic pillar of granite riding high above dark and angry clouds. Lightning briefly played around its base; and then it vanished as quickly as it had appeared—engulfed by black clouds that welled upward in some wind."

However, the first recorded climb was by Dr. R. H. Forbes and Jesus Montoya in 1898 after four previously unsuccessful attempts. On the successful climb, the good doctor had brought along a grappling hook fitted with an extension so that ". . . he was able to extend his arm. . . ." Forbes made his sixth and final ascent of Baboquivari in 1949 on his eighty-second birthday! He may have gone on and bagged the peak a seventh time . . . but his new bride nixed the plan.

The complexity of terrains and relative abundance of water support a wide variety of plants and animals. Many birds are attracted to the area, including the rare and unusual thick-billed kingbird, five-striped sparrow, northern beardless tyrannulet, and zone-tailed hawk. Vegetation varies from saguaro, paloverde, and chaparral communities to oak, walnut, and piñon at the higher elevations.

The Hike

This trail, constructed by the Civilian Conservation Corps (CCC) in 1934, takes you to the base of Baboquivari Peak, where the tecnhical climbing route begins. Hikers will need to turn around here.

Distinctive 7,734-foot Baboquivari Peak is a sacred place to the Tohono O'odham. The peak marks the center of the universe and the home of Elder Brother I'itoi, who taught the Tohono O'odham how to live in the desert. Although experienced climbers "free-climb" the three pitches, most climbers will want the security of a belay. The Tohono O'odham Nation controls access to the west side of the wilderness.

Miles and Directions

0.0 Start at the Summit trailhead in Baboquivari Park.

4.0 Reach the base of Baboquivari Peak, where the hiking ends and rock climbing begins. Retrace your steps.

8.0 Arrive back at the trailhead.

109 Sycamore Creek

There are many "Sycamore Creeks" in Arizona, all named after the native Arizona sycamore tree, a streamside, water-loving tree readily distinguished by its smooth-gray and cream-colored bark and large, five-pointed leaves. This hike follows a small but charming creek.

Distance: 12.0 miles out and back
Hiking time: About 7 hours
Difficulty: Moderate
Trail surface: Cross-country along the creek
Best season: Fall through spring
Water: Seasonal in Sycamore Creek
Other trail users: None
Canine compatibility: Controlled dogs allowed
Land status: Pajarita Wilderness, Coronado National Forest

Nearest town: Nogales
Fees and permits: None
Schedule: Open all year
Maps: USGS Ruby; USFS Nogales District, Coronado National Forest
Trail contacts: Coronado National Forest, 300 West Congress, Tucson, AZ 85701; (520) 388-8300; www.fs.usda.gov/coronado

Finding the trailhead: From Tucson drive about 55 miles south on I-19. Exit onto Highway 289; go about 20 miles, and turn left at the Sycamore Canyon sign. The parking area and the trailhead are 0.5 mile down this road at Hank and Yank Spring. GPS: N31 25.82' / W111 11.40'

The Hike

The route begins at Hank and Yank Spring Picnic Area, the site of an old post–Civil War ranch that was founded by Hank Hewitt and Yank Bartlett. There is no official

WILDLIFE CORRIDOR

There are dozens of Sycamore Creeks in Arizona, but none is as important as this particular one to migrating wildlife, especially birds. Black phoebe, vermilion flycatcher, common black hawk, several kinds of herons, and woodpeckers are but a few of the more than 130 species that frequent the canyon. Today people illegally crossing from Mexico into the United States also use the canyon. Be sure to contact the ranger district office to learn the latest on this potentially dangerous activity!

Part of the canyon has been designated as the Goodding Research Natural Area after biologist Leslie Goodding, who made extensive plant collections in the area between 1935 and the 1950s. He found 624 species of plants, including a rare fern, *Asplenium exiguum*, previously thought to grow only in the Himalayas and parts of Mexico.

Sycamore Creek, Atascosa Lookout

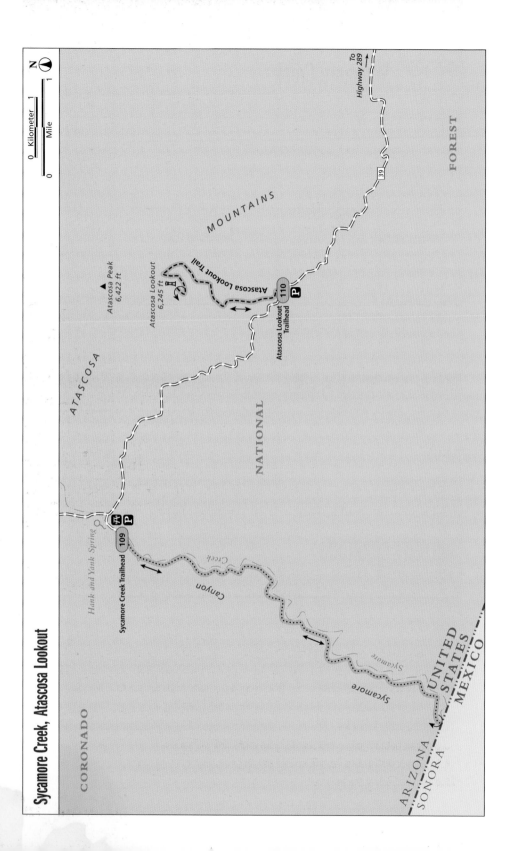

CORONADO

Hank and Yank Spring

Sycamore Creek Trailhead
109

ATASCOSA

Atascosa Peak
6,422 ft

▲

Atascosa Lookout
6,245 ft

Atascosa Lookout Trail

Atascosa Lookout
Trailhead
110

MOUNTAINS

NATIONAL

FOREST

Canyon

Creek

Sycamore

Sycamore

ARIZONA
SONORA

UNITED
STATES
MEXICO

39

To
Highway 289

N

0   Kilometer   1
0   Mile   1

Sycamore Creek, Coronado National Forest

trail—you just follow the stream. To avoid wading, especially when the creek is running high, you may have to do some fancy footwork along cliffs and ledges. Don't do this hike if there is any chance of flooding. The hike ends at the US-Mexico border.

Miles and Directions

0.0 Start at the Sycamore Creek trailhead and follow the stream

6.0 Reach the US-Mexico border, your turnaround point.

12.0 Arrive back at the trailhead.

110 Atascosa Lookout

This interesting day hike in the Atascosa Mountains leads to the site of a former fire lookout that offers sweeping views of the ranges of southern Arizona.

See map on page 322.
Distance: 4.4 miles out and back
Hiking time: About 3 hours
Difficulty: Moderate
Trail surface: Dirt trails
Best season: Year-round
Water: No water available
Other trail users: None
Canine compatibility: Controlled dogs allowed

Land status: Coronado National Forest
Nearest town: Nogales
Fees and permits: None
Schedule: Open all year
Maps: USGS Ruby; USFS Nogales District, Coronado National Forest
Trail contacts: Coronado National Forest, 300 West Congress, Tucson, AZ 85701; (520) 388-8300; www.fs.usda.gov/coronado

Finding the trailhead: From Tucson drive about 55 miles south on I-19. Exit onto Highway 289, and drive west 9 miles. Turn onto gravel FR 39, and go another 4.8 miles. Look for the trailhead on the right and a small parking area on the left. GPS: N31 24.32'/W111 8.84'

Atascosa Mountains

The Hike

The rocky, unmaintained trail climbs fairly directly to the abandoned fire lookout at 6,249 feet. From there you have wonderful views of the surrounding countryside—Sycamore Canyon to the southwest, Pena Blanc Lake to the east, and Nogales to the southeast. Way off to the west is the distinctive hump of Baboquivari Peak and the telescopes crowning Kitt Peak. For an even higher perspective, you can make your way north 0.75 mile to the summit of Atascosa Peak, which is about 200 feet higher than the lookout.

Miles and Directions

0.0   Start at the trailhead on FR 39.

2.2   Reach Atascosa Lookout, your turnaround point. (***Option:*** Hike north 0.75 mile to Atascosa Peak for an even higher perspective.)

4.4   Arrive back at the trailhead.

Western Deserts

This is another part of Arizona best explored from fall through spring. Many of the relatively small desert mountain ranges have been designated as wilderness areas since the publication of the first edition of this guide. There are few official trails, but experienced desert hikers can enjoy finding their own cross-country routes. This section gets you started on the few trails that exist.

Granite cliffs near Wabayuma Peak, Hualapai Mountains

111 Cherum Peak Trail

This is a day hike to the second-highest peak in the Cerbat Mountains and a good introduction to the type of hiking found in the desert ranges of northwestern Arizona.

Distance: 4.0 miles out and back
Hiking time: About 3 hours
Difficulty: Easy
Best season: Fall through spring
Trail surface: Dirt trails
Water: No water available
Other trail users: None
Canine compatibility: Controlled dogs allowed
Land status: Bureau of Land Management

Nearest town: Kingman
Fees and permits: None
Map: USGS Chloride
Trail contacts: Bureau of Land Management, Kingman Field Office, 2755 Mission Blvd., Kingman, AZ 86401-5308; (928) 718-3700; www.blm.gov/az/st/en/fo/kingman_field_office.html

Finding the trailhead: From Kingman at the US 93 exit from I-40, drive 22.1 miles northwest on US 93. Turn right onto the Big Wash Road, and drive 12.5 miles to the signed Cherum Peak trailhead on the left. (There are two small BLM campgrounds along the Big Wash Road—Packsaddle and Windy Point.) GPS: N35 24.93' / W114 9.01'

The Hike

The Cherum Peak Trail crosses a drainage, then works its way along small ridges and slopes, staying generally on the east side of the crest of the range. After passing through a couple of saddles on the main crest, the Cherum Peak Trail reaches the rocky summit.

From the summit are grand vistas. To the northeast are the Hualapai Valley, the Red Lake Playa, and the Music Mountains. Detrital Valley and the Black Mountains are to the northwest. On a clear day you can see Mount Charleston, near Las Vegas, Nevada.

PLANTS AND TREES OF THE DESERT

Along the lower part of the road to the Cherum Peak trailhead, you pass through a mixture of Great Basin and Mojave Desert plants. Joshua trees and creosote are two common species characteristic of the Mojave. Many of the smaller shrubs, such as saltbush, sagebrush, and snakeweed, are typical of the Great Basin Desert. The trail passes through piñon pine woodland and chaparral. There is no one plant called chaparral; this habitat is composed of primarily evergreen shrubs. In this area, look for manzanita, silk-tassel bush, and scrub oak.

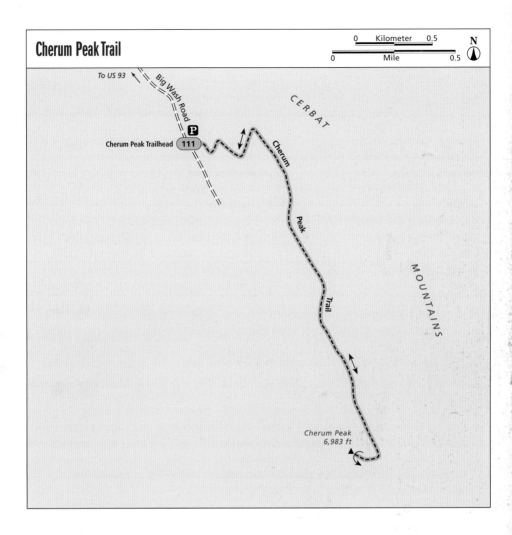

Cherum Peak Trail

To US 93

Big Wash Road

Cherum Peak Trailhead **111**

CERBAT

Cherum Peak Trail

MOUNTAINS

Cherum Peak
6,983 ft

Miles and Directions

0.0 Start at the signed Cherum Peak trailhead off Big Wash Road.

2.0 Reach Cherum Peak. Enjoy the grand vistas before retracing your steps.

4.0 Arrive back at the trailhead.

Looking southeast from Cherum Peak

112 Wabayuma Peak

This seldom-used route in the southern Hualapai Mountains takes you to the top of 7,601-foot Wabayuma Peak.

Distance: 6.0 miles out and back
Hiking time: About 4 hours
Difficulty: Moderate
Trail surface: Dirt roads and trails, cross-country
Best season: Spring through fall
Water: No water available
Other trail users: None
Canine compatibility: Dogs under control allowed

Land status: Wabayuma Peak Wilderness, Bureau of Land Management
Nearest town: Kingman
Fees and permits: None
Schedule: Open all year
Maps: USGS Wabayuma Peak
Trail contacts: Bureau of Land Management, Kingman Field Office, 2755 Mission Blvd., Kingman, AZ 86401-5308; (928) 718-3700; www.blm.gov/az/st/en/fo/kingman_field_office.html

Finding the trailhead: From Kingman go south on the paved Hualapai Mountain Road, which climbs through Hualapai Mountain Park and then passes through a summer home community. Turn right onto Flag Mine Road, a dirt road. Continue on this road through Wild Cow Campground to reach the signed Wabayuma Peak Trailhead, about 29 miles south of Kingman. GPS: N34 57.21'/W113 54.94'

Another, rougher access road leads to the same trailhead from the south. Leave I-40 at Yucca (exit 25), which is about 22 miles west of Kingman. Drive southwest on paved Boriana Mine Road. About 3.3 miles from I-40, turn left onto Boriana Mine Road, which starts as maintained dirt. After about 10 miles the road meets the wilderness boundary at its southeast corner. To continue, you'll need a four-wheel-drive vehicle. Snowdrifts may close the upper parts of the road during winter and early spring. The road crosses a saddle 20.9 miles from I-40; this is the Wabayuma Peak Trailhead.

The Hike

The trail starts from the Wabayuma Peak trailhead and climbs along the ridge crest to the northwest through low chaparral brush. This brush-plant community is indicative of a warmer climate, which is common on south-facing slopes at this elevation. The views are spectacular right from the trailhead. After a gradual climb the trail swings through a saddle with a few scattered ponderosa pines, which grow on cooler, north-facing slopes in the Hualapais. The trail turns sharply west out of this saddle and climbs over a small hill along the ridge. It now turns north along the ridge and climbs into a saddle at the base of the prominent granite escarpment. Here the summit trail forks left (leaving the jeep trail, which contours north) and starts to climb rapidly in a series of switchbacks. The trail fades out on the ridge crest, which is a pleasant, parklike mix of granite outcrops and pine trees. To reach Wabayuma Peak, work your

Wabayuma Peak

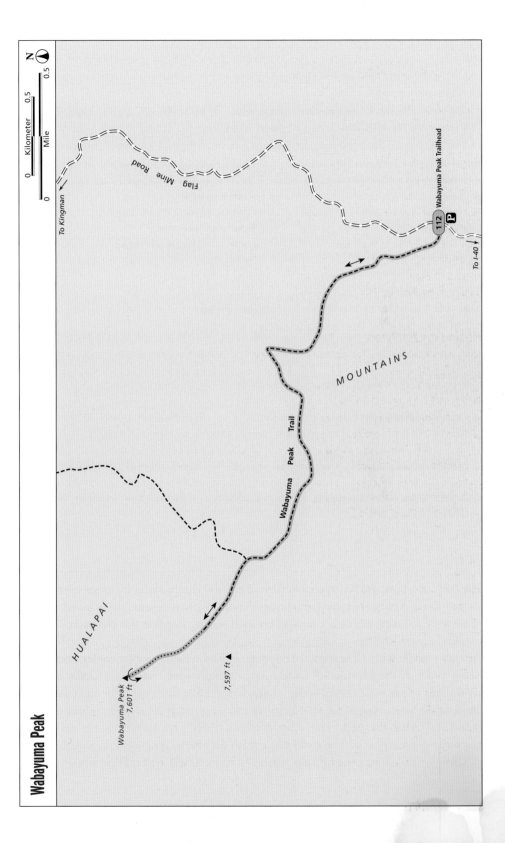

N

Kilometer
0   0.5
Mile
0   0.5

To Kingman

Flag Mine Road

112 Wabayuma Peak Trailhead

P

To I-40

Wabayuma Peak Trail

MOUNTAINS

HUALAPAI

Wabayuma Peak
7,601 ft

7,597 ft

way northwest cross-country to the foot of the peak. The steep summit block will require some route finding and rock scrambling to reach. Watch for hedgehog cactus growing in the cracks.

Alternatively, walk up the easier peak, which is only about 0.1 mile southwest of the end of the trail. This summit is only a few feet lower and provides the same incredible views. The desert ranges of Arizona and California's Mojave Desert stretch for miles to the west. To the northwest the 11,000-foot Spring Mountains are visible in Nevada. On a clear day you can see the 12,000-foot San Francisco Peaks 135 miles to the east.

Miles and Directions

0.0 Start at the signed Wabayuma Peak trailhead, past Wild Cow Campground.
1.0 Reach the first saddle.
2.0 Leave the jeep trail.
2.6 Start cross-country toward the foot of Wabayuma Peak.
3.0 Reach Wabayuma Peak. Retrace your steps.
6.0 Arrive back at the trailhead.

113 Harquahala Mountain Trail

This challenging day hike in the seldom-visited Harquahala Mountains leads to the site of a historic solar observatory station. It was also the site of a US Army heliograph station during the Arizona Indian Wars.

Distance: 6.4 miles out and back
Hiking time: About 6 hours
Difficulty: Strenuous
Trail surface: Dirt trails
Best season: Fall through spring
Water: No water available
Other trail users: None
Canine compatibility: Controlled dogs allowed
Land status: Harquahala Mountain Wilderness, Bureau of Land Management

Nearest town: Aguila
Fees and permits: None
Schedule: Open all year
Maps: USGS Socorro Peak and Harquahala Mountain
Trail contacts: Bureau of Land Management, Lower Sonoran Field Office, 21605 N. Seventh Ave., Phoenix, AZ 85027-2929; (623) 580-5500; www.blm.gov/az/st/en/fo/lower_sonoran_field.html

Finding the trailhead: From Aguila drive 13.6 miles southwest on US 60. Turn left (south) onto a four-wheel-drive road, and go 2.2 miles to the trailhead. GPS: N33 50.04'/W113 22.56'

The Hike

The first half of the trail climbs steadily southeast alongside a dry desert wash and into a rugged granite-walled canyon. At 1.5 miles the trail swings abruptly right and ascends the first of many steep switchbacks. The Harquahala Mountain Trail ends on the broad summit at the old observatory building. Take your time and enjoy the views.

ABANDONED OBSERVATORY

In 1920 the Smithsonian Institution built an astrophysical observatory on the summit of Harquahala Mountain to study the effects of sun activity on the earth's climate. Scientists believed that measuring the amount of energy reaching the earth (dubbed the "solar constant") would aid in forecasting weather. After five years the studies were inconclusive and the facility was abandoned; only ruins remain today. Since 1979 the observatory has shared the summit with a microwave communication facility that controls the water flows in the Central Arizona Project canals that bring Colorado River water to Phoenix. Long, adventurous backpacks can be mounted deep into the Harquahala Mountain Wilderness from the summit.

Harquahala Mountain Trail

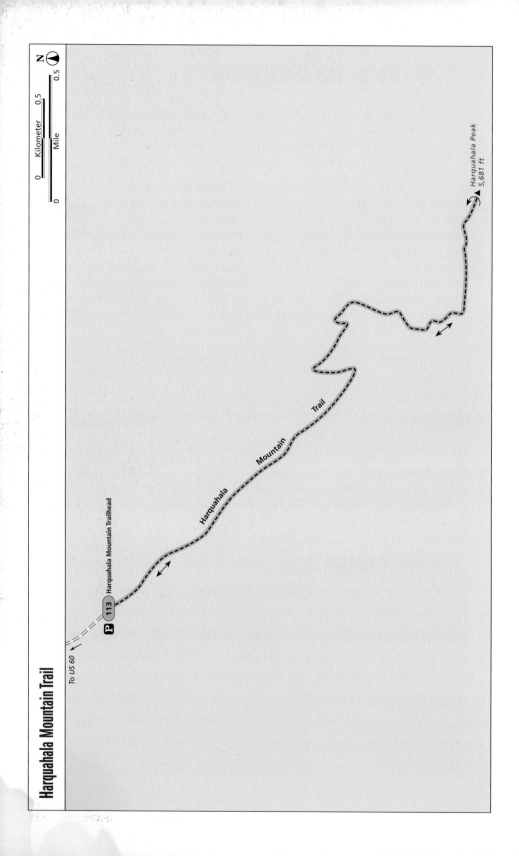

To US 60

P 113 Harquahala Mountain Trailhead

Harquahala

Mountain

Trail

Harquahala Peak
5,681 ft

N

Kilometer
0   0.5

Mile
0   0.5

Lone saguaro cactus, Harquahala Mountain foothills

Miles and Directions

0.0 Start at the trailhead and begin climbing.

1.5 Reach first switchback and start a steep ascent.

3.2 Reach the Harquahala summit. Retrace your steps.

6.4 Arrive back at the trailhead.

114 Vulture Peak

This is a fine day hike through gorgeous Sonoran Desert with a final rock scramble to the summit of a distinctive landmark peak near Wickenburg.

Distance: 4.0 miles out and back
Hiking time: About 3 hours
Difficulty: Moderate
Trail surface: Dirt trails, rock scrambling
Best season: Fall through spring
Water: No water available
Other trail users: None
Canine compatibility: Controlled dogs allowed
Land status: Bureau of Land Management

Nearest town: Wickenburg
Fees and permits: None
Schedule: Open all year
Maps: USGS Vulture Peak
Trail contacts: Bureau of Land Management, Lower Sonoran Field Office, 21605 N. Seventh Ave., Phoenix, AZ 85027-2929; (623) 580-5500; www.blm.gov/az/st/en/fo/lower_sonoran_field.html

Finding the trailhead: From US 60 in Wickenburg, drive south 7 miles on the Vulture Mine Road. About 0.7 mile past Milepost 30, turn left onto the signed Vulture Peak Trail Road. It's another 0.4 mile to the trailhead parking area. GPS: N33 52.66'/W112 49.10'

The Hike

The trail winds through wonderful Sonoran Desert. Saguaro, ocotillo, paloverde, jojoba, creosote bush, teddybear cholla, and staghorn cholla hug the trail. The first 1.6 miles or so is a fairly gradual climb. Then you meet the end of the four-wheel-drive road, and the trail begins to ascend more steeply. Take your time, enjoy the views, and before long you will reach Vulture Saddle. There are grand vistas from here, but if you have a little more energy, it's only another 240-vertical-foot scramble to the summit of Vulture Peak.

BIRDS OF THE AREA

Look for black-throated sparrows, North America's only desert bird that does not have to drink water (it gets moisture from metabolizing the carbohydrates, fats, and proteins in the seeds that it eats); delicate silky flycatchers known as phainopeplas that feed on mistletoe berries in the paloverde trees; and Say's phoebes "hawking" insects out of the air.

Vulture Peak and moon ▷

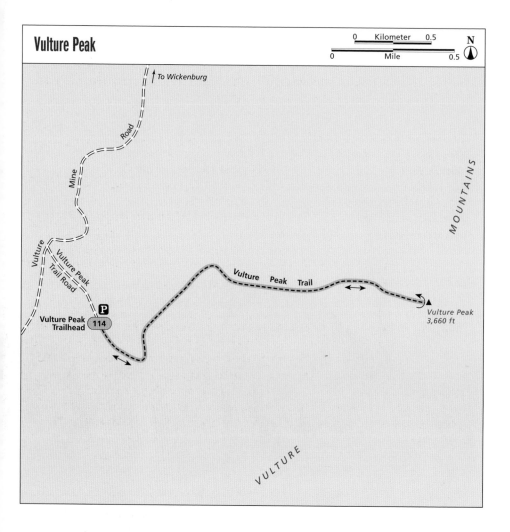

Miles and Directions

0.0 Start at the trailhead on Vulture Peak Trail Road.

1.6 The four-wheel-drive road ends.

2.0 Reach Vulture Peak. Retrace your steps.

4.0 Arrive back at the trailhead.

115 Ben Avery Trail

This day hike follows an old prospecting trail through classic Sonoran Desert to a rare desert spring in the Eagletail Mountains.

Distance: 7.0 miles out and back
Hiking time: About 4 hours
Difficulty: Easy
Trail surface: Old roads, sandy washes
Best season: Fall through spring
Water: No water available
Other trail users: None (Indian Spring is not reliable)
Canine compatibility: Controlled dogs allowed
Land status: Eagletail Mountains Wilderness, Bureau of Land Management

Nearest town: Phoenix
Fees and permits: None
Schedule: Open all year
Maps: USGS Eagletail Mountains West and Eagletail Mountains East
Trail contacts: Bureau of Land Management, Yuma Field Office, 2555 E. Gila Ridge Rd., Yuma, AZ 85365-2240; (928) 317-3200; www.blm.gov/az/st/en/fo/yuma_field _office.html

Finding the trailhead: Drive about 13 miles west of Tonopah on I-10, and take exit 81. Turn off for the Harquahala Valley, and drive south 5 miles to Courthouse Rock Road. Follow this road west about 5 miles to a major fork. Take the right fork, a gas pipeline maintenance road, and go about 6 miles to a marked road going south. Follow this track about 1.5 miles to the Ben Avery trailhead at the wilderness boundary near the looming hulk of Courthouse Rock. Some lands around and within the wilderness are not federally administered. Please respect the property rights of the owners, and do not cross or use these lands without their permission. GPS: N33 28.85' / W113 21.55'

The Hike

This trail, named for a well-known Phoenix outdoor writer, makes a nice day hike to Indian Spring. This is a good area to see wildlife and perhaps evidence of prehistoric cultures. This old jeep trail, now within the Eagletail Mountains Wilderness area and closed to vehicles, meanders gently through impressive Sonoran Desert set against rugged, rocky mountains.

The topo maps are handy, especially since the trail can be vague where it crosses or follows sandy washes.

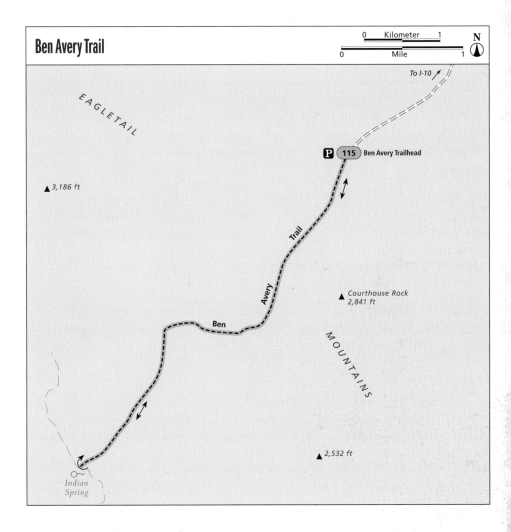

Ben Avery Trail

0 Kilometer 1
0 Mile 1

N

To I-10

P 115 Ben Avery Trailhead

E A G L E T A I L

▲ 3,186 ft

Ben Avery Trail

▲ Courthouse Rock
2,841 ft

M O U N T A I N S

▲ 2,532 ft

Indian
Spring

Miles and Directions

0.0 Start at the Ben Avery trailhead and head west on the old jeep trail.

3.5 Reach Indian Spring, your turnaround point.

7.0 Arrive back at the trailhead.

Courthouse Rock, Eagletail Mountains

116 Palm Canyon

This easy day hike takes you to a unique desert oasis featuring a stand of rare California fan palms in the rugged Kofa Mountains.

Distance: 1.6 miles out and back
Hiking time: About 2 hours
Difficulty: Easy
Trail surface: Dirt trails
Best season: Fall through spring
Water: No water available
Other trail users: None
Canine compatibility: Controlled dogs allowed
Land status: Kofa Wilderness, Kofa Mountains National Wildlife Refuge

Nearest town: Quartzite
Fees and permits: None
Schedule: Open all year
Maps: USGS Palm Canyon
Trail contacts: Kofa National Wildlife Refuge, 9300 E. 28th St., Yuma, AZ, 85365; (928) 783-7861; www.fws.gov/refuges/profiles/index.cfm?id=22570

Finding the trailhead: From Quartzite drive 18 miles south on US 95 (from Yuma drive 63 miles north on US 95). Turn onto the signed Palm Canyon dirt road, which heads east 9 miles toward the Kofa Mountains. GPS: N33 21.61'/W114 6.41'

The Hike

The trail follows the desert wash at the end of the road that eventually takes you into a deep, narrow canyon. Follow the most prominent trail to a small sign on a slightly elevated area near the middle of the canyon. By looking upward in the narrow, north-trending side canyon, you will see a grove of Washingtonia palms (also called California fan palms), the only native palms in Arizona. These remarkable trees also grow in other canyons cutting into the Kofa Mountains and at scattered locations in California and Baja California. Although the fruits were gathered and eaten by local

KOFA

Many people think that Kofa is an Indian word, but it actually is derived from the acronym for the King of Arizona Mine. In the 1890s prospector Charles Eichelberger discovered gold in these rugged mountains. To mark his property he had a branding iron forged that read "K of A." Later, when a post office name was being discussed, someone remembered the brand. The name Kofa resulted, undoubtedly a more genteel name than its earlier moniker—a name inspired by certain rectangular rock formations along the crest of the mountains that resembled an outhouse.

California fan palms, Palm Canyon, Kofa Mountains

Indians, this particular population wasn't "discovered" by botanists until 1923. The palm's name commemorates President George Washington, who probably never saw a palm, especially this species! Today this palm is commonly planted as an ornamental.

A trail brochure can be picked up from the Kofa National Wildlife Refuge office in Yuma.

Miles and Directions

0.0 Start at the trailhead on Palm Canyon Road, and follow the desert wash.

0.8 Reach a viewpoint overlooking the oasis. Retrace your steps.

1.6 Arrive back at the trailhead.

117 Squaw Lake Nature Trail

This short nature trail at Squaw Lake, near Imperial Dam on the Colorado River, is popular with birders.

Distance: 2.0 miles out and back
Hiking time: About 1 hour
Difficulty: Easy
Trail surface: Dirt trails
Best season: Fall through spring
Water: No water available
Other trail users: None
Canine compatibility: Leashed dogs allowed
Land status: Bureau of Land Management

Nearest town: Yuma
Fees and permits: None
Schedule: Open all year
Maps: USGS Imperial Reservoir
Trail contacts: Bureau of Land Management, Yuma Field Office, 2555 E. Gila Ridge Rd., Yuma, AZ 85365-2240; (928) 317-3200; www.blm.gov/az/st/en/fo/yuma_field_office.html

Finding the trailhead: From Yuma drive north over the Fourth Avenue Bridge into California. Take CA S-24 in Winterhaven north for 20 miles. Look for the informational signs on the right side of the road to locate the trailhead. GPS: N32 54.23'/W114 28.65'

The Hike

Like Betty's Kitchen Interpretive Trail, this is a favorite area with birders, especially in winter and spring. More than 200 species have been recorded in the area. Some of the summer residents include summer tanagers, southwestern willow flycatchers, vermilion flycatchers, and yellow-billed cuckoos. Frequent migrants include Townsend's and black-throated gray warblers, western tanagers, and Lazuli buntings. The lake attracts mallards, northern pintails, and common mergansers. The endangered Yuma clapper rail may nest here too.

A trail guide is available from the BLM office in Yuma.

Squaw Lake Nature Trail

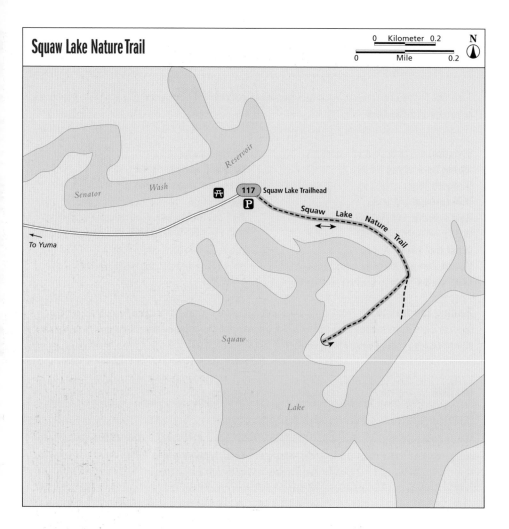

Miles and Directions

0.0 Start at the trailhead at the informational signs.

1.0 Reach Squaw Lake. Retrace your steps.

2.0 Arrive back at the trailhead.

118 Betty's Kitchen Interpretive Trail

This short but informative nature trail leads through another popular birding area near the Colorado River.

Distance: 0.5-mile loop
Hiking time: About 30 minutes
Difficulty: Easy
Trail surface: Dirt trails
Best season: Fall through spring
Water: No water available
Other trail users: None
Canine compatibility: Leashed dogs allowed
Land status: Bureau of Land Management

Nearest town: Yuma
Fees and permits: None
Schedule: Open all year
Maps: USGS Laguna Dam
Trail contacts: Bureau of Land Management, Yuma Field Office, 2555 E. Gila Ridge Rd., Yuma, AZ 85365-2240; (928) 317-3200; www.blm.gov/az/st/en/fo/yuma_field_office.html

Finding the trailhead: From Yuma take US 95 east to Avenue 7E (Laguna Dam Road). Head north for 9 miles just past Laguna Dam. Proceed another 0.5 mile and look for the Betty's Kitchen Interpretive Trail sign. (GPS location not available)

Desert flowers are common after wet winters, while alpine flowers bloom in late summer.

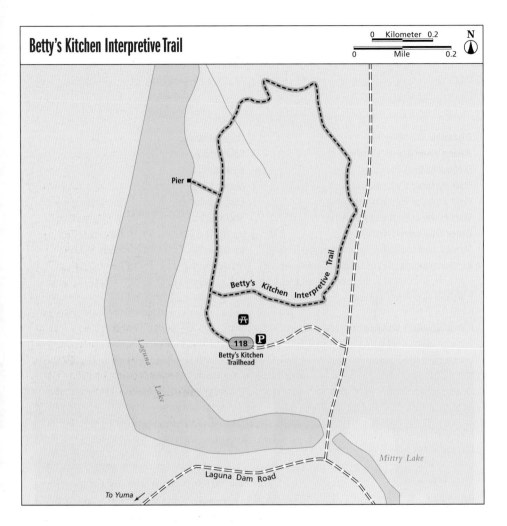

0   Kilometer 0.2

N

0   Mile   0.2

Pier

Betty's Kitchen Interpretive Trail

Laguna Lake

118 P

Betty's Kitchen
Trailhead

Mittry Lake

Laguna Dam Road

To Yuma

The Hike

The Betty's Kitchen area is named for a small cafe that once stood here. This short loop walk through a woodland of tamarisk, Fremont cottonwood, willows, screwbean and honey mesquite, and paloverde offers outstanding bird watching. Common shorebirds include killdeer and spotted sandpiper. In winter look for mallards and cinnamon teals. Anglers try their luck for bluegill, largemouth bass, carp, flathead and channel catfish, and tilapia. There is a box containing a trail guide at the trailhead.

119 Muggins Peak

This is a cross-country day hike to the highest point in the Muggins Mountains Wilderness.

Distance: 4.0 miles out and back
Hiking time: About 3 hours
Difficulty: Moderate
Trail surface: Cross-country through open desert and along sandy washes
Best season: Fall through spring
Water: No water available
Other trail users: None
Canine compatibility: Controlled dogs allowed
Land status: Muggins Mountains Wilderness, Bureau of Land Management

Nearest town: Yuma
Fees and permits: None
Schedule: Open all year
Maps: USGS Ligurta, Dome, Wellton, and Red Bluff Mountain West
Trail contacts: Bureau of Land Management, Yuma Field Office, 2555 E. Gila Ridge Rd., Yuma, AZ 85365-2240; (928) 317-3200; www.blm.gov/az/st/en/fo/yuma_field _office.html

Finding the trailhead: To reach the southwest boundary, take the Dome Valley exit off I-8. Travel 1.25 miles on the frontage road. Turn northwest and go to County Avenue 20E, then continue to County Seventh Street. Turn right (east) and drive to the foot of the mountains where Muggins Wash Road continues northeast and drops into Muggins Wash and the wilderness boundary. This route crosses some private land, so please stay on the road until reaching the wilderness area. GPS: N32 43.88' / W114 16.369'

The Hike

This relatively small but rugged 7,674-acre wilderness is dominated by Klothos Temple, Muggins Peak, and Long Mountain. Washes snake their way up into and around these peaks, making excellent hiking routes, and the desert slopes are relatively easy

HISTORY AND WILDLIFE

Signs of old placer mine workings from the late 1800s in the western half of the wilderness lend some historic interest to the area.

Typical Sonoran Desert vegetation covers the area. Along washes may be found blue paloverde, ironwood, mesquite, smoke tree, and bitter condalia. Other species of note are holly-leaved bursage, Hoffmannseggia, Wiggins' cholla, and a red-spined barrel cactus. Wildlife includes chuckwalla, Gila monster, cactus wren, desert bighorn sheep, possibly desert tortoise, and elf owl.

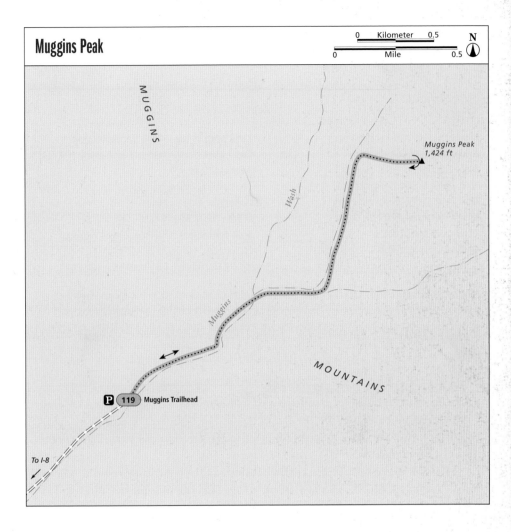

cross-country hiking. One such hike would be to continue up Muggins Wash about 1.75 miles to the west side of Muggins Peak. An uphill cross-country scramble takes you to the summit.

Miles and Directions

0.0 Start at Muggins trailhead on Muggins Wash Road.

2.0 Reach Muggins Peak, your turnaround point.

4.0 Arrive back at the trailhead.

◀ *Muggins Mountain at sunset*

120 Bull Pasture

This is a day hike to a desert "meadow" perched on the west slopes of the rugged Ajo Mountains.

Distance: 3.6 miles out and back
Hiking time: About 2 hours
Difficulty: Moderate
Trail surface: Dirt trails, optional cross-country
Best season: Fall through spring
Water: No water available
Other trail users: None
Canine compatibility: Dogs prohibited

Land status: Organ Pipe Cactus Wilderness, Organ Pipe Cactus National Monument
Nearest town: Ajo
Fees and permits: None
Schedule: Open all year
Maps: USGS Mount Ajo
Trail contacts: Organ Pipe Cactus National Monument, 10 Organ Pipe Dr., Ajo, AZ 85321-9626; (520) 387-6849; www.nps.gov/orpi

Finding the trailhead: From Ajo drive 33 miles south on Highway 85 to the Organ Pipe Cactus National Monument headquarters. Turn left onto Ajo Mountain Loop Drive. Drive 8 miles to the signed Bull Pasture trailhead at the Estes Canyon Picnic Area. GPS: N32 0.95'/W112 42.71'

The Hike

The maintained trail leaves the picnic area and climbs to a ridge overlooking Bull Pasture, a scenic basin high on the flanks of the Ajo Range. As the name suggests, Bull Basin was a favorite cattle pasture prior to the creation of Organ Pipe Cactus National Monument in 1937.

In 1971 a hiker wandered into Bull Pasture and was never seen again despite repeated searches, which continued off and on for years after the official search ended.

Miles and Directions

0.0 Start at the Bull Pasture trailhead at the Estes Canyon Picnic Area.
1.8 Reach the overlook above Bull Pasture. Retrace your steps.
3.6 Arrive back at the trailhead.

Organ Pipe cactus, Bull Pasture Trail ▶

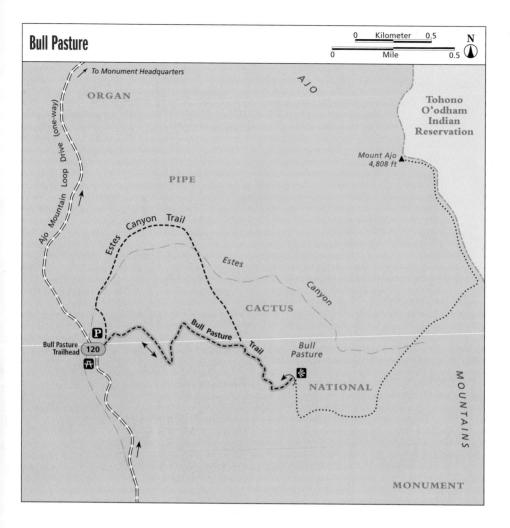

0 Kilometer 0.5
N

0 Mile 0.5

To Monument Headquarters

ORGAN

AJO

Tohono
O'odham
Indian
Reservation

Ajo Mountain Loop Drive (one-way)

PIPE

Mount Ajo
4,808 ft

Estes Canyon Trail

Estes

Canyon

CACTUS

Bull Pasture Trail

Bull
Pasture

Bull Pasture
Trailhead

P

120

NATIONAL

MOUNTAINS

MONUMENT

Options

From the trail's end at the overlook, a rough but rewarding cross-country hike leads to the summit of Mount Ajo—at 4,808 feet the highest point in the monument. The route goes from trail's end around the head of Bull Pasture basin, trending generally eastward toward the steep slopes on the far side. The route then goes up and to the right to gain the main north–south ridge. You will have to pick your way around some cliff bands. Once on the ridge, the route is a straightforward walk north about a mile to the summit.

From the top of Mount Ajo, you can see far into Mexico to the south, west across the monument, and north and east across the vast Tohono O'odham Reservation toward the Baboquivari Mountains. This option adds 3.6 miles to the hike.

Hike Index

About the Author

Bruce Grubbs is an avid hiker, mountain biker, paddler, and cross-country skier who has been exploring the American West for decades. He has used high-technology gear in the backcountry in his work as a professional pilot, an amateur radio operator, and a mountain rescue team member. Bruce holds Airline Transport Pilot and Instrument Flight Instructor certificates. He lives in Flagstaff, Arizona, and is the author of more than thirty-five books.

Other books by the author:

Grand Canyon Guide
Exploring Great Basin National Park
Exploring with GPS
Hiking Northern Arizona
Best Easy Day Hikes Flagstaff
Best Easy Day Hikes Sedona
Hiking Arizona's Superstition and Mazatal County
Mountain Biking Phoenix
Mountain Biking Flagstaff and Sedona
Backpacker Magazine's Using a GPS
Desert Hiking Tips
Hiking Nevada
Hiking Oregon's Central Cascades
Mountain Biking St. George and Cedar City

For more information, check the author's website at brucegrubbs.com.

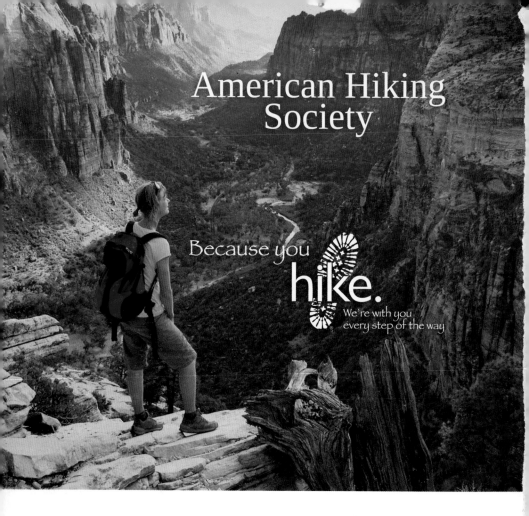

American Hiking Society

Because you **hike.**
We're with you every step of the way

As a national voice for hikers, **American Hiking Society** works every day:

- Building and maintaining hiking trails
- Educating and supporting hikers by providing information and resources
- Supporting hiking and trail organizations nationwide
- Speaking for hikers in the halls of Congress and with federal land managers

Whether you're a casual hiker or a seasoned backpacker, become a member of American Hiking Society and join the national hiking community! You'll enjoy great member benefits and help preserve the nation's hiking trails, so tomorrow's hike is even better than today's. We invite you to join us now!

American Hiking Society